SALT OF THE SEA

THE PACIFIC COAST COD FISHERY AND THE LAST DAYS OF SAIL

SALT OF THE SEA

THE PACIFIC COAST COD FISHERY
AND THE LAST DAYS OF SAIL

CAPTAIN ED SHIELDS

PACIFIC HERITAGE PRESS
Lopez Island, WA USA

HERITAGE HOUSE
Surrey, B.C. Canada

Copyright © 2001 Pacific Heritage Press

First edition 2001

Published in the United States of America by
Pacific Heritage Press
479 Old Homestead Road
Lopez Island, WA 98261

Library of Congress Cataloging-in-Publication Data
Shields, James Edward, 1916-
    Salt of the Sea: The Pacific Coast Codfish Industry and the Last Days of Sail / Ed Shields
    Includes biographical references and index. Printed on acid free paper
    ISBN 0-9673633-8-1
    1. Cod fisheries - North Pacific - History   2. Pacific Coast Codfish Company - History
    3. Fisherman - North Pacific. I. Title.

Library of Congress number 2001135705

Published in Canada by
Heritage House Publishing Co. Ltd.
#108 – 17665 – 66A Avenue
Surrey, B.C. V3S 2A7

National Library of Canada Cataloguing in Publication Data

Shields, Ed 1916–
    Salt of the sea

    Includes index.
    ISBN 1-894384-35-0

    1. Shields, Ed. 2. Cod fisheries – North Pacific Ocean – History.
3. Pacific Coast Codfish Company – History. 4. Fishers – North Pacific Ocean – Biography. I. Title.

SH214.2.S54 2001   338.3'727633'092   C2001-911031-6

Heritage House acknowledges the support of Heritage Canada, the Book Publishing Industry Development Program, and the British Columbia Arts Council.

Cover and book design by Jeremy Snapp
Edited by Audrey McClellan
Layout by Darlene Nickull

Printed in Singapore

DEDICATION

This book is dedicated to the maritime historians of the Pacific Coast of America.

Schooner *John A* homeward bound, 1922.

FOREWORD

Fishing for codfish from dories and the decks of sailing ships in the Bering Sea and North Pacific lasted approximately 87 years, from the earliest recorded date of 1863 to 1950. Within that long span of time, there were few changes made in the equipment used. The small schooners, brigs, barkentines, and four-masted schooners worked and sailed in the same way year after year. Navigation skills and local knowledge were passed on as lessons learned from one generation to another. Hand-line fishing from the decks of the ships and dories remained constant, aided only by the advent of outboard motors. In time, electric lighting and gasoline-powered auxiliary engines came into use and gave the fishermen a slightly easier life in their pursuit of codfish, but little else changed. God's own wind, tides, and currents, and wooden ships of sail were the primary hallmarks of an industry that remained traditionally bound to the same methods.

Captain Ed Shields is uniquely qualified to write this comprehensive history of the North Pacific codfish industry. He was born and raised in a family of this tradition, then seasoned with a mixture of going to sea and learning the management side of selling salted codfish that gave him the background from which this history is written.

Salt of the Sea is an objective history of an industry that was centered in the North Pacific waters of the United States. It is also the biographical story of Ed Shields' father, Captain J.E. Shields, a prominent ship-owner who outlasted all of his competitors and gave not an inch in his determination to produce a quality product and protect his lifelong ambition to remain independent. The inevitable passage of time took its toll on both body and drive, as well as on the planking and frames of his last active schooner, the *C A Thayer*, while the advent of frozen and packaged fresh fish was the death knell for the salt codfish industry.

In 1957 I made a fortuitous job change, leaving my career working around deep-sea freighters and going to work for the State of California, where I bought and oversaw the partial refitting of the *C A Thayer* for ultimate use as a floating museum in the state's Department of Natural Resources, Division of Beaches and Parks. Though I was aware of the existence of this 62-year-old schooner, I faced the prospects of having to learn quickly how wooden ships were built, how to guide this one through the quicksands of shipyard practices, and how to manage the survey reports and repairs recommended by my betters.

During the six months of refitting, repairing, and finally remasting this old ship in three shipyards of Puget Sound, I came to know every remote corner of her interiors. There were still traces of salt in the hold. The aromatic vapors of stale codfish slime rose from the bilges, and no amount of pumping could eliminate this. Yet the lingering atmosphere of the ship's long past hung like a spirit about her decks as the repair work progressed. The two Captains Shields paid periodic visits to the ship, with advice and reminiscences that were invaluable in the preservation work. Only seven years had passed since the *C A Thayer* had come home from the Bering Sea on her last fishing voyage. The ship was still very definitely alive, and so was her history.

Eventually the ship was refitted and sailed with an experienced and volunteer crew to San Francisco, where she was delivered to her new owners. More repairs were done to restore her to near original condition.

The ship slogged past her century mark and at this writing is 106 years old. Bilge pumps are working, pumping clear water, both rain and sea water, through the overboard hoses as a new owner, the National Park Service, struggles frantically to find funds to keep her sound and preserved.

Captain Ed Shields and his father, Captain J.E. Shields, on the *C A Thayer*, circa. 1957.

Now that the *C A Thayer* has lived through the entire 20th century and carried on into the 21st, it is fortunate indeed that Captain Shields brings to the fore this history of a long-lived, sailing-ship-dominated industry so deeply planted in the North Pacific. The preservation of family records, his own large collection of on-board photographs – as well as the varieties of pictures from other sources – and his personal recollections of those earlier years have combined to produce this history. The *C A Thayer* and her near sister *Wawona*, in Seattle, are the only surviving ships of this age. The written testimony in *Salt. of the Sea*, coupled with the existence of two aged ships, are fortuitously offered to new generations for their preservation and education.

Captain Shields has recorded this story completely, with passion and skill. No one else could have done it. If by some stroke of magic the salt codfish industry were to be revived, this book contains the blueprint by which it might be rejuvenated.

Captain Harold D. Huycke
July 2001

PREFACE

Codfishing was an occupation practiced for many centuries in various parts of the Atlantic Ocean. In the Americas this included the Grand Banks off the coast of Newfoundland as well as Georges Banks out off the New England shores. These brave fishermen sought the cod for the fresh fish markets of Boston and New York as well as the salt cod markets of the rest of America and the Caribbean regions. Tales of the Gloucester fishermen can be found in the history books.

With the settlement of the West Coast of America, fishermen began pursuing cod in the Pacific. As the cod banks were so far removed from the markets of San Francisco and other parts of California, the fishermen had to resort to preservation with salt. Refrigeration was not developed until early in the twentieth century.

By that time, commercial cold storage stations built in Alaska and the seaport cities springing up in Washington, Oregon, and Northern California made it possible for the fishermen to land fish preserved in ice and have the shore facilities process and deliver high-quality fresh product to the market. Salt preservation became a thing of the past.

Decades later, the development of the diesel engine for use in fishing vessels brought an end to the use of sail. Dory fishing from large sailing vessels will never again prevail as a major method of fishing. Hence, the importance of preserving the records of this industry so that they are not totally lost.

This book is primarily based on my own memory of the days of dory codfishing with sailing vessels after the turn of the last century. My father, Captain J.E. Shields, was the manager and later sole owner of the Pacific Coast Codfish Co. He also owned 18 sailing schooners over the course of his life. Many were employed in the South Sea island trade, freighting lumber from West Coast ports to fabled islands, as well as to the Bering Sea and the Arctic coast of North America. The tales of these voyages were firmly impressed on my young mind, and when I was a small boy, Father would take me to visit the vessels he owned, or those of the PCCC, that were in harbor.

After I finished high school in 1934, I made my first five-month voyage to the Bering Sea, continuing this tradition most of the years until 1950, the last codfish voyage, when I was the captain. I have therefore firsthand information on this industry, gained from personal experience with the men who had followed the fishery for many years, along with my own experience as a crew member.

I have attempted to chronicle the past days as I remember them and as I lived them, with a brief history of the early development of the fishery.

Captain Ed Shields

ACKNOWLEDGMENTS

Over the years I have collected considerable information about the sailing vessels of the West Coast, including a large collection of pictures. I had a good camera on the voyages and snapped many pictures. I have also acquired many from friends here and there. I have given credit for each picture where I knew the source. I would like to thank Harry Kirwin, long-time marine photographer; Joe Williamson, marine photographer; Gordon Jones, for loan of pictures and other materials; Harry Dring of San Francisco, for many pictures; Jim Cole and Hewitt Jackson, for their sketches; many friends who gave me pictures; and the *Seattle Times*. Thanks to Herman Grotle, for the loan of Captain Grotle's log books.

Thanks also go to the Puget Sound Maritime Historical Society; the National Maritime Museum in San Francisco; the Landmark Society of Tiburon, CA; the U.S. Federal Record Center, Sand Point, Seattle; John Kiwalla of Placerville, CA; and Harold Huycke of Seattle.

In writing this book I made use of the following documents:

Log books of *Sophie Christenson, Charles R Wilson*, and other codfish schooners, Ed Shields Collection,

Captain John Grotle's log books

A list of vessels documented on the Pacific Coast by the Fireman's Fund Register (an insurance company) in 1916

Family records of the Pacific Coast Codfish Co.

Letter by Mr. C.C. Hale of Union Fish Co. of San Francisco

John M. Cobb's 1915 report on the Pacific cod fisheries for the U.S. Commissioner of Fisheries

H.W. McCurdy's *Maritime History of the Pacific Northwest*

My own manuscript *Maritime Memories*, concerning Captain J.E. Shields

An interview with Captain "Codfish" Thomason, recorded in San Francisco about 1959 by Karl Kortum, Harold Huycke, and Fingal Larson, held in the archives of the San Francisco Maritime Library

CONTENTS

The Union Fish Co. plant at Tiburon/Belvedere, California, circa 1915. Note the extensive area devoted to the "flake yard," where cod are dried in the sun. The split cod will be placed flat on these racks, skin side down, while the wind and sun remove the moisture. The schooner *Galilee* and the barkentine *Fremont* are at anchor, while the schooner *Sequoia* is at the wharf.

CHAPTER 1

THE BEGINNINGS OF THE SALT COD FISHERY ON THE PACIFIC COAST

Codfish is a plentiful species of saltwater fish found in shallow coastal waters or on undersea banks (areas where the sea floor rises closer to the surface) around the world. They have long bodies, big heads, and dorsal and anal fins, and generally congregate in large schools.

The Scandinavian nations have harvested cod for centuries, taking advantage of the unlimited quantities available off their shores. The fisherman in these countries had good seagoing boats and the skill to catch the fish, but preservation for later consumption was a problem. Cooking serves as a short-term preservative only. During the winter months, ice was available from the lakes to preserve the fish for several days, but salting and drying were the only methods available for longer storage.

Fishermen brought the cod on shore, where they cleaned and split it. Some fish were lightly salted and hung to dry over wood racks for a month or more, at which time the cod resembled a split cedar shake. It was hard and very little moisture remained. In this form it would not spoil even in tropical countries. The other method was to literally bury the split cod in coarse salt, either on the vessel or in the sheds of the shore stations. Later they washed the salted cod to remove the natural fish slime, then dried it further to a moisture content of about 60% to 70%. In this form the cod was shipped to southern European countries. Before it was eaten, both the hard dried and the salted cod had to be soaked in fresh water to remove the salt and reconstitute the fish. The cod from the northern European countries became a staple food item and an important item of commerce.

The same method of cod preservation was practiced in the American colonies and later the American states, as well as in the Canadian Maritime provinces to the north. With the settlement of the American West there was an increasing demand for food for all these newcomers. Salt-cured or preserved cod was one source of food at a time when mechanical refrigeration had not been developed.

The first recorded West Coast fishery producing salt cod was centered in the San Francisco Bay area, where there were growing numbers of people, all needing food every day. The salted cod was soaked out and cooked and, together with boiled potatoes, served with a cream sauce. Many of the early residents of California were of Spanish or Italian descent and well schooled in the preparation of this food.

The earliest records of the U.S. Bureau of Fisheries show the *Timandra* delivered the first commercial quantity of salt cod from distant banks to San Francisco in 1863. The following history of these early days was included in a 1915 report written by John M. Cobb for Hugh Smith, the U.S. Commissioner of Fisheries.

In 1857, Captain Matthew Turner in the 120 ton brig *Timandra* sailed from San Francisco with an assortment of cargo for Nicolaevsk on the Amur river. He was detained, however, for three weeks at Castor Bay at the head of the Gulf of Tartary, because the Amur River was full of ice when he reached the Asiatic Coast. While the vessel lay there waiting, in three fathoms of water, the crew began fishing over the rail with hand lines, simply as a pastime. They were surprised to find plenty of cod averaging about two feet in length. Captain Turner had not previously seen codfish, but some of the crew were familiar with the species, and he, knowing their market value at San Francisco, appreciated the importance of the discovery, and became interested in the fishing. Two years later, Captain Turner made another trip to the Amur River. Reaching Saghalin Island off the Gulf of Tartary, he began fishing for cod and found them very abundant. Only enough were taken for the ship's use, however, for he had no means to cure them.

In 1863, Captain Turner once more sailed in the *Timandra* to the Amur River on a trading voyage. But this time he was prepared to catch and cure some cod on his return voyage. Besides fishing gear, he carried 25 tons of salt. Returning he stopped at the Gulf of Tartary. Cod were plentiful at first and ten tons were taken in a few days, and salted in kenches [bins of salted cod]. Suddenly the fish disappeared and none could be caught. Then the brig ran down the coast to southern Kamchatka, where fish were found in abundance and excellent success was met with on the first day. The vessel lay near the rocky coast, and on the second day during the prevalence of dense fog, both anchors were lost. This mishap compelled Captain Turner to abandon fishing and leave the coast. He reluctantly sailed for home. His fish sold at San Francisco for 15 cents per pound. His voyage would have been notably profitable if the loss of the anchors had not interfered with obtaining a full fare. This was the first occasion that salt cod were landed on the West Coast from Pacific fishing grounds.

In 1864, Captain Turner sailed on his brig on a codfishing voyage without trading goods. Thus the *Timandra* was the first vessel to engage in this industry from Pacific ports. On the same grounds visited the previous year a fare of 100 tons of codfish was obtained and the voyage was remunerative. The same year the schooner *Alert* made a trip to Bristol Bay, Alaska, in pursuit of cod. Her voyage proved to be a failure, for she took only 9 tons of fish.

Captain Turner states that since he made his voyage to the Gulf of Tartary, as he related above, no American vessels have gone there to fish for cod. His success, however, had a very decided effect on the codfishing business in the North Pacific. In 1865 six vessels sailed to the Okhotsk Sea in pursuit of cod. These were the first American vessels to visit that region on codfishing trips, and their sailing evidenced a resolution to begin the business upon a broad commercial basis.

But Captain Turner, who seemed to have possessed the spirit and enterprise of a pioneer or discoverer, determined to look for codfish nearer home. Not disheartened by the ill success of the *Alert* in 1863, he sailed for Alaska on the schooner *Porpoise* of 45 tons, March 27, 1865. He arrived at the Shumagin Islands on May 1st. He began fishing that same day. Cod were abundant and close to shore. As a result he returned to San Francisco on July 7th with a fare of 30 tons of fish, something less than a full cargo, only for the desire to market the catch in advance of the arrival home of the vessels that had sailed to the fishing grounds on the Asiatic side of the Pacific. This was the first fare of cod from the Shumagin Islands, a locality since famous in the annals of the Pacific codfishery.

The codfishing fleet of 1865 was composed of rather small sized schooners, most of which were originally built in New England for the Atlantic fisheries, but had sailed around Cape Horn to find employment in the business of the Occident. It is remarkable that one of these that crossed the Pacific, sailed about 5000 miles from home, was only 20 tons, a mere boat in which to make such a voyage and to return loaded nearly to the decks in the water. Following are the names and tonnages (in round numbers), of the fleet: *Equity*, 63 tons, *Flying Dart*, 94 tons, *R L Ruggles*, 75 tons, *J D Sanborn*, 71 tons, *Mary Cleveland*, 91 tons, *Porpoise*, 45 tons and *Taccon*, 20 tons.

This fleet returned with sizable catches, landing a total of 225,000 salt-cured cod. These cod would probably weigh 12 to 18 pounds when caught. After dressing and salting, 3 to 4 pounds of cured cod remained. There was not yet a market and

Pirate Cove codfish station of Alaska Codfish Co., circa 1905–1910. Note the dories at anchor as well as the small schooner.

distribution methods to absorb this quantity of salt cod, so the price fell and the trips were not profitable. This did not totally discourage the merchants, and in subsequent years other vessels were sent to the same area with varying degrees of profit.

The Shumagin Islands were still under Russian control at this time, but after the United States purchased Alaska in 1867, the fisheries were no longer in Russian territory. Still, several vessels continued to fish on the Okhotsk Sea, which remained under Russian jurisdiction, and on several occasions the Russian authorities seized ships' papers and detained vessels until the captains purchased fishing licenses.

In his 1915 report for the U.S. Commissioner of Fisheries, John Cobb described an 1895 incident concerning the *Hera*, which took place on the Russian coast.

> The three mast schooner *Hera*, 369 tons, of the San Francisco codfish fleet was the only American vessel that fished in the Okhotsk Sea. Her catch was all made from 10 to 30 miles off shore. While fishing, the vessel was boarded by a Russian officer, who ordered that fishing cease and that the vessel report at once to the Governor

Sand Point codfish station, circa 1905–1910.

of the district and there procure a license. The master of the *Hera* denied that he was fishing in waters of Russia, as he was fully 10 miles from shore. The officer threatened to seize the vessel if the order was not obeyed. The master complied, and on reporting to the Governor again protested as having any legal right or authority to interfere with him when fishing so far from land, no fishing having been attempted under 10 miles from shore. As before, a protest was not recognized, and $1,000.00 in gold was demanded for a license that must be procured before the vessel would be permitted to leave the port. A compromise was made by the master, giving under protest his personal order for $1,000.00 as the owner of the vessel at San Francisco. The vessel then returned to the fishing grounds, completed her cargo, and returned to San Francisco with a catch of 150,000 codfish, of a net

Dories returning to deliver cod to one of the Shumagin Island codfish stations.
Note the size of the fish in the lower dory, weighing approximately 20 pounds each.

16

Dories out fishing astern of the schooner. The near one is secured to the vessel by the long painter.

weight of 685,140 pounds. The order given by the master was forwarded to the Russian consul in San Francisco for collection; but the draft having been given under compulsion, its payment was refused.

In the following years there was one vessel in the Okhotsk Sea in 1896, none from 1897 to 1902, one in 1903, one in 1904, four in 1905, five in 1906, four in 1907, three in 1908, and one in 1909, the last year an American vessel fished for cod in the Okhotsk Sea.

The difficulties imposed by Russia on foreign vessels fishing off the coast of Siberia flared up again in 1907. Men from a Russian gunboat boarded *John D Spreckles* and *S N Castle*, taking the ships' papers and claiming they were fishing within 30 miles of the coast. The ships returned to San Francisco with small catches of 5000 and 18,000 fish respectively. A few days later, on June 12, the Russians boarded the *Fremont* and seized her papers also. Then on June 19 the gunboat came alongside the *City Of Papeete*, seized her papers, and ordered her to quit fishing.

Captain Sensland, master of the *City Of Papeete*, went on board the Russian patrol boat and showed the commander a letter written by the U.S. Secretary of State, John Hay, which stated that under international law, any nation has the right to fish three or more miles offshore. Alfred Greenebaum, president of the Alaska Codfish Co., had anticipated such an occurrence and provided the letter. The Russian officer then steamed off for advice and returned on July 10, restoring the ship's papers to the master.

On July 12 the Russian patrol boat steamed alongside the *Fremont*, returning her papers and those of the *John D Spreckles* and *S N Castle*. The *City Of Papeete* eventually returned to San Francisco with 120,000 fish, while the *Fremont* had 108,000 fish.

A fully loaded codfish dory with the fisherman at the oars, awaiting his turn to unload the morning catch.
Note the small freeboard on the side of the dory. This illustrates the great sea ability of this small boat.

Cobb's report to the Commissioner of Fisheries contains an extensive summation of the salt cod fishery of the Pacific, including both Alaskan and Russian shores. There are listings and tables of vessels and catches over the years. Beginning in 1865 there was a dramatic increase in the catch of vessels based in the San Francisco Bay area — from 54,000 fish caught in 1864 to 1,467,000 in 1870. From then on the catch diminished, and some years there was less than a third of the 1870 number. By 1891, the San Francisco fleet consisted of five schooners, ranging from 125 to 225 tons, and one brigantine of 328 tons.

That same year the *Lizzie Colby* of Seattle entered the fishery. This was a two-masted vessel of 143 tons, owned by Captain J.A. Matheson of Provincetown, Massachussetts. He had the ship brought around South America, although he came west to Anacortes by railway. This was the first vessel in the Puget Sound fleet to enter the Alaska salt cod fishery, and by 1906 the Puget Sound ships were producing over a million fish per year, all caught in Alaska waters. This overtook the production of the California companies with their combined catch from both the Alaskan and Russian shores.

The fleet grew and the market increased as merchants exerted additional effort to sell the cod. The size of the vessels also increased as the industry developed. Prior to 1900, many vessels had been purchased on the East Coast and brought around via the Strait of Magellan at the southern end of South America.

By the time codfishing off the Russian coast came to an end after the 1909 season, all the vessels were concentrating on the Alaska banks of the Bering Sea, south of Unimak Island, and around the Shumagin Islands (see Appendix III). Cod were to be found almost everywhere in the banks with less than 100 fathoms of water.

Vessels fishing in Alaska waters registered at the nearest Customs House, either Sand Point in the Shumagin Islands or Dutch Harbor on Unalaska Island. Captain John Grotle of Seattle was active in the area after the turn of the century. One

A fisherman returns with an extremely loaded dory. The fish are piled higher than the gunwale of the dory, possibly 250 cod. A load like this was only possible when the ocean was totally calm. This might occur once during the summer.

year when he was fishing in the winter at Unga, he had to take passage on the mailboat to Dutch Harbor, leaving his vessel anchored in Unga Harbor, in order to register at the Customs House.

Codfishing became divided into two different seasons. From late November to March the cod entered the shallow waters of the harbors to spawn, and the winter fishery took advantage of this activity. It operated from permanent shore stations and was primarily based in the harbors. The summer season took place on the offshore banks, and this fishing was conducted from the vessel. Cod were abundant in many locations, and during the summer they were found here today and elsewhere tomorrow. Thus the captain had to move from place to place to locate the schools. Then there were the required trips back to harbor to replenish the fresh water.

Shore stations were constructed in various harbors on the Shumagin Islands and Sanak Island, with the men living in bunk houses and curing and storing the salt cod in open warehouses. Each station might employ from six to a dozen fishermen. By 1915 there were 17 shore stations in operation, taking over a million fish each year, and in the following years they produced approximately a third of the total Alaska catch. Of the total, 14 were owned by California fish packers and three by Alaska residents. The stations in Unga Harbor, Falmouth Harbor, and Eagle Harbor, previously owned by the Seattle and Alaska Codfish Co., had all been sold to San Francisco companies by 1910.

A fisherman waiting to unload the morning catch.

At the shore stations, the men had breakfast in the company mess hall, launched their dories, weather permitting, and rowed a short distance to a spot each considered good. At this time, the dories did not have engines. They were sailed or rowed by oars. Once the fisherman reached his spot, he anchored the dory and cast one hand line over each side of the dory. When the dory was loaded with cod, the fisherman rowed or set his sail and returned to the station wharf, where he unloaded his catch, had dinner, and returned for a second trip.

At the end of the day, all the fishermen working together had to dress and salt the cod. When the weather was cold, many of the fish would be frozen. The fishermen broke off the head and removed the entrails, after which the splitter split the fish from head end to tail and, on the return stroke with the knife, removed that portion of the backbone behind the belly cavity. The fish were washed and trucked into the warehouse, where the salter laid each fish open in a large wooden tank and applied a generous amount of coarse salt, sufficient to cure or preserve the fish.

The companies that owned the stations each had supply schooners, which would arrive in Alaska in November with the fishermen, unload the salt and supplies for that station, and possibly sail to another station with supplies. When unloaded, the schooner would normally anchor in a safe harbor for the winter. Then after the cod had departed from the shallow harbors, the winter's catch was loaded on the vessel and transported to either San Francisco or Puget Sound. This same vessel often returned later for the summer fishery.

Starting in about 1915, there was an unexplained change in the migration pattern of the codfish, and the result was that the fish began to disappear from the harbors. By 1930 there were not sufficient numbers to support the inshore winter fishery, so the shore stations were closed. From then on all of the cod were caught by the offshore vessels, primarily in the Bering Sea.

In 1915 there were six Alaska vessels, all under 35 tons, in the offshore fishery. Washington companies had eight vessels, while California had seven. These ranged in size from the smallest, the 138-ton, two-mast schooner *Fortuna* of the Northern Codfish Co. of Seattle, to the 413-ton *Wawona* of Robinson Fisheries Co. in Anacortes. The majority were over 225 tons and had been constructed in California and Washington for the lumber trade.

A fisherman returns with a poor catch for the morning – about 40 or 50 cod.

In the San Francisco Bay area, the principal companies were Alfred Greenebaum's Alaska Codfish Co. at Redwood City, and the Union Fish Co. at Tiburon, managed by Chris Hale and later Charles C. Cox. There were other men and firms involved that came and went as the profits varied.

In the Puget Sound area, the first records of the codfishery name Captain J.A. Matheson, who came from Provincetown, Massachusetts, and established his plant in Anacortes with his schooner *Lizzie Colby*. Later he added the three-mast schooner *Fanny Dutard*. This vessel operated until 1930. Captain Norman Matheson, nephew of the owner, was master for many years and known among fishermen as "The Squealer" because of his high-pitched voice.

A loaded dory is returning to the schooner. The fisherman has been under sail and then took out the oars just before coming alongside the vessel. The oars give him more control. There are probably 1500 to 2000 pounds of fresh cod in this dory. This represents half a day's catch. He will pitch the fish onto the schooner, then move the dory aft out of the way. After the dories have been unloaded from the second fishing trip and the fishermen have had their dinner, all of the dories will be hoisted on board and secured for the night.

The schooner *John A* at anchor in the Shumagin Islands.

In 1896, Tracy E. Robertson established the Oceanic Packing Co., with a plant in West Seattle. He outfitted the schooner *Emma* and sent it north. In 1897 the company dispatched the schooner *Swan* and the brigantine *Blakeley*. It operated for several more years. In 1902 the Seattle and Alaska Codfish Co., which was founded by Captain John Grotle among others, took over the plant of the Oceanic Packing Co. In 1910 the Seattle and Alaska Codfish Co. sold the vessels and shore plants in Alaska to California interests and immediately formed the Pacific Coast Codfish Co. This firm, later purchased by my father, Captain J.E. Shields (see Appendix I), operated in the codfish trade until 1950. Its three-mast schooner *C A Thayer* was the last vessel to fish for cod.

West Seattle was also home to the King and Winge operation.

In 1904, W.F. Robinson purchased the two-mast schooner *Alice* and established Robinson Fisheries Co. in Anacortes. He added the three-mast schooner *Joseph Russ* in 1905. Charlie Foss was captain of the *Russ* until it was lost on Chirikof Island in the spring of 1912. The *Joseph Russ* was replaced by the three-mast schooner *Wawona*, and Captain Foss continued until his death on August 14, 1935, when he was entering Unimak Pass on the Bering Sea side, homeward bound with a full cargo of cod. His body was buried on Akun Head overlooking the Bering Sea where he had fished for so many years. Captain Tom Haugen then took command of the *Wawona*. Robinson's son-in-law, John E. Trafton, later took over management of the firm and continued until 1947.

―――――◈◈◈―――――

For the commercial codfishing companies based in San Francisco and Puget Sound, the dory was the basic tool for fishing. The fishermen on the Grand Banks, the Labrador Banks, and Georges Banks out of Gloucester developed it, and no other

The *Maid Of Orleans* with a full load of lumber prior to her days in the codfish industry.

small craft was its equal. The Pacific Coast companies generally purchased their dories from shops located in or near Gloucester.

The dories used on the West Coast were called 14-foot dories because the bottom was 14 feet long. There was an overhang both fore and aft to make the overall length about 18 feet. The dory flared out in every direction and accordingly rose with each swell. Between 1910 and 1925 the dories were rowed by hand with oars. Some also had a small sail. In the bow was the wooden anchor windlass, commonly called the gurdy, for hoisting the anchor.

Each fisherman had to row his dory from the vessel to his selected location, possibly as far as a mile from the mother ship. When he was satisfied about the location, he would cast the anchor to hold him there against tide and wind action. If he had used the sail, at this time he would furl it and stow it on the starboard side of the dory.

After the anchor was cast, he would toss fish lines with several baited hooks over each side of the dory. To retrieve the line, the fisherman would stand facing aft. As he hauled in each fish line by hand, the slack line fell at his feet. There were kit boards or dividers across the dory. When the fish came to the surface, the fisherman would take it on board in the after portion and remove the hook. He'd cast the line over the side again, then cut the throat of the fish so it would bleed. After

The *Charles R Wilson,* loaded with lumber, at the discharge wharf prior to codfish period.
Note the size of the deck load and how deep in the water the vessel lies.

maybe 50 fish were in the after section, he would transfer some of them to the bow space so as to keep the dory on an even keel fore and aft.

This would continue until the dory was loaded to capacity for the weather conditions or, if fishing was slow, until it was time for dinner. At that point the fisherman would row back to the schooner, unload the catch, and come on board to eat, after which he would return for a second attempt at fishing.

In the evening, after all of the fish had been pewed onto the deck of the vessel, the dories were hoisted on board regardless of how good the weather might appear. Each dory had a rope strap in both the bow and stern, and the hoisting hooks were slipped into them. The first dory was landed on deck with blocking beneath to fit the sheer contour of the bottom fore and aft. Then the kit boards, seats, and loose gear like the fishing reels and bailer were placed on the bottom. The bait bucket, anchor gurdy, and other larger items were taken from the dory and placed on deck. When the dory was fully open, the next one was placed inside and all of its equipment likewise stowed on the inside bottom or removed. Five or six dories were thus nested one inside the other. The stack or nest was lashed securely to the deck to prevent damage should a sea cross the deck. The *John A* carried up to 22 dories, which meant there were four nests or stacks of five or six each.

The dories were launched, weather permitting, each day at about 4:30 a.m. and returned after the second daily fishing trip at about 5 or 6:30 p.m. This appears to be an awfully long day, but it must be remembered the fishermen lived on the

Schooner *C A Thayer* at a wharf in southern California, off-loading a cargo of lumber from Washington or Oregon mills. The vessel has considerable freeboard as the deck load has already been removed.

vessel. They had breakfast within a few minutes of waking in the morning. Likewise, after the dories were hoisted on board and secured each night, there was immediately dinner and then they were off to the bunks for sleep. Therefore, in almost every case there was adequate time for sleep and rest.

———⊰◈⊱———

Most North Pacific codfishing was conducted from sailing vessels, which acted as mother ships for the dory fishermen. In the earliest days before the turn of the century, many of the vessels in this fishery were two-mast schooners from the East Coast, where they had formerly been employed in the codfishery out of the New England states. These vessels suited the industry well. Codfishers needed a ship that could float all the equipment required and still have space for the cargo of fish. An engine would have consumed a considerable portion of the cargo space, and the fuel would have further limited the carrying capacity, but with a sailing schooner, an engine was not required for the passage to and from the Alaska grounds.

On the Pacific Coast there was a demand for lumber to be shipped from the mills of Northern California, Oregon, and Washington to San Francisco and Los Angeles area. Specially designed two-, three-, or four-mast schooners were developed for this trade, and several hundred such vessels were constructed. They had wide beams and somewhat blunt hull lines, designed to carry large loads southbound and to return north without need for ballast. They had capacities of

The *Joseph Russ* of the Robinson Fisheries Co. of Anacortes, homeward bound. Note all of the patches on the sails and the missing fore topmast, which was carried away. Several dory sails are set to dry as the season was over. This vessel was similar in size to the *John A* and was fishing at the same time period. In 1912 she was lost on the rocks of Chirikof Island in the spring when bound for the Alaska Banks.

from 200 to 800 tons. The West Coast lumber carriers did not have the fine streamlines on the hull body typical of the vessels of Atlantic Ocean commerce. Here speed was secondary to cargo capacity and ability to operate with smaller crews.

Shortly after the turn of the century, however, steam replaced sail and the steam schooner was developed to carry lumber on the West Coast. These were considerably larger and had a steam engine for propulsion rather than depending on sail alone. Thus the sailing vessels became obsolete and were available on the market at any price a purchaser might offer. Many of these fine schooners were bought by ship breakers and burned, but the codfish and other fishery companies soon recognized this bonanza for obtaining good vessels at minimal costs and purchased many of the schooners. The *John A*, the first schooner purchased by the Pacific Coast Codfish Co. of Seattle, was a typical small three-mast schooner, no longer economical to operate in the coast lumber trade.

Several changes were necessary when a ship was converted from the lumber trade to codfishing. Typically, the forward steam donkey engine was removed from the forward deckhouse, and the galley was installed instead. The after cabin remained unchanged except for the addition of several more bunks. The after cabin on the *John A* was extended forward about 20 feet to allow additional bunks for the dressing crew. On many of the other schooners, the foc's'le in the forward

Hall Brothers shipyard built many schooners at Port Blakely, Washington, from 1881 to 1903, including the *Sophie Christenson* and *Wm H Smith*. Note the minimal facilities. The shed contains the band saw and planer. All other work was done in the open.

portion of the hold was made large enough to accommodate most of the fishing and dressing crew . On deck, several wood and steel tanks were secured to hold fresh water for the extended fishing voyage. Some of these vessels had a new gasoline or distillate engine installed to hoist the anchor. Otherwise, the vessel remained as before. There was no space required for engines or fuel, so the main portion of the hold was available to cure and store the salt cod.

Many fine schooners had been constructed in the shipyards on Humboldt Bay, California, by either Hans Bendixsen or Peter Matthews. All were very similar except in size. *Maweema*, *Wawona*, *C A Thayer*, *Charles R Wilson*, *Azalea*, *Vega*, and *Louise* were some that entered the codfishery. Many were somewhat larger than the *John A* and were relatively good sailers. Similar schooners were constructed on San Francisco Bay, on Puget Sound, and at other locations. By 1910 to 1915, most of them had been replaced by steam schooners.

Captain J.E. Shields' *Sophie Christenson* and *Wm H Smith* of the Union Fish Co. of San Francisco were two of the vessels constructed in the yard of the Hall Brothers at Port Blakely, Washington. These two four-mast schooners had been previously employed in the offshore lumber trade to South America and the South Pacific islands before entering the Alaska salt cod fishery.

Anchoring the vessel was no small task. At this time the codfish vessels used a patent or Navy anchor with no protruding stock. The schooners were fitted with a windlass to hoist or heave in the anchor. The windlass on the port side was used for all the normal anchoring. The windlass had a drum on this side adapted to handle both chain and cable. The *John A* had a 2000-pound anchor that could be hauled into the enlarged hawse pipe, allowing the patent anchor to be secured there.

When the schooners were built, the anchor gear was intended for use in harbors and consisted of a horizontal drum. The anchor cable and chain were wrapped three times around the drum. The anchor chain was made in lengths of 15 fathoms (90 feet), and a sufficient number of these lengths, called shots, were shackled together to provide the necessary "scope" of chain or cable to safely anchor the vessel. These early 1900 cod schooners generally had one or two shots of chain attached to the anchor, and then perhaps 60 fathoms of "cable laid" or four-strand rope was attached to the chain. Next there was another shot of chain, so when the vessel was at anchor there would be 15 to 30 fathoms of chain, then 60 fathoms of cable, and the next 15-fathom shot of chain was held on the windlass so there was chain in the hawse pipe to prevent chafing of the cable rope portion. In bad weather, the captain would pay out the chain in the hawse pipe and another 60 fathoms of cable, leaving a last shot of chain to wear in the hawse pipe. As soon as the weather permitted, this last 60 fathoms of cable had to be hauled in to prevent the first 60 fathoms of cable-laid rope from chafing on the bottom.

When anchoring, first the chain next to the anchor and then the cable had to be overhauled over the drum to allow the anchor to reach bottom. The drum holding the chain or cable did not have a mechanism that allowed it to rotate backward under control of a brake as normal windlasses did. When heaving the anchor in, several men were required to hold the slack portion of the cable tight on the drum to provide the necessary friction. The wet cable was exceedingly stiff, and the seamen used great quantities of ashes to provide additional friction – something like sprinkling ashes under automobile tires in the snow.

There were rocks on the bottom in many locations where fishing was conducted. These rocks would chafe on the rope portion of the anchor line and at times wear through. At other times the rope would break when a strain was applied. In either case, the vessel was adrift. After the 1920s the vessels had all-chain anchor lines.

In the Bering Sea, the cod banks are far enough offshore that the vessel could drag the anchor several miles without being in danger of drifting ashore. Further, in the Bering Sea most of the storms either blow parallel to the shore or are from the southeast and hence would blow a vessel away from the beach. During these storms the vessels fishing around the Shumagin Islands in the North Pacific either had to remain wherever they were or make sail and seek shelter. Many times the schooner would lie broadside to the sea and roll the rails under, flooding the deck with water.

The codfish schooners *Maid of Orleans* and *John A* (right), moored at the West Seattle pier. To the left is the West Seattle ferry, circa 1912. The Pacific Coast Codfish Co. purchased the *John A* in 1911 and the *Maid of Orleans* the following year. The latter vessel had been employed in codfishing by the Seattle and Alaska Codfish Co., and John Grotle had been captain.

Captain John Grotle at the steering wheel of the schooner *C A Thayer*, moored near the Ballard Bridge in Seattle, circa 1930.

CHAPTER 2

EARLY CODFISHING DAYS FROM PUGET SOUND WITH CAPTAIN JOHN GROTLE

Captain John Grotle, a Norwegian-born fisherman, came to Seattle about 1890. He made many trips north in various vessels, transporting men and supplies for the gold fields. He was also engaged in the salt codfish industry for 36 continuous years, beginning with the 1899 season.

In 1900, Captain John traveled to Boston and purchased the 110-foot *Carrier Dove*, a two-mast schooner of 83 tons that had previously been employed in the codfishery of the Grand Banks and Georges Banks. Captain John sailed the vessel to South Amboy, New Jersey, and took on a cargo of blacksmith coal for transport to Seattle. The 18,000-mile voyage took the vessel around South America via the Strait of Magellan.

In Seattle, John Grotle and several others had formed the Seattle and Alaska Codfish Co., which also included the two-mast schooners *Nellie Colman* and *Lizzie Colby*. The latter vessels were of comparable size.

On April 22, 1901, the *Carrier Dove*, under Captain Grotle, departed Seattle for the Bering Sea and conducted one-man open-dory fishing there. On May 9 they stopped at Cape Mordvinof, on the north side of the Alaska Peninsula, to obtain fresh water. Here they took on board four men desiring passage north along the shores of the Bering Sea. On June 6 these four new crew members deserted and rowed a dory ashore. This was during the time of the Alaska gold rush. On June 19, several members of the crew of the *Lizzie Colby* came on board for a visit and reported that they had been ashore where the deserters had landed and found two of them shot to death on the beach. The other two miners were never found.

The *Carrier Dove* completed the fishing trip, returning to Seattle on August 24 with 50,000 large salted cod. As there were only seven fishing dories on the vessel, this was a good catch.

On November 22, Captain Grotle took the *Carrier Dove* north with fishermen and supplies to construct a shore fishing station at Falmouth Harbor on Popof Island in the Shumagin Island group. After construction was completed, the fishermen operated from both the shore facilities and the anchored schooner. The cod came into the shallow waters of the harbors to spawn during the winter months and thus were plentiful. The fishermen launched their one-man dories and rowed up to two miles to a location each man considered favorable. On many days the fishermen could not proceed as the ice on the harbor was too thick for them to break with the oars. On other cold days, some of the fish would freeze in the dory and the fisherman would have ice on his mittens or gloves. Nevertheless, Captain Grotle and the vessel returned to Seattle with 34,967 salted cod. He would only accept fish with a minimum length of 28 inches, which would weigh 14 to 18 pounds.

The Seattle and Alaska Codfish Co. also constructed shore stations at Squaw Harbor and Unga on Unga Island and at Eagle Harbor on Nagai Island. There were many other shore stations on islands in the vicinity, owned by codfish companies with plants and offices in the San Francisco Bay area. The Seattle and Alaska Codfish Co. was the only one that had shore stations in Alaska and plant and headquarters in the Puget Sound region.

West Seattle plant of the Seattle and Alaska Codfish Co., circa 1905, with salted cod drying in the sun.
Note the masts of two of the schooners at the wharf.

Captain Grotle continued in this fishery, making at least two voyages to Alaska each year, one winter and one summer trip. He was married and had three children, but with this occupation there was very little home life during those years. He was captain for the Seattle and Alaska Codfish Co. from 1901 to 1910, then spent another 22 years with the Pacific Coast Codfish Co., where my father was first the sales agent and later owner. Over the years, Captain Grotle was in command of many different vessels owned by both companies, including the *Nellie Colman, Maid Of Orleans, John A, Charles R Wilson, C A Thayer,* and *Sophie Christenson.*

Navigation at this time depended on the captain's skill at using his chronometer, sextant, and navigation tables from the nautical almanac, which predicted the sun's location every day. He also had a taffrail log, similar to the odometer on a car, which registered distance traveled.

The vessels had no engines and were propelled only by the wind in the sails. There was no reverse gear, so the approach to land was precarious. It had to be made during daylight, with sufficient visibility to recognize the local landmarks. Further, there were no towboats for assistance. Many times a vessel had to "heave to" or, in landsman's terms, just wait where it was. These small vessels, however, were good sailers and could beat offshore, provided the wind was not too strong.

Another view of the Seattle and Alaska Codfish Co. West Seattle plant.

Great skill was required on entering a harbor, as the shores were very rocky. Should a vessel strike bottom or the shore itself, there was generally sufficient sea or waves running that the vessel would immediately be damaged beyond salvage. The crew had to be ready to lower the sails and to drop the anchor. Many times they entered these western Alaska harbors during snowstorms and freezing weather. Some of the sails would be stiff with ice and could not be lowered easily. Still, the vessel had to be brought to a wharf or to anchor.

On returning to Seattle, the captain sailed the vessel into Seattle Harbor without towboat assistance. Occasionally the vessel was anchored in the inner harbor between where the shipyards are now and Duwamish Head. Then a dory was launched to run a line or hawser to the company wharf on the West Seattle shores, and after heaving the anchor, the vessel was hauled to the wharf.

These years of fishing were not without occasional loss of life. The worst disaster occurred after the *Nellie Colman*, a two-mast schooner owned by the Seattle and Alaska Codfish Co., departed Unga, Alaska, on November 19, 1905, with a cargo of salt cod. The vessel was under the command of Captain Andrew Johnson. There were 12 crew members; the captain's new wife; Miss Aune, sister of Captain Chris Aune, a long-time codfish captain; and the fishing crew from the station,

The three-mast schooner *John A* on the Bering Sea cod banks about 1916. Note the vessel is riding deep in the water, which indicates this is at or near the end of the season. The main deck is about the level of the white line, so the vessel has only about two feet of freeboard. The vessel is at anchor and the riding sail is set to hold the schooner heading into the wind rather than possibly lying broadside to the swells and rolling considerably.

The starboard side of the *John A* during the 1921 season, showing the fish dressing crew. The planks on edge are called "checkers," and they contained the fresh fish and prevented them from sliding across the deck as the vessel rolled.

numbering 29 persons in total. The wreckage and 15 bodies were found on the shores of Yakatanga Bay the next February. No one knows what occurred, but the North Pacific Ocean has most severe storms in the winter.

———⟫◆⟪———

In the fall of 1910 the Seattle and Alaska Codfish Co. sold all of its holdings to San Francisco firms. This included both the vessels and the shore stations in western Alaska. The southern companies made this purchase to eliminate some of the competition. There still remained the Matheson Fisheries Co. in Anacortes with the vessel *Fanny Dutard*, and the Robinson Fisheries, also in Anacortes, with the schooners *Alice* and *Joseph Russ*. Further, the schooners *Fortuna* and *Vega* were employed by King and Winge of Seattle. However, none of these Puget Sound firms at that time owned or operated any shore stations in Alaska. The sale of the Seattle and Alaska Codfish Co. eliminated the last Puget Sound company owning or operating a shore station in Alaska.

The former owners of Seattle and Alaska Codfish Co. then formed a new firm, the Pacific Coast Codfish Co., and sent Captain Grotle south to San Diego to search for a vessel for the firm. He purchased the *John A*, a three-mast schooner of 131 feet and 282 gross tons.

Captain John Grotle mentions many times in the daily log that the vessel is "rolling the rails under." Here we see this action as the seas sweep the decks while the *John A* is at anchor and lying broadside to the seas. Under these conditions, much damage was done on deck. Often the checker boards and pens were destroyed by seas cresting over the rails. Note the stack of dories and their lashings.

The *John A* was built in Fairhaven, California, on Humboldt Bay in 1893 for the Pacific Lumber Co. of Scotia, California. The vessel was to haul the company's lumber from Humboldt Bay to Southern California, and for this trade she served well. However, by 1911, the John A, like the rest of the sailing vessel fleet, had been displaced by the steam schooners and was on the distress market.

Captain Grotle took command of the *John A* in San Diego for the new company, sailed to San Francisco, loaded a cargo of bulk salt for curing codfish, and continued to Seattle, where the vessel was outfitted as a codfish schooner. The steam donkey engine in the forward deckhouse was removed and the space converted into the galley and mess room. A new distillate engine was purchased and installed to hoist the anchor in lieu of the former steam donkey engine. The windlass was modified somewhat, but the former drum with the anchor rope remained on the port side. The conventional windlass with the wildcat to grab the links of chain remained on the starboard side. Also the former small hawse pipe and stock anchor were retained on the starboard side. A new large hawse pipe was installed on the port side to accommodate a Navy or patent style anchor.

The forward wall of the after cabin was extended forward and bunks were added for the codfish dressing crew. A new foc's'le was constructed in the forward end of the hold, with bunks for 20 dory fishermen. Freshwater tanks were added and other changes made for the new fishing trade. All the necessary equipment, supplies, and dories were loaded on board.

One of the early codfish schooners of the Seattle and Alaska Codfish Co., possibly the *Lizy Vance*.

The *John A* under command of Captain Grotle departed from the Seattle wharf at 10 p.m. on April 20 in tow of the tug *Mystic*. They passed Port Townsend at 5 a.m. on April 22, and at 6 a.m. the tug let go of the schooner with a light southwest wind off Point Wilson. From there the schooner had to sail on her own the full length of the Strait of Juan de Fuca, 90 miles before passing Cape Flattery. In his log, Captain Grotle wrote, "Fresh southerly wind. At 7:00 A.M. blowed away the flying jib."

It required four days from Seattle to reach Cape Flattery and the open ocean. Next there was the crossing of the North Pacific Ocean. This was a distance of 1800 miles by the Great Circle route, but it was much longer in a sailing vessel battling westerly winds. First stop after 22 days was in East Anchor Cove on the southwest corner of Unimak Island. The vessel was prepared for fishing and the freshwater tanks filled. Fishing was conducted off the Ikatan Peninsula at Cape Pankof, where 52,558 large cod were caught. They had to return to East Anchor Cove after 33 days to refill the freshwater tanks. (See Appendix III for charts of the North Pacific Ocean and Alaska Peninsula.)

The next fishing location was east of Caton Island, where they remained until the vessel was fully loaded with 162,931 salted cod. Many storms were encountered and Captain Grotle mentions several times in his log that the vessel was rolling excessively and lying broadside to the seas, with swells cascading across the decks and causing considerable damage. They departed from Caton Island on August 17 for Seattle.

I have included the daily log entries for this trip in Appendix II so that the reader might obtain a better understanding of the difficulties encountered on a codfishing voyage. Otherwise it might appear that the vessel just departed Seattle in

The schooner *John A* Loaded with salt cod. All sails are set for the homeward voyage.

mid-April, fished in Alaska, and returned with a full cargo of salted cod. The log entries show that Captain Grotle fished with the schooner *John A*, first on the banks off Cape Pankof, where he caught 52,558 codfish. Then he took on fresh water and sailed a few miles to the grounds east of Whale Point on the east end of Caton Island, where he completed the voyage on August 17 with 162,931 salted cod on board. On this trip Captain Grotle lost 13 days to unfavorable weather when he was coming from or going to East Anchor Cove to take on fresh water. There were 34 days when the vessel was anchored on the fishing grounds but the weather did not allow dory fishing. Captain Grotle launched the dories a total of 49 times, of which only 27 were full days. Some days the dories were not launched until 9 or 10 a.m., and other days, even though they were launched on time in the morning, the weather deteriorated and fishing had to be terminated before evening.

During this season, two men deserted on two different days by taking a dory and rowing for shore. On one day one of the fishermen failed to return and was presumed to be lost. The weather that day would not have allowed him to row to a safe landing.

Several times during the 1911 season, Captain John notes in his log books that the vessel was rolling unmercifully. When at anchor, a vessel will most times head into the tidal current. When the wind is strong, the vessel will lie facing the wind. However, if the tidal current is particularly strong during a storm, the vessel will lie broadside to the swells and roll the rails under. When this occurs, the decks are filled with sea water and much of the gear stowed on deck is smashed or damaged. On one occasion in 1911, several of the dories nested on the deck were damaged severely.

This excessive rolling was quite common on codfish schooners. They were built with a somewhat shallow draft and fairly wide beams so they could carry a large deckload of lumber as well as that in the hold and not be top heavy. Then when they were empty, they could sail north without ballast. In the codfish trade, however, there was no deck load, and when they departed from Puget Sound or San Francisco there was a considerable quantity of bulk salt in the bottom of the

Deck scene on the schooner *John A* when sailing for home.

hold. During the season this salt was expended in curing the cod, which was then placed in the hold. In both instances the heavy cargo was in the bottom of the hold, which made the vessel bottom heavy or, in seamen's terms, "very stiff." This meant that when the vessel rolled, the return from a roll was far too fast and resulted in its rolling the other way, moreso than if there had been a deck load.

Captain Grotle also makes several entries concerning the rough sea conditions. During a severe storm at Cape Pankof, the schooner *Fortuna*, anchored only a mile to the west of the *John A*, began to drag anchor and drift close. There was danger of collision at anchor in rough seas. On several other days the captain attached a second shot of cable and payed this out to assist the anchor in holding. When the vessel was dragging the port-side anchor and all of the chain and cable were out, the starboard anchor was also set. It was very precarious being at anchor this close to shore.

The *John A* was the largest codfishing vessel Captain Grotle had commanded up to this time, and possibly part of the problem was that the vessel was too large to be fishing in these waters close to shore with the violent storms.

Notwithstanding the difficulties Captain Grotle experienced during the fishing season, 1911 was a successful year for the new company. The catch of salt cod was disposed of, and in the late fall the Pacific Coast Codfish Co. purchased the two-mast schooner *Maid Of Orleans*. The owners were familiar with this schooner as she had previously belonged to the Seattle and Alaska Codfish Co. She was outfitted for the 1912 season with Andrew Slatstrom as captain. He continued on as captain of the *Maid Of Orleans* through the 1914 season.

Captain J.E. Shields taking an observation on the sun while on the *Sophie Christenson*, 1935.

A nest of dories on the deck of the schooner.

After the *John A* was securely moored to the Poulsbo codfish plant wharf, the fishing crew left the vessel and took the passenger steamer to Seattle. My father's office was on the Colman Dock in Seattle, near where the Poulsbo passenger steamer landed. The crew walked to the office to make a draw on the summer's pay. They could not draw the total pay until the vessel had been unloaded, which required about two weeks.

Back at the codfish plant, the sails were cut loose from the masts and rigging, taken on the wharf, and opened to dry before they were shipped to the sail loft of Sunde and d'Evers in Seattle. A crew of local men unloaded the cargo. These men opened the hatches, and using fish pews, a tool similar to a pitchfork but with only one tine, they first pewed the fish to the deck, then to the wharf, and then onto the steelyard beam scale, where they were weighed. Men scrubbed the fish in a dory filled with water from the bay to remove the excess salt and the dried fish slime on the outer skin. Then they placed

In the salt cod industry, the fishing dory has many uses. Here it takes the place of a tank in which to scrub the slime from the skin of the cod. The cleaned cod were then placed in a bucket hanging from the steelyard beam scale to record the catch. This was later replaced by a platform scale. The loaded hand cart was wheeled right onto the scale and its weight recorded. The crew was paid the agreed compensation for the weight delivered.

the fish in two-wheeled carts and took them to the storage tanks in the warehouse buildings. These wood tanks would each hold 20 tons of salted cod. The fish were held there until orders were obtained and then were removed and packed for shipment.

As mentioned, the *John A* returned to Poulsbo at the end of the 1911 season with 162,931 salted cod, which weighed out at 382 tons. The average weight per fish was 4.7 pounds. As the dressing of the fish removed about 50% of the live weight, and the salting shrank the weight in half again, these fish must have averaged 18 pounds when caught.

After the cod was unloaded, the *John A* was thoroughly washed with sea water both on deck and in the hold. The galley was scrubbed and the utensils placed in storage. The halyards and other running ropes were dried and hung in the foc's'le for the winter.

Schooner *John A* moored at the Port of Seattle Fisherman's Terminal (facing page).

The crew unloading the *John A* at the Poulsbo plant of Pacific Codfish Co. in 1911, the first trip of cod delivered to the new company plant. The fish were pewed (forked) from the hold of the schooner to the wharf, weighed on the steelyard scale, scrubbed, and wheeled to the storage sheds (overleaf).

The *John A* has been unloaded and shifted from the face of the wharf to a mooring, with the stern secured to a pile dolphin driven in the sandy bottom of the bay. The bow is secured to the wharf. The packaged fish and all supplies were shipped to or from Seattle on a steam-powered passenger and freight boat, so the wharf face had to be open for this boat to land and discharge or take on merchandise.

The next problem was where to moor the vessel until the beginning of the next season. The Pacific Coast Codfish Co. plant was constructed in Poulsbo in 1911. At that time, all of the packaged cod was shipped to Seattle by steamer from the wharf at the new plant. The wharf had to be available for the steamer to land, so the schooner could not be moored at the face of the wharf. A cluster of piles was driven a short distance east of the wharf, and the vessel was moored with the stern lines going to this dolphin or pile cluster and the bow lines leading back to the wharf.

The salt water of the oceans, and of Puget Sound in particular, are loaded with marine organisms, far more than are found in fresh water. Some of these are teredoes and limnoria, wood-boring creatures that devour any untreated wood in the salt water. Teredoes bore holes in the wood about the size of a lead pencil. They are always beneath the surface of the wood; there is no outside indication of the extent of damage. If the worm by chance comes to the surface on the inside of the vessel, water immediately leaks into the hull. Limnoria are about the size of a sand flea and chew away on the surface, giving an "eaten away" look. The only way to repair the damage is to replace the plank that has been chewed. If the vessel is moored in fresh water for a prolonged period, both of these creatures will be killed, but in the 1910s, freshwater moorage was not an option. Other kinds of marine nuisances are barnacles, clams, mussels, seaweed, and the like. They attach to the surface without damaging the wood. However, they create a large drag on the vessel and will greatly slow its speed. To counteract these creatures, the bottoms of vessels were coated with a paint that inhibited them. In 1911 the commonly used paint contained copper compounds that have since been prohibited due to the harm they cause the environment.

The three-mast schooner *John A* at the Pacific Coast Codfish Co. plant in Poulsbo after completion of the 1911 fishing season.

In 1917 the Chittenden Locks and the Lake Washington Ship Canal were completed, allowing transit of vessels with a draft of up to 30 feet into the fresh water of Lake Union. A vessel moored in Lake Union for 30 days or more would find all of the marine wood-boring creatures dead, but the cells still attached to the underwater body of the vessel. The underbody of wood hull vessels were safe from further action by these creatures while they remained in the fresh water. However, the bottom still had to be cleaned at least once each year the vessel operated again in salt water.

After the Chittenden Locks were completed, Father kept all of the vessels, both his own and those of the Pacific Coast Codfish Co., in fresh water during the off season. Many years the vessels were moored at the Port of Seattle terminal on the Canal, just west of the Ballard Bridge. At other times they were anchored in the middle of Lake Union. Here they were secured side by side, with one heading east, the next one west, and the next east again (see page 182). There would be as many as six vessels thus anchored, not all of the same ownership.

Vessels moored in Poulsbo at the Pacific Coast Codfish Co. wharf.
Next to the wharf is *John A*, *Maid of Orleans*, and *Charles R Wilson* (overleaf).

The *Charles R Wilson* moored to the West Seattle mooring buoy after the return from the 1913 season.

The codfish schooners based in Anacortes were all moored in the fresh water of the Lake Washington Ship Canal or Lake Union after construction of the Chittenden Locks. The San Francisco vessels did not have any freshwater location for off-season moorage and were anchored off the Belvedere/Tiburon plant of the Union Fish Co.

◂◆▸

Sailing day in 1914 for the schooner *Charles R Wilson*, moored at Pier 1, Seattle.

The schooner *Maid Of Orleans* in Seattle Harbor. This vessel was built in San Francisco in 1882 by Dickie Bros. She was 120 feet long and 180 gross tons.

In the 1912 season, Captain John Grotle continued in command of the schooner *John A*, which was outfitted as before, departed from Seattle in mid-April, and was towed to Cape Flattery. The previous year the tow line was cast off at Point Wilson outside Port Townsend, so this year they did not have to sail westward the length of the Strait of Juan de Fuca. During the ocean crossing they met with the same storms and periods of calm with slatting. (Slatting is the term to describe the violent swinging of the gaff on the upper edge of the sail as it moves from side to side with the rolling vessel when there is no wind to fill the sail. When this occurs, most often the throat and peak halyards are slacked to minimize the stress on the sail and rigging.) They stopped in East Anchor Cove for fresh water and to fix the dories and the fish dressing equipment. Again nearly a whole week was lost when they could not sail out of the harbor due to unfavorable weather.

The first stop for fishing was at Cape Pankof. The first day a storm occurred and three dories did not make it back to the vessel. After the storm had subsided, Captain Grotle sent two dories to search for the other fishermen. Two men were located but the third was never found and presumed drowned.

A classic picture of the *Joseph Russ* of the Robinson Fisheries Co. of Anacortes, under the command of Captain Charlie Foss. The vessel is at anchor with most of the dories on the "long painter," a rope attached to the stern of the vessel. There is a slight tidal current in the Bering Sea, and this is enough to string the dories out as shown in the picture. Otherwise they would be alongside the vessel pounding into each other. Note that the inner jib sail has been set halfway up. This is a signal from the captain to each fisherman to return to the vessel. The schooner is deep in the water, indicating this is the last day of fishing and there are enough fish on board to fill the hold or to use up all of the salt. In either case, the season is over. The previous season the fore topmast carried away and was not replaced, thus the odd appearance. The *Joseph Russ* was a successful schooner for Robinson Fisheries until she was lost on the rocks at the west end of Chirikof Island on April 21, 1912. She was replaced by the *Wawona* in 1913.

After about two weeks of fair fishing the vessel left Cape Pankof for the Caton Island banks east of Sanak Island. A return to East Anchor Cove was necessary near the end of June to replenish the fresh water. While in harbor the crew discovered the rudder was cracked. This necessitated sailing to King Cove, where there was a salmon cannery and machine shop. The rudder was removed, iron reinforcing made, and the rudder replaced. The vessel was placed on the beach at high tide once to remove the rudder and again to reinstall it. This operation cost nearly the entire month of July.

Captain Grotle returned to Caton Island and finished the season. His ship's log tells of much stormy weather and rough seas when the deck was filled with water. They caught only 134,000 cod. Again Captain Grotle expresses frustration over the weather and is more than happy to complete the voyage in Poulsbo.

The three-mast schooner *John A* was the first vessel owned by the new Pacific Coast Codfish Co. Here the vessel is homeward bound in 1911 with the first cargo of salt cod. She is "down to the marks," as they say. The white line is at the deck level so there is practically no freeboard between the sea and the deck other than the bulwarks or rail. The stern davits show the falls down to the water, indicating that the dory normally hung there had been launched to take this picture. The cargo weighed out at 382 tons The number of cod on board was 162,931. This year all of the fishing was conducted on the Pacific Ocean side of the Alaska Peninsula. Some of the locations were Cape Pankof near the southeast corner of Unimak Island, east of Caton Island in the Shumagin Islands group, and farther east near Seminof Island. These locations were exposed to the storms of the Pacific Ocean. At times the vessel had to heave anchor and sail to a more protected location.

The *Maid Of Orleans*, under Captain Andrew Slatstrom, also fished these grounds for the Pacific Coast Codfish Co. and returned with 101,000 salted cod.

Ultimately the year proved successful, even though the catch from the *John A* was far less than that of the 1911 trip. In the fall of 1912, Captain Grotle was sent to Southern California to again search the market of idle sailing schooners formerly employed in the lumber trade. He purchased the *Charles R Wilson*, a three-mast schooner of 150 feet and 328 tons, constructed in Fairhaven, California, in 1891 by Hans Bendixsen. This vessel was about one third larger then the *John A*. She was brought to Seattle and fitted with a fisherman's foc's'le in the forward portion of the hold. The steam donkey engine was removed and a 12-horsepower, one-cylinder gasoline engine installed to drive the anchor windlass and a deck winch. An enlarged galley and mess hall were constructed in the forward deckhouse to accommodate a total crew of 35 or more men.

From 1912 to 1916 the Pacific Coast Codfish Co. had a contract with Beardsley Co. of Newark, New Jersey, to supply 500 tons of skinned cod each year, which was part of the reason for the increase in the number of vessels fishing. In 1913 the company had three vessels on the Western Alaska banks – the *Charles R Wilson*, *John A*, and *Maid Of Orleans* – and the catch was respectively 187,000, 140,000, and 105,100 cod.

A dory fisherman returning to the schooner with half a day's catch of cod. He has possibly 150 cod in the dory.

The San Francisco companies and those in Anacortes also had good sales. From the San Francisco Bay area there were the schooners *Galilee*, *Vega*, *W H Dimond*, *City Of Papeete*, and the *Ottillie Fjord*, with a combined catch of 717,000 cod. The Puget Sound schooners *Alice* and *Fanny Dutard* from Anacortes, and the *Fortuna* from Seattle were also on the fishing grounds in 1913, but the *Joseph Russ* was lost in the spring of 1912 on Chirikof Island when bound for the Bering Sea. The Puget Sound catch was 764,000 cod.

In 1914 there were eight vessels from Puget Sound and six from the Bay Area. The total catch was 2,183,000 cod. The Pacific Coast Codfish Co. had four vessels fishing and landed 435,000 fish: the *John A* had 100,000 cod; the *Charles R Wilson* 187,000; the *Maid Of Orleans* 52,000; and the company also chartered the *Fortuna*, a two-mast schooner, which landed 96,000 cod. At this time almost all the fishing was conducted in the Bering Sea on the banks north and east of Unimak Island. There was no fishing west of Unimak Pass.

The fall of 1914 brought major changes. War had been declared in Europe. Food was required and there was an enlarged market. There was also a new demand for lumber in the South Sea islands including Tonga, Fiji, Raratonga, Hawaii, and Samoa. The larger codfish schooners in the Puget Sound fleet, after they returned from the Bering Sea, were cleaned up and loaded with lumber for the offshore voyage. From 1916 to 1921 the *Charles R Wilson* and *John A*, as well as the *Wawona* and *Azalea* from Anacortes, were thus engaged. On the return voyage they brought a cargo of copra (dried coconut) or raw sugar. These winter offshore voyages were quite profitable, but it was a struggle to get the schooners back to Puget Sound in time for the forthcoming fishing season.

Dories tied to the "long painter" behind the schooner
John A, waiting to be hoisted on board for the night.

The dory fisherman pewing the catch onto the schooner.

In 1915 the *John A* under Captain Grotle sailed to Squaw Harbor for fitting out. They tried fishing off Cape Pankof, with poor results, and departed for Slime Bank in the Bering Sea. Fishing there was minimal and the schooner returned to the banks east of Caton Island to complete the trip with 154,000 cod. The *Maid Of Orleans* had 110,000, and the *Charles R Wilson* had 181,000 for the PCCC. The *Azalea, Fanny Dutard, Wawona, Alice,* and *Fortuna* fished from home bases on Puget Sound, and seven vessels fished from San Francisco.

In 1916 the PCCC had the same three vessels. The *John A* under Captain Grotle made the first stop at Sand Point, as there were already three vessels at the harbor at Unga. Supplies, including salt, were transferred to the *Maid Of Orleans*. Eight days were consumed there, mostly on account of unfavorable wind that prevented their sailing south out of the harbor. This year Captain Grotle did not attempt to fish on the Pacific side but headed directly for the Bering Sea. Here he found sporadic fishing during the first portion of the season. The weather was less severe when at anchor than that previously encountered on the Pacific side, but the vessel appeared to be at the wrong location many days. The other vessels found better fishing. On June 10 there were only 13,191 cod on board.

On July 19 Captain Grotle recorded in the log book a catch for that day of 7658 cod. It must be understood that these fish were all over 28 inches long and would each weigh 16 pounds or more, which means a catch of 122,528 pounds of fresh cod for that day – not a small accomplishment. All of those fish had to be split and dressed that day. When landed in Poulsbo they would have shrunk from the cleaning and salt to approximately 30,631 pounds. This was the record day. Most good daily catches were 3000 to 4000 cod, although the were several days with over 5000 cod.

The schooners *John A* (outboard) and *Maid Of Orleans* (foreground) moored
between the company wharf and the pile dolphin, circa 1912–13.

They required one stop for fresh water at Bear River, northest of Port Moller, which consumed nine days from the cod banks. They completed the season with 165,340 cod.

During the period from 1910 to 1926 there was no material change in the operation of this fleet of codfish vessels. The dories were all one-man operations and the fish were dressed and salted on the vessels by a dressing crew. There were no electric lights and therefore the foc's'les were very dark. In the daytime the skylights provided good illumination for normal duties but not enough for reading in the bunks. After dark all illumination was by kerosene lamps. Still the vessels operated very efficiently, producing good catches.

Olaf Kittle returns with his morning catch, circa 1935, after engines were installed in the dories. Olaf is standing among the fish and controlling the engine. Note the cover over the engine and the strap showing in the bow for hoisting the dory at night (there is a similar strap, not shown, in the stern). The extra reinforcing of the side of the dory is visible here, as well as the increased capacity resulting from these additions. At this time the original gunwale of the dory is just above sea level, and without the additions the dory would fill with water. Each dory had a number – even on the starboard side and odd on the port side. The anchor line is thrown over the spray cover. The gurdy for hoisting the anchor is hidden under the spray hood.

CHAPTER 3

THE POWER DORY

In the spring of 1927, the dory fishermen came to the companies and asked for engines to be installed in each dory. Past attempts to install engines involved placing an outboard motor on the stern of the dory, as on other small open boats, but this didn't work because the dory differs in construction. Its stern is very narrow and there is no conventional transom on which to mount the engine. Looking at the problem today, it would have been logical to use a small, one-cylinder, Briggs and Stratton air-cooled engine, but that engine had not yet been invented. One-cylinder gasoline engines of 1 to 3 horsepower were available, but they were quite heavy and required cooling water. One of these installed in the 14-foot dories would have taken up most of the space needed for holding the fish. Further, they were not considered reliable in the wet conditions to be expected in the dories, with fish piled all around the engine. They did not use sparkplugs, but rather the make-and-break magneto system that was often cantankerous.

Some people had installed outboard motors in other open boats by placing the engine in a well constructed near the stern of the skiff. The codfishing companies explored this idea, and I remember Father had a steel well constructed and installed in a dory and tried in Seattle's Elliott Bay. Several other models were tried, each with a flange on the bottom of the well bolted to the dory bottom – one with the flange inside the well and one with the flange outside.

Finally they resolved the problem by constructing the well out of clear-grained spruce. By 1927, most of the dories of the Pacific Coast Codfish Co. and the Robinson Fisheries Co. were modified with a well for the engine, though some of the fishermen chose to remain with the oars and no engine.

Dories fitted with a well could no longer be nested on the deck of the schooner at night, so the companies purchased enough steel davits to hang most of the dories over the side of the vessel. A few were still stowed on deck, blocked up to protect the engine. Unless the weather on the fishing grounds was near perfect, each fisherman removed the engine from his dory every night. Enclosed engine boxes came later.

The first engines used by dories on Father's schooners were Evinrude one-cylinder machines. They were mounted on top of the forward side of the well. The fishermen would steer by rotating the lower unit of the engine in its own brackets. They operated the dories at a speed of about 5 knots. The machine was not protected from weather or salt spray, and when there was a fair load of fish in the dory, there was danger when the engine was running that the bow of the dory would scoop a large quantity of water and possibly fill the boat. Some of the fishermen made modifications that first year, constructing a spray hood on the bow to prevent the boat filling if the bow dipped under a swell.

During winter at the home bases, the companies modifed all the dories by making permanent spray covers, or as we called them, foc's'le heads. They also enclosed the engine so that it could remain in the dory overnight and did not have to be removed and reinstalled every day. There were pockets alongside the engine box where the fishermen stored cans of gasoline and spare hooks and sinkers. Under the foc's'le head was a pocket for storing oilskins when they were not being used.

This dory is bucking into the seas, and the advantage of the spray cover on the bow and the raised sides is evident. This rough water was an everyday experience in the Bering Sea when returning to the vessel.

Olaf Kittle returning to the schooner in a dory loaded with the morning's catch.

The next step was to order 15-foot dories – that is, a dory 15 feet long on the bottom and possibly 19 feet overall. This size increase occurred about 1929, when the *Sophie Christenson* was converted to a codfisher. The larger dories with the engine covers and the foc's'le head could carry 50% more fish.

The Johnson Engine Co. came to the codfish companies with proposals for better engines. First we tried a two-cylinder engine of 2° horsepower with opposed cylinders. This was a great improvement. Next the Johnson Co. made an alternately firing two-cylinder, 4 horsepower model with both cylinders in the same block. Still later they produced a 9.8 horsepower model, which was a larger version of the 4 horsepower engine. We used these until the end of codfishing in 1950. The engines were very dependable, and we were able to get up to ten years of service from each machine. They had to be thoroughly torn down and cleaned at the end of each season.

Later the gunwales of the dories were reinforced with a 2-inch by 12-inch plank secured to the top rail and shaped to the contour of the dory, and a 1-inch by 8-inch board was secured on edge to the inner side of the plank. The ends were fastened forward to the spray hood and aft to the engine box. Thus the dory sides were effectively raised at last 10 inches and greatly reinforced.

Captain J.E. Shields, forward in dory, and Dan McEchern return after visiting another schooner.

Charles R Wilson at a Seattle pier in preparation for the next codfish season in Alaska.

Chapter 4

Preparations for a Codfishing Voyage

In late March or early April, about three weeks before their departure to the fishing grounds, the codfish schooners were moved from Lake Union to the central Seattle waterfront. There was a stop at the Standard Oil Co. wharf to take on gasoline for the deck engines and outboard motors in the dories, stove oil for the galley stove, and lubricating oil to mix with the gasoline as required for the two-cycle outboard motors. Then they would continue the trip through the government locks separating the fresh water of Lake Washington and Lake Union from the salt water of Puget Sound. The drop at high tide was about 12 feet, and more with a lower tide. A towboat was moored alongside and in control.

Before World War II, the piers were numbered from Pier 1 (which is now Pier 51), with numbers increasing to the north. Colman Dock and Grand Trunk Dock were not numbered. Many times Father selected Pier 4 or 5 because they were convenient and not otherwise in use by vessels.

It was quite an occasion for a sailing vessel to be moored on the central waterfront, and they drew crowds of visitors and onlookers. The *Seattle Times* and *Post-Intelligencer* often ran stories concerning the forthcoming voyages to the "Far North." A reader might easily gather that the vessel would set sail from the dock and travel away past Nome, past the Bering Sea, even to the North Pole.

The primary purpose of having the vessels on the waterfront was, I believe, to recruit a crew for the summer fishing voyage. The men who went to Alaska in the summer or those who just followed the sea, so to speak, were accustomed to taking a daily walk up and down the waterfront to see what was going on and to pass the time. Some were scouting the field for a job for the summer.

Many fishermen worked in the logging camps during the winter. They would stay at these remote camps for several weeks or several months, then come to the city for a few days or a few weeks, taking a room in a flophouse on the so-called Skid Road, remaining in the city as long as their money lasted. These men were good workers, the finest, and this was their way of life. The camps were closed in the summer because of the fire hazard, so those jobs were unavailable during that time.

The sidewalk along Railroad Avenue (now Alaska Way) was the place to meet friends and tell tall stories, and the schooner was a fine place to stop and look for people they might know and to swap tales with the onlookers. Men were allowed to walk out on the pier to where the vessel was moored. This was the chance for the schooner captain – who was there in charge of activities like bending sails to the spars, painting the last spots, and scraping down the masts – to recruit a crew.

The men would give the captain a promise that they would sign on to fish or be a fish dresser for the season. It was always quite a worry for the company whether it could recruit a good crew. It was of utmost importance that the men be able to work together and also catch codfish. The whole purpose of the trip was to produce a cargo of salt cod. Only those men who were effectively working when on the fishing grounds were adding to the final catch. Any fisherman or other crewman who did not work on a fishing day did not contribute to the total catch, and a day lost could not be made up.

Charles R Wilson on the Seattle waterfront.

Sophie Christenson moored to the wharf in Seattle (left).

The schooners of the Robinson Fisheries Co. of Anacortes were likewise looking for the better fishermen, so there was some competition. During the Depression years, when jobs were not available elsewhere, there were many men seeking a berth on a vessel as this would provide food and lodging plus some money. In better times, many of these men would have had employment on shore. Day by day over a period of several weeks a crew was shipped for each vessel.

With all the curious people on the dock, it became necessary to have a night watchman on board the vessel moored to the pier. He could sleep in one of the bunks in the after cabin. With the stove there he could heat up something for dinner, or go to one of the local cafes. Just having someone on board was the principal requirement.

One night, at least the story was told to me this way, there were several men living on board one of the schooners. They had gone uptown for the evening with money in their jeans. Apparently they were working during the day and could draw pay, so there was plenty to jingle in the jeans, at least when they left the schooner. Several hours later they returned as a group, having in the interim acquired a goodly quantity of that hot stuff that came in the flat bottle. Needless to say they were feeling no pain.

Out on the wharf they marched to where the schooner lay. The method for getting on board was to take a long step from the wharf to the rigging of the vessel, then climb down the ratlines to the rail and thence to the deck. Each of these happy

The three-mast schooner *John A* in winter moorage on the Lake Washington Ship Canal in Seattle, circa 1935 (facing page).

fellows stepped to the edge of the wharf and then grabbed for the rigging for the next foothold. All was well except the returning fishermen's thoughts were on that day last summer when the codfish were literally jumping into the dory. They forgot that the old man, the captain, had told them that the vessel would be moved over to the salt dock that night. She was gone! As each man in turn reached for the rigging that was not there, into the bay he went, still singing and joking about last summer and the fish they had to let go because there was no more room in the dories.

The three men in the bay, being good Scandinavians, had no trouble swimming, nor did they suffer from the cold water. The *C A Thayer* was moored to the next pier, and two of her crew were standing on the adjoining wharf and heard the commotion. They likewise were not feeling the chill of the night due to "good spirits." The poor fellows in the water must need help, they thought. Down the ladder on the pier they went, only to find the wood steps were covered with seaweed and as slippery as the proverbial greased pig.

"Joe the Blacksmith" was first, and thinking himself strong of arm he grabbed the first swimmer. His hold on the seaweed gave way. Now there were four in the water. Next "Digger Sam" (he used to be a grave digger) tried the same ladder with the same results, and now there were five in the bay. None suffered from the cold as yet. Someone made the remark afterwards that the chorus was rendering all the verses of "Clementine," with the special accent on the foaming brine. At any rate, Big Nick, the Seattle policeman on the waterfront beat that night, finally heard the commotion and went to have a look-see.

By now the happy quintet had drifted across the open slip where the schooner had been moored, then under the next pier and into the slip where the schooner *C A Thayer* was moored. In a little while the watchman on the *Thayer* heard the music arising in his vicinity. He welcomed Big Nick on the schooner to help in recovering the happy swimmers from the brine. They brought the Jacob's ladder out on deck and the two men had it over the side in jig time. Big Nick then made a flying leap from the deck to the top of the vessel's rail, a distance of at least four feet. Before the watchman could stop him, the fearless Seattle policeman was descending toward the water. Now a Jacob's ladder is made with wood treads, but the risers are of rope so the ladder can be coiled up when not in use. Further, the wood treads are somewhat tippy, and some care is required of the person using same. Before Big Nick knew what the score was, one of the swimmers had gripped his shoe. This was just sufficient to tip the tread, and to the great surprise of everyone, there was now one more swimmer in Elliott Bay.

The watchman finally produced a long-handled boat hook, and while keeping himself firmly planted behind the bulwarks, he pulled the men one at a time to the ladder. From there each had to climb the ladder and jump down to the deck. Big Nick, being the closest, was first up and gave assistance to the watchman as the other men reached the top of the ladder.

When all of the men were safely on deck, the watchman led the Scandinavian crowd to the after cabin of the schooner, where a brisk fire was burning in the heating stove. They all stripped off their dripping clothes and hung up the outer garments on the hooks around the stove. The underwear was wrung out and also hung to dry. There were sufficient bunks in the cabin to accommodate all the fishermen, who climbed in between the blankets, shivering every inch of the way. By morning the fishermen were refreshed, the clothes somewhat dry, and they rolled out of the bunks and donned the same damp duds.

How the Seattle policeman made out his report to cover the incident has always been a mystery. Supposedly the story appeared in one of the Seattle newspapers under the heading "The Bay Was All Cluttered Up."

———◆———

All of the supplies for the forthcoming season had to be obtained now. The salt came from California, where it had been evaporated out of the bay water. Until about 1942 it usually arrived as cargo on a steam schooner. It was in bulk in the hold of the steamer and transferred by clamshell bucket to the schooner, which had been moved to the pier where the steamer was moored. The salt was dumped over the open hatch on the codfish schooner and fell into the hold and over the deck. When enough salt had been placed in the first hatch, the schooner was moved so the salt would be dumped in another hatch. All the salt that had spilled on deck was later shoveled into the hold. There was then a tedious job of shoveling the high mound of salt under the hatches into the wing pens – wooden pens that had been constructed in the hold to allow the

Before World War II the piers in Seattle were numbered from Pier 1 (Pier 51 today), with numbers increasing as you travel north. Colman Dock and Grand Trunk Dock were not numbered. Many times Father selected Pier 4 or 5 for mooring the schooners prior to sailing.

salter to remove only enough salt for the day's needs, without having the entire quantity exposed and running down into the excavated area where the salter was placing fresh cod. In the end the salt was nearly level in the hold and was covered with clean canvas. The largest of Father's schooners, the *Sophie Christenson*, required about 500 tons, while the *Charles R Wilson* needed at least 350 tons.

Coal was used in the galley stove, at least until the late 1930s. After that date the *Sophie* had an oil-burning galley stove. The foc's'le stove (there were two in the *Sophie*) and the stove in the after cabin were also fired with coal, which was stored under the floor in the foc's'le. It was delivered in bulk, about five tons, and dumped on the deck at low tide. From there it was shoveled through the skylights on each side of the foc's'le, and by chute down to the coal locker under the foc's'le floor. A great mess was made even though the coal had been well wet down ahead of time. Coal dust was everywhere. It would have been much cleaner if we had loaded the coal before the foc's'le was painted each year. The clean-up job necessitated everything be washed.

Groceries were delivered by truck and stowed in the store room under the after cabin. The after portion of the hold had been closed off with a double-ply tongue-and-groove board bulkhead so as to keep the moisture of the fish hold out. Within this store room, a smaller room was made, with its own door and lined with galvanized iron sheets. The flour was stored in this room, and the metal was to keep rats and moisture out. Normally there were no rats, but along the waterfront they were plentiful and might come on board before sailing day. Should a family of rats get on board, there was no way to get rid of them. All the crew could do was make sure they did the least damage.

Fresh water was contained in steel tanks located in various places both above and below deck. We had at least one tank on each side of the vessel just aft of the foc's'le and separated by a wooden bulkhead from the fish hold. Those below deck were connected to the hand pump in the galley. The pipe entered the tank at the top and extended down to the bottom inside, so if the pipe broke from the working of the vessel, the tank of water would not be lost. The tanks were covered on the inside with a heavy coat of Portland cement and water, mixed to a paint-like consistency and applied when the tank was first installed, then renewed about every three to five years. A man entered the tank through the manhole and applied a coat to all the inside surfaces with a large paint brush. This coat was allowed to dry, the tank was entirely filled with fresh water at the dock, and this water was then discarded. The tank was filled a second time just before it left for the fishing trip. Each tank was filled to about 95% capacity. This left some air space, and there was a large vent at the top of the tank so air entered freely. All of the tanks were equipped with baffles or splash plates, and as the vessel rolled, the water surged through the holes and was aerated. The baffles prevented the water from surging violently from one end to the other and possibly rupturing the tank. The net result was the water remained aerated and sparkling almost like a mountain stream. When water is stored in this manner it will never spoil or turn sour. Water stored in tightly stoppered wood casks, on the other hand, does not have the aeration and will usually sour and spoil within a month. Many of the early explorers lost fresh water through improper storage in tightly stoppered casks. They did not have steel tanks to use as we did. The availability of aerated fresh water contributed greatly to the comfort of men living aboard ships in more recent years.

Gasoline was in steel tanks both on deck and below. They would never pass Coast Guard inspectors today.

All these supplies were each in turn stowed away. Then with about two weeks remaining before the selected sailing date, the sails were brought on board. For many years Father used Sunde and d'Evers Co. on the Colman dock for the storage and repair of the sails of all the vessels. The only other sail loft in Seattle was that of George Broom. There was no particular reason I knew for Sunde's doing the sail work, other than the fact that Dave Dannamen, one of the stockholders of the Pacific Coast Codfish Co., was also an officer of that firm. Then in about 1930, Father purchased a heavy-duty sail maker's sewing machine and set up his own sail loft in the second floor of one of the warehouse buildings in the Poulsbo plant. He would make an arrangement with one of the Poulsbo seine boats or use his own *Phyllis S* to bring the sails from Poulsbo to the waiting schooner. Then the crew would bend the sails, which was the job that attracted the most attention from onlookers walking along the waterfront. Every afternoon there would be a crowd watching. Nothing attracts attention like a large sail partially hoisted on a tall mast. This work on the vessels provided a paying job for a considerable number of the crew and assisted in recruiting fishermen.

Near the end of the days in port, usually on a weekend, the dories would be launched in the bay in Poulsbo, tied in several long strings, then towed to the side of the schooner in Seattle. The dories were last to be loaded because of the room they consumed on the deck of the vessel. The *Sophie Christenson*, with 22 fishermen, carried 24 dories. The *Charles R Wilson* required 16. A few might be lowered down into the hold, but only a few. This was after the installation of the well in the dories meant they could no longer be nested one on top of the other as had been done previously. After the vessel departed for sea, some of the dories would be hung from the davits swung inboard. On the larger *Sophie Christenson*, up to five dories were swung outside on each side.

There were numerous other items required for the trip. All the fishing gear had to be on board. We used hand lines, which were heavy, tarred, cotton fish line. The hooks were of Norwegian manufacture. Lead for the sinkers came in five-pound chunks. Tools of all variety were needed: planes, chisels, drills, hammers, cold chisels, wrenches, etc. You name it,

Deck view of the *Sophie Christenson* with dories on board.

and some day it would be required. In the captain's quarters was the slop chest, a store of clothing and similar items the men would need, especially those who made a "pier head jump" (meaning they decided to go on the voyage the day the vessel was sailing, so they had no clothes with them other than what they were wearing). The medicine chest had to be well stocked, with the contents kept under lock and key, and since the trip lasted for five months, the men required sufficient tobacco to see them through. The company purchased cigarettes "in bond," that is without federal tax stamps, so they had to be sealed by the U.S. Customs agent. This was legal because they would be consumed outside the three-mile limit of the coast.

By agreement with the fishermen, each man owned his own engine. This meant Father had to be convinced there actually were enough engines on board for all the fishermen on the day of departure. Some of the fishermen had taken their engines to a First Avenue hock shop to borrow money. Father had to get the hock slip or receipt from the fisherman, then go to the hock shop, pay the charges, and retrieve the engine. Many of the fishermen did not bother to clean up their engines after the previous trip, so they were not in working condition and Father had to have them overhauled. Other fishermen did not have an engine at all, so it was necessary to purchase one or more new engines from the local dealer,

Sophie Christenson, moored to the wharf in Seattle. Dories were stowed
over the main hatch and on the skids alongside the forward deckhouse.

Pacific Marine Supply Co. We used Johnson engines with longer drive shafts than regular, so had to special order them from the factory in advance. Once the engine arrived, we extended the length five more inches by installing an intermediate shaft with supporting housing. When all assembled, the engine was more than 10 inches longer than standard. This was so the dory could be loaded deeper with cod.

All engines had to be retrieved, overhauled, and bought prior to sailing day, and we also had to have a good supply of spare parts to make repairs during the season, as well as at least two spare engines. With 22 dories on the *Sophie Christenson*, fishing from 45 to 70 days each season, some engine breakdowns were inevitable. When I was captain I used spare parts to repair everything from a broken crankshaft to stripped gears. A fisherman without an engine was not producing fish. On several occasions a fisherman was towed back to the schooner, unloaded his morning catch, and went in for dinner. While he was gone I removed his engine and slipped a spare one in his dory. Then he could continue fishing that day. The engine was repaired when I had the time.

In the end, when sailing day rolled around, the vessel had to be outfitted completely for all that was necessary to run a city of 30 to 50 people for five months. It was a self-contained entity that would not be able to obtain help or supplies from the outside once it left the wharf. It was not until 1932 that any of the schooners had a wireless set.

I believe that the preparations for the 1929 fishing season were the most difficult for Father. The previous year the three-mast schooner *Maweema*, owned by the Alaska Codfish Co. of San Francisco, had been lost on the return portion of its voyage with a full cargo of salt cod. The vessel was sailing from the last fishing position towards Unimak Pass. In dense fog she ran ashore on St. George Island in the Pribilof Islands of the Bering Sea, a total loss. To fill its needs for 1929, the Alaska

Dories were stowed on top of the main hatch.

Codfish Co. gave Father a contract to produce and deliver two vessel cargoes of salt cod to the plant in Redwood City, California. This contract was to be fulfilled with the schooner *Charles R Wilson*, a long-time codfisher then owned by Father separate from the Pacific Coast Codfish Co., and also with the *Sophie Christenson*, a four-master that had recently returned from delivering a cargo of lumber to Suva and was laid up in Lake Union, facing the bleak future of many former proud ships that were sold foreign or burned to recover their metal fastenings. The *John A*, the first vessel the PCCC had purchased, was taken out of layup for the season, and the *C A Thayer* under Captain Grotle completed the fleet. This made four vessels to prepare at the same time, two for the personal account of Father and two for the PCCC. It was an awesome task.

Father hired a crew of carpenters and sailors to work on the *Sophie Christenson* all winter, converting her into a codfisher. This required the construction of a foc's'le below deck, a new galley and mess hall on deck, new pumps, electric plant for 32-volt electric system with batteries, electric wiring throughout, water and gas tanks, etc. On the *Wilson*, which he had purchased from the Pacific Coast Codfish Co. the year before, Father had the after house extended full height out to the rail, thus increasing the available inside space for crew. Captain Jack Kelly was the master.

It was necessary to look beyond the local area for fishermen for the *Sophie Christenson*, since she was new to codfishing from Puget Sound. Captain Bob Firth, a rugged Nova Scotian, was hired. Though it was he who had lost the *Maweema* the previous season, he had a reputation for producing large cargoes of cod, and when Father hired him, Captain Firth brought forth from San Francisco a goodly portion of his former crew. All this required extensive effort on Father's part. I do not know how he arranged for the transportation of all those men to Seattle, as they would not have had the funds themselves to purchase the ticket. I do remember when Hjalmer Larson hit the Seattle waterfront. There was great excitement among the crews of all the vessels as a result, and many men who were working on the vessels took off for several days on one grand spree. Hjalmer and several others made the big house (the city jail) and the court of Judge Gordon, the police judge. Father eventually had to bail out those in jail.

All the purchasing for the four vessels, the hiring of crews, and the coordination of all necessary work being done was conducted from the small office of Room 66, Pier 1. In that office were George Shields (Father's brother) and Esther Strahm. How it was all accomplished was a wonder. And the preparation of ships was not all, for the processing plant in Poulsbo was still working on fish from the previous year, the sales of which were continuing. Lent, which usually falls in March and April, was one of the most important times of the year for the sale of salt cod and could not be lost. Collections had to be made for fish sold, and all the books of each account kept separate. On top of all this, Father was involved in other operations, including being the Seattle sales representative of a large California salt company.

Esther lived in Father's home with our family in the Madrona district at this time, and I remember Father and Esther spending many evenings making out purchase orders for supplies. At that hour of the day they were free from interruptions in the office, especially interruptions by the crew members who came there to bother him for this or that and to make a draw on the summer's wages.

⟫◇⟪

Each voyage of a codfish schooner to the Bering Sea or to the Shumagin Islands took at least five months. The vessel did not put in at any port in Alaska for resupply, so it had to carry, when departing from Seattle, all the necessary food to feed the crew over this entire time. (There were 45 men in the crew of the *Sophie Christenson*. The other schooners had smaller crews.)

The crews were fishing in the Bering Sea, where the air temperature was only slightly above freezing most of the time. The sea temperature in April was about 28°F and warmed up in August to 34°. There was no refrigeration equipment, so they had to take supplies that would keep without cold storage rooms. They carried a generous supply of salt beef and salt pork, newly cured just before the start of the voyage. These were packed in 250-pound barrels, and a daily supply could be removed when needed and placed in clean sea water to remove the excess salt. There was also sweet pickled picnic (pork shoulder) and ham that was very good, and a considerable quantity of smoked hams and bacon. These were hung from nails in the deck beams in the store room, spaced carefully so they did not touch each other. They were of a special cure for the Alaska trade with more salt and smoke.

There was also what was called "fresh meat." Before the start of the trip, the cook would report for duty on board. Each morning Father would bring on board several hundred pounds of fresh beef or pork. The cook cut this up into proper size pieces for cooking. The beef would be cooked in pieces of about two pounds. The pork had to be cut in smaller chunks, generally as pork steaks or chops, and these were baked until thoroughly done. This meat was then placed in metal buckets or tubs, the size for 30 to 50 pounds of shortening, and covered with a hot melted lard or shortening. This excluded all the air and made a tight seal when cooled off. The cans were stowed on top of the salt in the hold, where it was cool. One can was taken to the galley as needed on the voyage. Usually this prepared meat was served twice a week. During the cooking the juice was carefully preserved and stored in quart Mason jars, and a portion removed as necessary to make gravy. This was far superior to any commercial artificial gravy product.

On sailing day, several beef sides were delivered and hung in the rigging. When the schooner reached the Pacific Ocean, the air was much cooler and the meat would keep for at least ten days.

There would be a large quantity of fresh Fleischman's yeast on board. This was broken into grain-size pieces and packed in glass Mason jars with water that had been boiled. This preserved the yeast, necessary for bread baking, for the entire trip.

Butter was packed in half barrels of 100 pounds each. The butter did not need to be soaked to remove the salt.

Eggs were given a special treatment that the produce houses performed for the Alaska trade. Each egg was coated with paraffin so as to close the pores and prevent the egg from breathing through the shell. The coat was so light it could not be detected by the eye, and the cost was only about one cent per dozen. The eggs were then packed in the usual double-end,

36-dozen wood cases and were stored on top of the salt in the hold. The cases were turned every week to prevent the yolk from settling to one end of the shell. If the yolk touched the shell, the egg would spoil shortly after.

Canned fruits and vegetables were stowed at the far aft portion of the store room, with fruit on one side and vegetables on the other. There were fresh apples and oranges, as well as dried fruit for pie filling and to serve on the table, including dried apples, apricots, peaches, prunes, and raisins.

There was a generous supply of flour, as the cook had to make bread for the crew. Father purchased the finest hard wheat flour from Alberta, Canada. This was far better than the soft wheat of Washington. Further, potatoes were in good supply as the crew were mostly meat and potatoes men, and they often turned down the canned vegetables. Six to seven tons of potatoes were required on the larger vessel, and they were stowed near the canned fruit and vegetables, in the store room under the after cabin. Dry peas and beans were a must. Pea soup with salt pork and baked beans with pork were favorites.

There was sufficient quantity of everything to feed the crew for five months, with some remaining in case the voyage was longer. Some cooks were good at budgeting supplies, while others soon ran out of some items.

On the fishing grounds, fresh fish was served as often as possible for the evening meal (supper). Fresh codfish was most often used, as there was always a good supply caught that day. The men never turned down halibut fresh out of the water and sliced and fried. Naturally the need for halibut as bait came first, and only when there was an oversupply did halibut show up on the table. Salted cod, either fully cured or lightly salted, was a staple. It was served with boiled potatoes and a cream sauce.

CHAPTER 5

SAILING DAY

Sailing day for a codfish schooner headed for the deep sea banks of the Bering Sea of Alaska was one of those events a person never forgets. This is the climax of the winter's work of preparation and those days on the Seattle waterfront, loading supplies. If you were a bystander, this day was one long show, the likes of which were sometimes depicted in the most fanciful movies. If you were an old-timer crew member, you might be having a last fling or spree, enjoying the last drinks plus a last visit to the ladies uptown. However, if you were the captain or owner, it was something else indeed.

Sailing day was usually set over a week in advance, but never on a Friday. Not no-how! Saturday was usually not acceptable because the business houses worked half a day and were not open after noon. All the last-minute supplies had to be delivered, including those that were kept under lock and key. The captain had to lock up cigarettes and some other items for the food supply that had been purchased "in bond" and could not be used or opened until the vessel was at sea. It was not safe to have these on board ahead of time as someone might break in and steal them.

Likewise the slop chest clothing came at the last minute. Up until the day before, Father did not know how much to order, as all of the crew had not been shipped. When a man was shipped he gave Father an order for his clothing, oilskins, tobacco, blankets, etc. Father ordered these from the supplier the day before sailing, and the captain handed them out after departure. If there were no slop chest with clothing and gear, each man would have had to go to an outfitter for these items. Since many of the crew had no money before the voyage, some would have gone without the necessary goods. When they took goods from the slop chest, they were normally charged the same price they would have paid in the stores. These charges were deducted from their pay at the end of the summer.

When the groceries came on board several days earlier, the captain took all of the flavoring extracts and cached them in a safe place or a corner of his cabin. Most extracts contain alcohol, and more than once in years past, when the cook had stocked the galley with supplies for daily use including extracts and spices, someone who needed one last drink had downed a whole bottle of almond, vanilla, or maple extract on the first night out or even earlier. It was generally no problem to find out who was guilty, for even several days later the aroma was still present on his breath. But to be short of extracts meant pastries, pies, and cakes would not have the proper taste.

Other items delivered that day were new navigation charts; a supply of fresh bread and meat for two weeks (the latter was wrapped with burlap and hung in the rigging); and the chronometer from Northwest Instrument Co., which had kept it over the winter and finally checked the "rate," the amount of time the instrument gained or lost each day, down to one tenth of a second per day. The office always sent a packet with writing materials, stamps, invoices for the goods on board, a new log book, several previous years' logs for the information of the captain, and a farewell note.

Sophie Christenson at the Bell Street pier in Seattle, circa 1935.

Schooner *Charles R Wilson* on sailing day, circa 1925. Note the starboard anchor
is of the old "stock" type and must be hoisted to the cat head before going to sea.

The captain and one or more experienced men who were not under the influence had to take charge of everything that came on board and stow it where it belonged, as the next day the vessel would be at sea and rolling, possibly with some water on deck from a large swell or wave. They usually had the assistance of several men who were shipping out for the first time and not engaged in the bottled spirits. The old-timers were enjoying the festivities at the local bootlegger or, after the repeal of prohibition, at some nearby tavern.

Father had the names of crew members listed in a book he kept safely tucked in his pocket, and he checked it over frequently to verify all were present. First thing in the morning he came down to the vessel and, along with the captain, checked off in his book the name of every man who could be accounted for. Some had made an earlier appearance and drifted off. Others were known to be dependable and there was no worry about them at this time. There were usually several who landed in jail the night before. No need to get them out yet; they were safe there. Arrangements had previously been made with the Seattle Police Department to deliver them at the last minute, their bail having been assured. Father made his rounds of the taverns and bootlegger joints to see who was at each. At this time, all he needed was to know where they were. Then he was able to go back to the office to complete last-minute work for the vessel. In the later years, when he went out as captain on the *Sophie Christenson*, things were even more hectic, as he would be leaving port and would be

The start of the voyage. The tug has taken the vessel away from the wharf and
is proceeding to the open water of Elliott Bay, Seattle Harbor.

unavailable for at least five months. Back and forth between vessel and office he went, always under a full head of steam. By 12 noon he would set the sailing hour, say 3 p.m. Then he would phone the towboat company to confirm the time, call the Seattle jail to inform them to deliver the men being detained there, go to the jail to pay the fines of those being held, stop at the taverns to pass the word. Until the end of prohibition, he would send a messenger to the bootlegger.

Oh, yes, one other place not to be forgotten was the King County Jail in 1934–40. They had the cook, a man by the name of Bert Van Vreeden. He was a very good cook when off the bottle, but could not control himself in port. (He was such a good cook that the cooks in both the Seattle Jail and the King County Jail offered a reward to the patrolman who brought Bert in each fall. Then Bert was placed in charge of the jail kitchen while the hired cook took life easy.) It was no trouble to get the sheriff's office to make the delivery, and always the deputy at the wheel told Bert that his job would be available again in the fall when the schooner returned. The galley of the schooner would have been put in order and cleaned up by others under the direction of the captain. A good fire was burning in the stove, and a new outfit of cook's clothes was waiting on Bert's bunk. He put them on and strutted like a kingpin in his galley quarters, or up and down the deck. He might even be able to get a stew going on the stove for supper that night before his friends introduced him to the joy juice that some crew member had smuggled on board without being caught by the captain.

The tug is moored under the starboard bow of the schooner and slowly moves the vessel out of the slip and into the harbor.

As the assigned hour approached, the tug pulled alongside and tied up. Several taxis would arrive from the local places where a few fellows had congregated, the doors opened, and the fishermen literally rolled out on both sides. I have often wondered how all those large men were able to squeeze into that small space. A taxi in 1929 was not as roomy inside as today's models are, and at that time it was not at all comfortable for more than two to sit side by side on the back seat. Still, that taxi might disgorge up to six bulky fishermen.

By this time Father was standing at the gangplank, if there was one. Otherwise he'd be at the ladder. Each man was frisked up and down for that last bottle he intended to take along. When Father pulled the bottle from his pocket, there would be a strong cry that this was needed for sobering up on. Father knew otherwise. It would all be killed that day and add to the problem of getting the entire crew sober. The bottles never got that far, because with one sweeping motion Father would snatch it from the fisherman's pocket and send it sailing out over the side and into the bay.

The men brought their sea bags and placed them in the foc's'le to stake out a bunk or just left them lying on the deck. I do not remember a sailing day when it was raining hard, so usually nothing got wet.

Back and forth Father went. One more trip to the office for something he needed if he was to be the captain. His notebook with the crew list was in and out of his pocket many times as the names were checked and rechecked. Each time someone had slipped away when Father was not looking. It was not always the same person. After the taverns were legal this did not concern him as much, as the wandering fisherman could be found at the nearest watering place. The big problem was those men who had not yet put in an appearance. Everyone would be given the quiz: had he seen Three Finger Pete or Big Nick or whoever? Father knew where each would hang out. Then a frantic call disclosed that the man was asleep in his room. His landlady would give the information. Someone would make the trip to retrieve the poor fellow.

Finally Father would let out the cry "SINGLE UP!"

These were the words everyone was waiting for. There would be a scurry, by those in condition, to take in all the mooring lines between the vessel and the wharf except one manila line fore and aft. The other lines were generally steel wire so they would not chafe and wear on the cleats or edge of the wharf.

Father would go over his book one last time. Each name was given the final mark. First the dory fishermen, who were most important for the voyage; then the cooks; next the splitters and salters; and last the ordinary dress gang men, those that could be replaced if needed. It often happened that a fisherman could not be located at the last minute, so someone who had been in the dress gang for several years and was known as a possible fisherman was shipped in his place. The place in the dress gang would be filled by someone who was on the dock, hoping and waiting for just such a chance. This man would jump on board without any sea bag or other clothing. He'd purchase his clothing, blankets, oilskins, and other necessities from the slop chest. The men who got these last-minute jobs were said to be "taking a pier head jump."

Then Father would call, "LET GO!"

The last mooring lines were cast off. The tug would slowly move the schooner out of the slip backwards, as they were always moored with the bow towards the shore.

After clearing the end of the wharf and any other vessels moored there, the tug would let go of the mooring lines and place the main towing line on the bow of the schooner, swing around, and tighten up. The schooner would follow. They were now off and away for Alaska!

There were several farewell wishes from those left behind as the vessel departed from the pier. How you felt now depended on where you were, whether on the vessel or on shore. On shore it was a relief to most of us, except for Father. Possibly he had one or two more schooners to sail within the next week. If this was the only one, or the last one, there was a tremendous letdown in the level of activities for that day. Even though there might be another vessel due to depart the next week, there was no more work for that day. Rest was needed.

If you were the captain on the vessel, it was a different story as the voyage was just beginning.

⋙◆⋘

After the vessel departed from Seattle in the years up to 1945, or from Poulsbo after 1946, the first chore for the captain was to assign someone to steer the vessel. Even though the towboat was ahead on the tow line, it was still necessary to use the rudder of the schooner for steering so she would follow in a straight line behind the tug. Generally two men were assigned this task: one of the mates if he were sufficiently sober, and one other man. Only one man was required at the wheel, but it was better to have a second man available as lookout and to attend to any trouble that might arise.

The captain usually had other duties to perform. He had to keep close watch in the galley to be assured the cook would have something on the table for dinner. There were always some in the crew who wanted to eat. At times there were many others still drinking, consuming that last bottle they had sneaked past the captain at the gangway. During the days of prohibition, I saw some of the men bring whole gallons of moonshine on board. This would keep many men under the influence for a whole day.

Those bottles, whether gallons, pints, or half pints, all had to be rounded up. This was possibly the most important job of the minute. Some were held by the captain to be doled out over the next several days as the men sobered up. These bottles were kept safely locked up in the captain's cabin. He was never able to round up all of them, as some of the crew, with the knowledge of past experience, cached bottles in their bunks in the foc's'le. These would all be consumed before the drinking was terminated. However, it was to the advantage of all that the supply in the possession of the crew members when departing should be as small as possible. The more men who could be prevented from consuming additional alcohol and made to eat some food, the better. Others were put to bed to sleep off the next several hours.

The *Wawona* of Robinson Fisheries Co. of Anacortes on sailing day at the Port of Seattle Bell Street pier, circa 1940.

I believe it was in 1934, the first time I went to sea with Father, that one of the fishermen attempted a head-first transit from the deck to the foc's'le. The good old *Sophie Christenson* had sailed from the Port of Seattle Fisherman's Wharf across the ship canal from Ballard. We experienced no undue problem in the passage through the locks, and none of the crew escaped. But when this man took his header, he sustained a severe cut under one eye. The other men brought him back to Father, the captain. The man was suffering no pain, although blood was streaming from the wound. Father attempted to apply a bandage to hold the edges together, but the gash was too deep for this simple treatment. There were needles and sterile cat gut in the medicine chest and these would have been used had the vessel been at sea where no doctor was available, but the vessel was at the time passing through the channel and below the locks with the tug still alongside. Father had the tug stop the vessel off the Golden Gardens where the Shilshole Marina is now located. The *Sophie*'s anchor was dropped and the man was taken to the U.S. Public Service Hospital, also known as the Marine Hospital. Here the proper stitches were taken and the man returned to the vessel. It was not until the next day that he experienced pain from the accident.

Tragically, more than once a man jumped over the side of the vessel while the towboat was ahead on the long tow line. There was no way of getting the attention of the towboat for a stop, and the poor men were never found again. In 1929, the splitter on the *Sophie Christenson* jumped over the side while the vessel was towing out the Strait of Juan de Fuca under the command of Captain Bob Firth. He was never found. I remember Father received a phone call late one night informing him of George's accident. He was the head splitter, so Father had to round up another man, Tony Larson, who lived near Silverdale. Father drove to that town, convinced Tony that he was needed, rounded up his clothes, and drove him to Neah Bay where the schooner was waiting.

So much for the condition of the crew on leaving. The captain had to oversee that all the dories on deck were made secure and that supplies delivered earlier in the day were stored in their appropriate places, so that on the following morning, when the vessel reached the Pacific Ocean and sea conditions, nothing would be damaged. Watches had not yet been set, so there were no regular mates on duty to take charge. Further, the mates, being old-timers, were possibly as far under the influence as others and not in condition to perform duties. There were always enough men not under the influence to perform the necessary tasks, so everything was attended to in some condition or fashion. All they needed was direction, and to this end they looked to the captain.

As the evening wore on and darkness fell, things became more quiet. Many of the men were asleep by now. Dinner had been served. The captain would spend most of this night on the poop deck, watching the steering, walking forward every so often to be sure all was under control in the galley and foc's'le. It was a night of stress with the towboat ahead and no communication between the two vessels – radiotelephone was not developed until the late 1930s. There would be several men staying up who did not want to go down in the foc's'le due to the noise of those still inebriated. The night was not without company for the captain, and at this time he could become somewhat acquainted with the new crew members who were not celebrating.

The lights of the various towns along the Strait of Juan de Fuca would shine in the distance. First Port Townsend, then Victoria on the Canadian side, Port Angeles, Pysht, Neah Bay. The lighthouses would each show their own characteristic flash pattern, and by consulting his charts from time to time, the captain followed the progress. The vessel's log book started with an entry noting the ship's departure from the dock, then West Point, Point Wilson at Port Townsend, and so on. I have examined several of the log books from the 1910s and 1920s, where entries show the towboat cast off the line at Dungeness or Port Angeles, and from there the schooners had to set sail and beat their way out to the Pacific Ocean, taking two or three days as the winds were usually from the westward. From the earliest days of my memory, the towboat did not cast off the tow line before reaching the open ocean. I have at times felt empathy for the captains of vessels departing San Francisco, as they were in the ocean within two hours of departing. Moonshine was equally available there, so the crew did not have the 24 hours to sober up.

At any rate, by the 1930s, the tug towing the Puget Sound vessels continued all the first night, proceeding westward along the south shore of the Strait of Juan de Fuca. It was well past daylight before the vessel cleared Cape Flattery. Sometimes the tow was continued for 50 miles into the ocean before there was sufficient wind for the schooners to continue on their own.

Then came the whistle from the tug. One long blast to indicate the tug captain was ready for the schooner to cast off the tow line. Someone would be sent to the foc's'le head of the schooner to signal that the whistle had been heard. All hands were called out and the gas engine winch started. The old-timers knew what to do. The forestaysail was set first, followed by the foresail and then the spanker. By this time the towboat had shortened the tow line and had the vessel heading into the wind, so the schooner would not gain enough headway to overtake the tug. Then the tow line was cast off and the schooner fell off on the wind under her own power from the sails. The tug went ahead to clear the schooner and wait while the remaining sails were hoisted. No topsails were set on the topmast schooners during the westward portion of the voyage. Most times the tug would circle the schooner as a farewell gesture and give three blasts of the whistle that were followed by three blasts of the foghorn of the schooner.

The schooner was now on her own and had 1800 miles of open, stormy North Pacific Ocean to cross before reaching Unimak Pass, the entrance to the Bering Sea.

Hoisting one of the sails on *Sophie Christenson*, 1934.

CHAPTER 6

THE TRIP NORTH

On my first voyage as captain on the *C A Thayer* in 1949, the log book reads: "This day came in with a slight mist as we were towing out of the Straits of Juan de Fuca. Daylight came as we were passing Neah Bay at the western end of the Strait." The cook had prepared something for breakfast, although not a full meal. I had been up all night for security reasons. On departing from Poulsbo the day before, many of the men were more or less under the influence of alcohol, especially the old-timers who were the most experienced seamen. The cook was no exception.

We continued on west with the towboat ahead, and at about 9 a.m. passed Cape Flattery. By now the ocean swells were affecting the motion of the vessel and she was reacting with a slow roll. The mist was increasing and a light southerly wind began. The towboat continued until we were about 20 miles offshore from Cape Flattery, at which time the towboat captain blew his whistle, indicating his desire for us to let go of the tow line.

The crewmen were called to deck and the "engine man" started the gas engine winch, which was used to hoist the sails. This was a one-cylinder gas engine with a hopper water tank over the cylinder to provide cooling. It had 12 horsepower and was connected to the winch on the top of the forward house with a chain drive. The crew members were now able to set the sails.

They set the foresail first, and this gave us a little headway and steerage. The tow line was let go, after which the tug sounded the customary three blasts of the whistle as the "farewell and good voyage," then headed back east. We were now on our own. We set the forestaysail and the two jibs, then the spanker, and lastly the mainsail was hoisted. After all sails were set, the halyards were coiled up and hung in the rigging, leaving the deck clear. The wind being in the south, we were able to steer for the entrance to the Bering Sea at Unimak Pass. Now the schooner was reacting to every swell and became alive, so to speak.

In the crew of 35 men we had two cooks, an engine man, one of the fish dressers assigned to the galley to assist during the trip to the grounds, and the captain. The remaining 30 men were divided into three watches. (This number can handle the vessel easily. When the three-mast schooner *C A Thayer* was new and engaged in hauling lumber, she carried a crew of only eight men.) As captain, I had already selected who would be in each of the three watches. The first was under the direction of the first mate, the second under the second mate, and the third under the splitter. Once we were underway, the first mate and his watch took over the duty. Each watch was on deck for four hours, except the 4 to 8 p.m. watch, which was split into two sections of two hours each. Thus the watches rotated duty time each day. (The *Sophie Christenson* was an exception to this pattern, as she had a larger crew and therefore had four watches. The head salter was in charge of the fourth watch.)

The watch now on deck proceeded to secure everything that was loose and to clean up the deck. The engine man was called and started the deck pump, another small gasoline engine, and the deck was washed down. The mate assigned a man to the steering wheel, where he remained for one hour. At this time the bilge was pumped and the amount noted.

As captain, I noted in the log book when the tug let go of the tow line and our exact location at that time. For example, "Let go of tug 17 miles WSW of Cape Flattery Light, from which position I take departure." The taffrail log was attached to the stern railing and the current number was written on the slate board in the cabin, along with course, wind, sea condition, and visibility. At the end of each watch, the mate made a new entry of these items.

Noon dinner was served in two settings, at 11:30 and 12:00. The watch on deck waited for the second setting, while the next watch took the first setting. By now the wind had increased in strength and we were making about 5 to 6 knots. Most of the crew had sobered up by this time, but now a few of the first-time crew members were starting to experience the effects of sea sickness.

Everything was well under control, and I decided to take a short nap as I had been up since we departed. At about 3 p.m. I let it be known that the slop chest would be open. This meant the crew could come to pick up the clothing, oilskins, rubber boots, tobacco, and other items they had ordered through the home office when they agreed to ship out. Any man who had made a pier head jump could also outfit himself.

The watches changed at 4:00, and the third watch took over until 6:00. Supper was, as always, in two settings: the first at 5:30, followed by one at 6:00. We were sailing well and the wind remained in the south direction and not too strong, so we continued with all sails set. As twilight deepened, we lit the side lights. With the 120-volt electric system on the *C A Thayer* in 1949, this involved only the snap of a switch. In previous years the side lights and compass light were kerosene lanterns, which were most difficult to light with a match when the wind was blowing. There were no lights on deck. And so the first day at sea came to an end as the sun set in the west.

The log book for the second day of the voyage reads: "This day came in with a fresh S.W. breeze and moderate westerly swell." By now the crew was in better condition to perform the routine tasks. The morning watch from 4:00 to 8:00 began the daily chore of washing down the deck at 6:00 and checking everything from bow to stern.

Breakfast was served at 7:30 and 8:00. Right after the second setting, I had the mate call all hands on deck to lower the spanker sail and both of the jibs. The wind had increased and hauled more to the west, and under these conditions there was nothing to be gained by driving the vessel hard against the westerly swells. The *Thayer* was at this time 55 years old and not as solid as when new. Under reduced sails we steered as close as possible to the wind and were practically "hove to."

The weather being somewhat clear, I took a morning sight on the sun with my sextant to determine the longitude. After breakfast, the 14 dory fishermen came aft to the cabin to draw their fishing gear. This consisted of the tarred fish line, which was in a skein of 100 fathoms; the non-tarred white line, used as the leader attached to the hooks; a supply of fish hooks; a bait knife or eight-inch butcher knife; a file to sharpen the hooks; and anything else each needed from the slop chest. The slop chest items were charged to each man, while the fishing gear was supplied.

The fishermen also each required several fish line reels. These were made from slats of hardwood we had for that purpose. Each fisherman operated two fish lines, one over each side of the dory, and had one or two spare ones to use if one line wore out or was lost overboard.

Immediately after noon dinner I took the noon sight on the sun to determine latitude. Then with the necessary books and navigation tables I calculated both the morning longitude and noon latitude. I took the slate with all of the times and courses and calculated the dead reckoning noon position, which I compared with the log to determine if the log and courses were calculated correctly. The log might be recording too many miles or too few, and now was the best time to catch errors. The day's run or distance traveled was always calculated from noon to noon and was called "the day's work." In this case we had progressed 117 miles since the previous day.

Now was also the time to check over the old-timers concerning the progress of sobering up. Some of the men had been under the influence of alcohol for many days, and total withdrawal leads to the D.T.'s. I had one man who heard singing birds when he left the after cabin. After a radio call to my home doctor for advice, I began dispensing small quantities of whiskey at intervals, and several days later he recovered. Until he was sober I asked one man on each watch to guard him at all times for fear he might jump over the side of the vessel or do something else to harm himself.

C A Thayer setting sails off Cape Flattery, 1949.

There were always jobs to be done while underway.

After noon dinner and the navigation calculations, I was able to take a short nap. The fishermen, with their jack knives and other tools, proceeded to construct the fishing reels and attach the hooks to the white cotton leader line. They could do this work in the foc's'le, as there was some rain on deck and a little spray flying. At all times between meals, the coffee pot was on the stove and the table was set with food left from previous meals. The crewmen could come in and help themselves. This was called "mug up." The crew members on watch and not at the steering wheel could rest in the dining room or mess hall out of the weather. However, they had to be available should the mate in charge call them for some task. If the weather was agreeable, the men walked forth and back on the deck from the after cabin to the foc's'le head, always on the weather side of the vessel. This was a time to tell stories of past experiences on shore or at sea.

After the evening supper, I obtained another sight on the sun for longitude. We had progressed another 15 miles, and as we were now farther west than Seattle, I adjusted the clock 20 minutes back. We were by ourselves on the ocean and not dependent on any of the standard time zones. This adjustment of time continued as we progressed westward until we were

Schooner *C A Thayer* in the spring of 1950
with a fair wind and the square sail set.

Captain Ed Shields taking a sun sight.

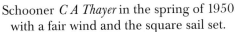

three hours behind Pacific Standard Time. The crew members were becoming accustomed to the movement of the ship and the separation from the moonshine or other alcohol products some had been indulging in during the winter. And so the second day passed.

One spring, I think it was 1935, when the sails on the *Sophie Christenson* were first set, the winch on top of the forward house was broken. The man controlling the halyard had continued to hoist after the throat halyard was full tight. From there on there was no more hoisting. Something had to give, and it was the teeth in the gear drive on top of the house.

These gears were made of cast iron; the small one was probably one foot in diameter and the larger one two feet. Several teeth were completely sheared off at their base, and several others had half the tooth missing, while the hold-down bolts had broken the base of the bearing frame. The damage had to be repaired or the winch could not be used for hoisting sails or dories.

Oscar Franson and I undertook the task. On making the appraisal, we found what we thought was a possible solution: we could drill holes $5/8$ inch in diameter in the hub of each gear where the tooth had been, then tap it with a   inch bolt tap and form a new tooth by filing the bolts to conform to the shape of the former tooth. Where a full tooth was missing, we had to provide two bolts, or studs as they should be called, after the head was cut off. The same was the case for the bearings; we would drill new   inch holes where there was solid metal and make new bolts to hold the bearing to the wood blocks that held the shaft off the deck. These bolts had to go all the way through the top of the house, so they were over two feet long;

fortunately we had several long rods that we could thread for the hold-down bolts. The plan looked possible, but the damaged gears were under the lower edge of the foresail, where there was more than enough cold wind to freeze a person.

We gathered the tools and found we had all that were needed. First we drilled a pilot hole into the gear hub with a small drill bit powered by the newly acquired 32-volt electric drill. In the process we broke several drills, as holding the electric drill by hand while the vessel was rolling was not the easiest thing to do. We had a ratchet set Father had scrounged several years earlier from one of the other old sailing vessels moored in Lake Union and bound for the scrappers. This was fortunate. We had a few taper shank drills that fit this hand ratchet. We turned the winch so that the hole to be drilled was horizontal and in a position where we could get a solid backing for a thrust to shove the drill. The first electric-drilled hole was about $3/16$ inch. Next, with the hand ratchet, we first used a drill that was about $3/8$ inch, then one a little over ° inch, following up with what we had in several steps until the $5/8$ inch hole had been made. The ratchet was turned about one-eighth of a turn with each stroke of the handle, and as the drill made some progress with the hole, the screw in the thrust end was tightened to apply more pressure. With good luck we could drill one finished hole in about one hour. There were 14 holes to make, as I remember. This took several days and many trips to the galley for a cup of coffee to help warm us.

Next we took the ▢ inch tap and threaded the drilled holes for the threaded bolts. Then we took the ▢ inch bolts and screwed them very tightly into the holes so they would not unscrew themselves as the winch was operated. We used a hand hacksaw to cut the bolts off to the right length, then filed them to the shape of the teeth. Surprisingly, when it was completed, the new teeth made from bolts engaged the remaining teeth. They turned, as I remember, about 20 revolutions per minute, a slow speed for gears. The job was successful and the winch was operated, but carefully, for the entire season. Needless to say, when the schooner returned to Seattle, new gears and bearings were purchased to replace the patched ones. Considering the tools we had to work with, I felt this was a remarkable feat.

⋯◆⋯

The course from Cape Flattery to Unimak Pass by compass is west by south. This seems strange to the novice, but the compass variation – that is, the angle between true north and magnetic north – is 23 degrees at Cape Flattery, so actually the true course is more to the north. Our first concern, though, was to gain sea room and get away from the land. The situation when you depart from Cape Flattery in a sailing vessel can be compared to climbing out of a funnel formed by the shores of Washington and Vancouver Island, with the island most feared. If you are lucky enough to have a strong southeaster for the first full day, you can count your blessings. This will put you sufficiently offshore to give a little sea room. However, if the wind is from the west, either southwest or northwest, you may find that you cannot clear land on either tack. The wind always blows in the mid quadrants, never from north, east, west, or south. It may vary from SSW to WSW while remaining in the southwest quadrant. I found it more to my liking, on departing Cape Flattery, to head somewhat south, even if not gaining much westing, rather than allow myself to be caught without sufficient sea room and the lee shore of Vancouver Island close by. That is a most difficult position from which to attempt to claw yourself off the beach.

After several days there was relief from the lee shore. We might have to shorten sail one or more times right off the bat on going out, but this was no more worry than the lowering and hoisting of the sails. The crew were sailors of the highest caliber. With 35 men on the *C A Thayer*, or 45 men on the *Sophie Christenson*, there were more than enough to handle the vessel. Besides, we had gas engines to hoist the sails, whereas when the schooners were new in the lumber trade, the steam donkey engine would not have steam up and was therefore not available. The crew of nine, including the captain, on the *Sophie Christenson* in the days of offshore lumber freighting would have hoisted the sails by hand, standard practice in all of the sailing vessels.

Ben Shanahan (right), an old-time codfisherman, teaches Leon Golay,
a first-time codfisher, how to splice rope on the *Sophie Christenson*, 1935.

On a typical day, the morning watch was called out at 3:45 to relieve the mid watch. Coffee was on the stove in the galley, and the crewmen helped themselves to this and any other food left on the table for night mug up. At 4:00 they relieved the previous watch. The watch mate took over from the mate on the previous watch. The retiring mate gave the course and, as is the custom on vessels at sea, the watch mate repeated it so the first man knew the proper order was received. Likewise the wheel was relieved, with the course being given by the helmsman and repeated by the man taking over: "Southwest by a quarter west and watch her carefully, do not let her go any to the southard if you can avoid it." (This presumes the vessel is on the starboard tack with the wind in the northwest quadrant.) The mate going off watch took his flashlight and read the taffrail log, then went below to enter this on the slate. He also noted the weather, wind direction, sea conditions, and distance made during his watch. Only then could he go forward for a cup of coffee before retiring.

For the next two hours, the mate on watch would spend considerable time on the poop deck with the helmsman, depending on how much experience the helmsman had. When I had the *Thayer*, there was a pilothouse over the steering wheel and this gave great protection, so most of the men on watch spent time there. Father put a wheelhouse on the *Sophie Christenson* about 1935. Before that time there was no protection for the man at the wheel, or for the mate for that matter. It was sure cold there, especially on the *Sophie Christenson*, as her poop deck was flush out to the rail and clear to the stern. The wind would sweep across there and right through the wool clothes and oilskins you were wearing and draw all of the heat from your body. None of the other codfish schooners had a wheelhouse. On the schooners that were built by Bendixsen in Fairhaven, California, the man at the wheel stood about three and a half feet below the top of the trunk cabin, so at least half of his body was protected. No one worried about a cold fair wind as that never occurred on the westward crossing.

At 5:00 the helmsman was relieved. The watch on deck tended only to necessary duties until 6:00. The best way to spend the time was to walk back and forth on the weather side of the deck of the vessel. Strange as it may seem, this is the side with the least wind. The lee side has all the wind spilling out from under the boom of the mainsail, and whatever sea water is on deck is always on the lee side. You would never pass time there. On the weather side, the bulwarks provided protection from the wind, as this solid rail was over four feet high. The crew usually paired off and walked forward and aft side by side, sometimes telling stories and then making several trips in silence. These night watches on deck have a fond place in my memory. In the spring of the year it was cold, but the exercise of walking provided the necessary body heat. The man at the wheel could not walk, but had to keep his hands on the spokes of the iron wheel, all the time trying not to shiver.

Just before 6 a.m. the watch went into the galley for another cup of coffee. By now the cook would be up and the fire in the galley stove burning well, as the cook had shaken down the grates and added a new charge of coal.

At six o'clock the wheel was relieved, as always, on the hour. Then the mate led his watch through the daily chores. Two men were given the task of cleaning the ashes out of the galley stove and dumping them over the lee side. Many times green hands tried to dump the ashes over the windward side, only to have them blow back on top of them. The best method was to spit first. If this came back in your face, you got the message. Then the crewmen went down to the foc's'le and cleaned out the stove there the same way. Coal was stored under the foc's'le floor, so they opened the hatch and one man went down while the other passed the buckets to him and took the full ones back. The coal box in the foc's'le was filled, then the box on the deck outside the galley, and last the one in the after cabin.

When this was accomplished, these two men would go with the flunky (the cook's assistant) to the store room under the floor of the after cabin for the day's supply of groceries: a sack of spuds, a case of eggs, one or two slabs of bacon, and such canned goods as the cook had ordered. They opened the small hatch to gain access to the salt meat, which was stored on top of the salt in the hold. Generally there would be one open barrel of each kind of meat, so they would take out the amount needed, such as salt pork or corned beef.

On each side of the galley we had several wood barrels lashed down, which we used to freshen up the salt pork, salt fish, and corned beef. The barrels stood on end with the top open and were filled with sea water. There was a small wood plug at the bottom to drain the barrel, and a canvas cover made to fit the top. The flunky and his helpers placed the salted meat in one of these barrels and soaked it for a day or two to rinse out the salt. The barrels were filled with clean sea water twice daily. There was another barrel that the cook used to rinse out the coffee pots and other dirty pots, this being followed by a

Schooner *Sophie Christensen* under sail in the Bering Sea, circa 1934.

light rinse with fresh water. Potatoes were also washed in salt water after peeling. Sea water was used whenever possible to save fresh water.

The day man would also be up at 6 a.m. to start the deck pump, the one-cylinder engine with a belt drive to either the pump or the dynamo for lights. With the pump running, two or three men of the watch would start forward on the foc's'le head with hose and brooms for a clean scrub down, working their way aft first on one side of the forward house and then the other. Of course salt water was used for this chore. Sometimes they took the hose into the galley to wash down the floor. It was cement and at times became quite dirty. Food spilled from the stove and other grease accumulated there until the deck became very slippery. If a bad spill occurred during the day, the cook often scattered salt on the deck to reduce the chance of a fall. All of this had to be washed out every day, because the vessel had to be kept clean. The foc's'le had to be swept as well as the after cabin.

The duty of the mate in charge of the watch was directed to the vessel itself. He would start forward with at least one other good sailor. They slacked off the throat and peak halyards of each mainsail a few inches, just enough that the portion of rope in the blocks, called the "nip" was changed to minimize wear in one spot. On the opposite end of the halyard was the purchase for that halyard, called the "jig tackle." The purpose of this was to make the halyard tighter than was possible by simply hoisting it. The mate and his men would set up the purchase to compensate for what had been let out on the halyard.

The mates kept a small pot of beef tallow that the cook had rendered out of corned beef. Into this pot they added a little lubricating oil, just enough that the mixture was not too hard. They would thrust a swab made from rags on a stick into the

Oscar Franson and Ed Shields working on the damaged gears of the winch. Note several of the new screwed-in bolts are showing before being cut off.

Fabian "Pjoiken" Johanson, second mate on *Sophie Christenson*, 1933–1941.

pot. Then the mate would go around to the jaws of each boom, on the lower edge of the sails, and swab some of this mixture of tallow to serve as a lubricant between jaws and mast. Someone else would be sent aloft to swab the jaws of the gaff likewise. If the day were nice, this man would be lowered in a bos'n's chair, swabbing the mast hoops along the way. Lubrication prevented the mast's becoming worn, which would create a slivery surface. Tallow was added everywhere else where chafing occurred. The mate checked to be sure none of the running gear was chafing, as this would wear through a piece of rope in short order.

When the deck had been washed, the pump was switched to the bilge and this was pumped dry. All wood vessels experience a certain amount of leaking, and most often this is greater during stormy conditions. Under normal sea conditions, not more than ten minutes were required to pump the bilge dry. Then the pump belt was taken off and the engine began running the dynamo to charge the batteries. With a clean deck, dry bilge, and galley stove burning with a full draft, things were ready for the day to begin.

The man at the wheel sounded the bell every hour according to ancient tradition: two bells added every hour and one added on the half hour, starting at 12:00 noon, 4:00, 8:00, and midnight. At 7:20 a.m., the helmsman sounded seven bells. This was the signal for those still in the bunk to get up for breakfast.

The cook rang the first breakfast call with his hand bell at 7:30, and the second call at 8:00. It took two settings to feed the entire crew. Everyone ate forward on the codfish schooners, not in the deep water style practiced in the freighting trade, where the captain and two mates ate aft. The watch on deck during the morning ate at the second table, while the relieving watch ate at the first setting. We never had a regular meal during the time we were standing a watch. We always waited until after the watch was over, as we might be called to duty while eating.

During the day or night, much time was spent walking back and forth on the deck. The weather was most often fairly wet on deck, and outer clothing was the rule. Some of the crew would merely sit on anything available just to pass the time. This is on the *Sophie Christenson*, 1936.

Sewing a sea bag with palm and needle.

After 8 a.m., if the weather was other than terrible, the men would slowly begin the work of preparing their own fishing gear for the summer's work. Everything had to be in readiness when we reached the fishing grounds.

Each fisherman had a dory assigned to him. If he had been on that vessel the previous season, he had the same dory. Each dory had an outboard motor in a well that was completely enclosed in wood. The dory bow was protected by the foc's'le head, a canvas covering supported by wood slats, which kept out water when the fisherman was bucking against a swell. The dories had all been painted yellow with a dark green gunwale, engine box or cover, and foc's'le head. They looked "neat."

The dories stowed on deck were placed bottom up against the bulwarks so that if a sea were shipped aboard the schooner, the dory would not fill with water and be damaged. They were unlashed in the morning and righted, allowing the fishermen to work inside their dories. Other dories were stowed on top of the hatch and were left upright. Because they were near the center of the vessel, they were not subject to danger from a sea shipping over the rail.

It seemed that every fisherman had some thoughts about how to improve his dory. The kit boards needed reinforcing, the bait board sides were too low, or some other detail should be changed. The men enjoyed getting into the dories and thinking of past years when the fishing was super. A few of them chose this time to overhaul their engines, and they'd generally perform this work on deck in the open rather then in the shop.

Two fishermen working on a dory engine.

The fishermen had to get an anchor from the store room and secure it in the dory. These were small stock anchors, about 20-pound size. This in turn was fitted with a 10-foot length of twist-link chain, then 100 fathoms of nine-thread hard-twist manila rope, called "dory rode." Each dory had a hand-powered windlass or gurdy with which to heave in the anchor line. The gurdy consisted of a spindle with four cleats mounted around the shaft so as to confine the line when it was being wound in. There was a handle on top. The whole gurdy was placed in the forward thwart. There was a wood block on the dory bottom to receive the lower end of the gurdy shaft, while the hole in the thwart was fitted with a large ball bearing assembly that had been salvaged from an auto wrecking yard. This made hoisting the anchor easier.

Each fisherman collected his new rope from the captain, who controlled everything new. Two men would split a coil between them. They would then wind the rope on the gurdy carefully, because if it became loose, one coil might slip down over another and make a tight knot.

The men had to check the anchor and reattach the length of chain. Possibly they'd need one or two new shackles. Also, the anchor might be worn where the cross shank went through the hole in the stock. We had a forge on board, so the men would bring this out and light a fire. They were very adept at making repairs and would place the anchor in the fire, heat it, and, using a heavy hammer, make the necessary adjustment.

Then the fishermen would turn to their fishing gear. Each fish line required a sinker. We called them leads. When the forge was out with a good fire burning, the men went again to the captain to get lead, which came in five-pound chunks.

Ben Shanahan winding his fishing line on the wood frame reel. Each fisherman had two similar fishing reels for holding the active fishing lines and two spares ready for use should the active line break or become damaged.

These were placed in a ladle and heated to the melting point. The men checked for the proper heat by thrusting a folded piece of paper into the hot lead. If it did not char or burn too rapidly, the heat was right. The fishermen made a wooden form in the shape of the fishing lead, wrapped a sheet of paper from a slick magazine around it, and tied it with sail twine. With a sharp knife they'd cut off the paper just below the top of the form, then place the paper-encased form in a bucket. While one man held the form, another filled the bucket with salt. When it was packed, the form was removed, leaving the paper ready to receive the hot lead. The men would slowly pour the lead into the mould, allow it to set, then remove it from the salt so another fish lead could be cast. Each dory fisherman required two leads, one for each active fish line. He also needed at least three spares. Those men who fished from the deck of the vessel also required like gear, although not in as large quantity.

Another piece of fishing gear was the spreader. This was made from bar copper ° inch by $1/8$ inch. The men would cut a length of about six to eight inches off the bar, then bend it to form an arc and drill one hole at each end and one in the center. A swivel specially made in Seattle for codfishing was then riveted to each hole. The center swivel was attached to a like swivel cast in the end of the fishing lead. The end swivels were for attaching the gangions with hooks attached. The fishermen took great care assembling their gear, as if the codfish knew how the fish lines and bait should be put together, and if theirs did not look just like the gear of the best fisherman, no self-respecting codfish would bite – although I have seen some sloppy gear in the dories, and that fisherman seemed to bring in just as much fish as the man with the pattern gear.

All of the fish were caught with hand lines. The men came to the captain and checked out enough skeins of tarred cotton line to make at least four fish lines each. The line was then wrapped on a wood frame called a reel, made from hardwood slats and with a swivel in the middle on top. The fisherman would hold the swivel and the line would unwind. These reels had to be made new unless the man saved his from previous years. If not lost, each reel would last several years.

Each man obtained fish hooks from the captain, just enough for his needs. The hooks were made in Norway and cost a lot of money, so they were not to be wasted. The hooks had a flattened end where the snoot line or gangion was attached. Then the end of the gangion was attached to the swivel so there were no loose ends. There were no knots as such at either the swivel end or the hook end of the gangion; instead they were spliced. This required the men to untwine the three strands of the cotton line and, using a sail needle, to thread each strand through the standing part. Hooks with an eye were not acceptable as they caused the splice to be bulky. This was a drawback because at times there were enormous amounts of jellyfish in the water, and the tentacles from these would become entangled in the fish line and gangion. If the line were smooth, with the end spliced back, the accumulation of slime could be wiped off. This slime could be terrible. I have seen it caught in the anchor chain, and when the anchor was hoisted there would be a ball of accumulated jellyfish, possibly 10 feet in diameter, sliding down the chain just at the water's surface.

Each hook had to be sharpened with a file, not just to have a sharp point, but so there were two knife-sharp edges from the top of the hook down to the barb. The purpose was to cut the bait. In other words, when the point of the hook was pressed against the bait, this sharp edge would cut through the skin. Otherwise, it was too difficult to get the hook through the bait. (The bait was halibut with a skin on one surface, which allowed the bait on the hook to withstand catching several fish before it was worn out or otherwise damaged by the teeth of the codfish. It is always necessary to have a neat-appearing piece of bait.) Each fisherman would make up probably a dozen sets of hooks with gangions attached. Then when the fish teeth chewed one, he had a spare handy to slip on the line with no lost time.

The dress gang was so called because it remained on board the schooner and dressed the fish brought in by the dory fishermen. There were two head men: the chief splitter and the chief salter. The former was responsible for those of the dressing crew who worked above deck, while the salter was responsible for the salt curing of the pack (the caught fish).

Splitting was done with knives specially made for the job. For years we purchased them from J.H. Baxter and Company in Boston. The knife blades came in a box wrapped in oil-soaked paper, but there were no handles. Each man had to make his own handles, so the splitter and header would take a piece of straight grain pine and whittle out the handle. There was a long spike-like stem on each blade for inserting into the handle. This was carefully fitted, and then a recess was cut into the wood handle all the way around at the blade end to prevent the wood handle from splitting. When all was ready, the splitter took a sheet of paper from a slick magazine and wrapped the handle with this, allowing the paper to extend toward the blade by about half an inch. He also obtained a small potato from the galley, made a cut so the potato would fit over the knife blade, and slid it down to the top of the paper. He placed the knife and handle in the bucket of salt, as was done with the fish lead form. Hot lead was poured into the opening in the paper so it would fill the spaces around the wood handle. Then the potato was slid down to the top of the still-hot lead so as to form a smooth surface and, most important, to cool the blade. The heat from the hot lead was not to be allowed to affect the temper of the steel in the knife! When the knife was removed from the salt, the splitter removed the paper and then, using a file, smoothed the lead down to the desired shape. Along the way the knife would be taken into the grip many times to gain the right feel. Both splitting and heading knives were made this way. These knives were carefully kept by the splitter and taken into the cabin after each day's use. Under no circumstances was one to be left out, where it might fall on the deck or be stepped on and the blade broken.

Each man using a knife in fish dressing wanted to have at least four. Out of this number he would find one to his best liking, a second that would not hold a good sharp edge, and another two that were usable but not the favorite. Another reason to have several knives was that each handle was different, and a change in the grip was something of a rest for the hand when working all day.

Each first-class splitter was expected to be able to split 6000 fish per day for several days in a row. There were times, especially when fishing near the entrance to Port Moller or along the coast northeast from there to a place known as Bear River, where we found heavy fishing. The codfish were chasing a small fish called candlefish and another called hooligans (eulachon), a smeltlike species. These small fish were on the bottom and even in the sand. Naturally the codfish did not bother to wash the sand off, but ate fish and sand together. Hence, the entrails were loaded with sand. This was dynamite for a sharp knife. The splitters hated the sand because it damaged their knives. It was impossible to keep these blades sharp under that condition. After the end of World War II, I found that I could make a more resilient knife by grinding down the blade of a power hacksaw. This steel would stand up far better when there was sand in the entrails of the cod.

Some fisherman took on other tasks. On each side of the schooner there were at least three Jacob's ladders, which the men used to climb from a dory to the deck. These were made new each year. The rungs were wood and the verticals were new rope. There were seizings above and below each rung to prevent it from sliding.

The bridles for hoisting the dories also had to be made on the way north. When on the fishing grounds, each dory would be slung from davits. The dories were hoisted from the water to the davits by means of a bridle hung from either the masthead or a boom. On the ends of this bridle were two hooks to engage the straps in the bow and stern of the dory. In order to use the apparatus, wood poles about 10 feet long were attached to each hook, thereby allowing two men, one on each end, to hook this bridle into the dory while standing on the deck of the schooner.

At 5 p.m., most of the men were ready to call it good for the day. Any dory that had been unlashed had to be placed inverted against the rail and secured. All tools were returned to the workshop, and items like the forge were stowed. Nothing was left loose on the deck for the night. We knew that the North Pacific Ocean in the month of April could be depended on to dish out some of the worst storms of any ocean, and we were determined never to be caught short. On the other hand, between the severe storms there were normally some few days when work could be done on deck. The main thing was to be prepared and not have to make preparations after the gale was upon us.

Dinner was served at 5:30 for the first table and at 6:00 for the second setting. The cook would have a good hot meal to satisfy the hearty appetites generated by working in the cold.

After evening supper there was a marked change in the activities. In early April, the long days associated with summer in the north had not yet arrived, so by 6:30, darkness would be upon us. The side lights were turned on and the general hoopla atmosphere of the day would be replaced by the quiet of the evening. The men having the mid watch would turn in shortly after dinner, while others would pass the time at a game of cards or reading in their bunks in the foc's'le. The atmosphere in the foc's'le was always on the quiet side, as no matter what hour of the day it might be, someone was asleep or at least resting. No loud noise was allowed.

The cooks had the galley put to rest by seven o'clock, and a few men would be there enjoying another cup of coffee and some tale of the past winter. Not that they were thirsty for a drink of coffee, but there was nothing else to do. No card playing was allowed in the mess room. The watch on deck would be up and most of them out on deck. If the day had been one of bad weather, then no work would have been done outside. The evening hours were a good time for the fishermen to file hooks and attach the white cotton gangions. It was time-consuming, but then there was an almost unlimited supply of time. It was a good time to tell stories while sitting on the benches of the foc's'le doing this work. "Do you remember that time when we were in the *City Of Papeete* with Captain McPhee, when..." or some other tale from the past. Fishermen are like all other sailors, long on stories.

After eight bells, when the 8:00 to midnight watch had taken over, there was a different serenity about the deck. By then it was dark, and the best place to be at night if you were on watch was on deck. This way our eyes became accustomed to the minimum light and you had no difficulty moving about. After a trip to the galley, it took up to 15 minutes before our night vision returned. Should the mate need help someplace, those whose eyes were not yet adjusted stumbled all over the place, tripping on everything on deck. Some of the worst objects were the ring bolts, formerly used to secure the deck load of lumber or a tank. So we stayed out on deck and enjoyed nature.

After the end of the 1935 season, Father had a pilothouse constructed on the poop deck of the *Sophie Christenson*, with enough room inside for most of an eight-man watch to sit on something, including the steering-gear housing box and the raised hatch to the lazarette. This gave the men shelter from the wind and a good place to pass the time. No stove was included in the furnishings, as who needs heat on a cold night? It was better to take on enough clothes so you were dressed to go on deck should there be a need.

During my first trip to the Bering Sea with my father in 1934, I stood watch duty along with all of the crew. My favorite place to spend the time was walking forth and back on the weather side of the main deck. There was no engine noise to jar the nerves, only the creaking of the rigging and sails as the vessel rolled. It took only a few days for everyone to have his sea legs, so the motion of the deck, first sloping to windward and then sloping farther to leeward, was taken in stride.

We walked in pairs. More fish were being caught in the stories that were told, and we would recall the good times last year when we were anchored off Port Moller or way out to the westward on the Middle Grounds. The fishermen were bringing in more cod than the dress gang could handle. Then the captain put all of the fishermen on a limit, each man being allowed only so many fish per day. We would dream of finding the same school again and contemplate the long hours of work and tired muscles. Which year was it when the *Wawona* had to leave right when we had the best fishing and take one of the men to Dutch Harbor because of an injury? This was before the vessels had radio to call for the Coast Guard cutter with the doctor to come. We felt sorry for them and the time lost, but were glad it did not happen on our vessel. There was always some form of rivalry between the various vessels, and most especially those belonging to the other companies.

Then old Charlie recalled the memory of that game of cribbage with four players, when the opponents were double skunked. Many were the stories of a night spent with the girls on Howell Street in Seattle. These men worked hard for the money they received, but when it came to spending money, all they asked for was a good time. Most of the men would be broke after two weeks ashore, but no matter, they had the memory. Being rolled in some alley did not leave the bad memory one might expect.

There was the time old Slippery Tom got his name. He had been caught by Big Mike, the Seattle bull (policeman), and was being held by his coat collar at the corner of Yesler and the alley between Second Avenue South and Occidental Avenue. While Mike was calling for the wagon, Tom slipped out of the coat and made off down the alley minus that outer garment so essential on a cold winter night. Mike was a big man and not to be made fun of by anyone, most especially another member of the police force. Should the Black Maria arrive and Mike be found without some reason for calling same, he would be the laughingstock of the force. There was a small gathering of men nearby who had been in one of the local joints, and they were feeling no pain. One poor fellow became the fall guy as Mike's enormous hand fell on his shoulder. There was no escape from the grip, and the others were let in on the hint that it would be better for them to be elsewhere when the wagon got there. Since it was only three blocks to the jail, time was of the essence. The group departed that area post haste, while the one poor small fellow was held captive and later escorted into the vehicle so familiar to that region of the city. No one knew his name or how he made out with the judge the next morning. All any of the fishermen remembered was Slippery Tom.

Night after night we walked along the deck and enjoyed the sight of the tough seas on the weather side of the vessel. At times we could look over her rail and find the horizon blocked by a large swell. The moon was in the last quarter and only now and then did it show through the clouds as they scudded past. Still it was back and forth. The deck was relatively smooth, but here and there an old ring bolt or other object caused us to alter the straight track we were walking. Occasionally we forgot and one of our toes would come in contact with an immovable object. The rubber boots we wore provided little cushion. How many times we discussed painting all the ring bolts white. Still, night after night we stubbed our toes on them, less often as their location became more firmly fixed in our minds.

Now there is the story being told by old Ben Shanahan about the time he was a dory fisherman on the halibut schooner *King And Winge*. It was a stormy night in Lynn Canal. The *Princess Sophia* departed from Skagway just before midnight on October 23, 1918, and four hours later struck Vanderbilt Reef. The vessel was hard aground on the rocky shoal with 268 passengers and 75 crew members on board. The *King And Winge* was alongside before daylight and made the offer to remove all the people the stout little fishing vessel could carry. Captain Leonard Locke on the large passenger vessel declined the offer, suggesting it was too dangerous to transfer people by the dories in the dark. So the *King And Winge* took shelter behind Benjamin Island. The U.S. Lighthouse Service tender *Cedar* arrived at the site the next morning, but the *Sophia* was high and dry, clear out of water at low tide. The *King And Winge* remained in the shelter where the *Cedar* also waited more favorable conditions. Late in the afternoon the *Cedar* received a wireless message that the passenger vessel was slipping off the ledge. Both *Cedar* and *King And Winge* returned to the open waters of Lynn Canal and ran out their time in a blinding snow storm. When they reached Vanderbilt Reef, it was dark and the *Princess Sophia* was nowhere to be seen. When daylight came several hours later, both vessels found the masts of the *Princess Sophia* projecting above water, but the only evidence of people were the bodies floating in the sea. *King And Winge* retrieved many bodies and took them to Juneau.

Ben Shanahan was an Irishman through and through, and was quite a man, a genuine dory man of the finest kind. He spent 50 seasons in a dory. Some record! He began fishing in Gloucester and was one of a group of men that came to Seattle about 1914 after a trip by Captain J.J. "Codfish" Kelly to the east coast to recruit fishermen for the Bering Sea codfishery of the Pacific Coast Codfish Co. Ben was an enormously powerful man, weighing well over 220 pounds and standing nearly six feet tall. He had only one eye; the other one had been lost during a barroom brawl over who belonged to some chick. How the others looked after the fight was a question never answered, but we all figured that if Ben lost an eye, the other men fared much worse. Ben also had false teeth when I knew him on the *Sophie Christenson*. I can recall many times, as he came over the rail after he had pitched his fish from the dory to the deck, he took his false teeth out and rinsed the snuff off them in the barrel of salt water for soaking the split cod, then took a handful of the water into his mouth to rinse it out, spitting out the remnants of the snuff. Then he gave the teeth a good shake to remove all surplus water before reinserting them in his mouth. He was quite a guy.

As we continued to walk the deck, telling stories, the man at the wheel struck the bell for the next hour. Whether it was 9:00 with two bells, 10:00 with four bells, or 11:00 with six bells, it was time for a change of wheelman. Someone would go aft to relieve the former helmsman, and we might all go back into the galley and mess hall for another cup of coffee. On the *Sophie Christenson*, Father had old Harry Oosterhuis in the crew as the night watchman on the fishing grounds. When we were sailing to and from the fishing banks, he took charge of the galley at night and saw to it that the coffee was always hot and somewhat fresh. He also assisted the cooks in the morning with breakfast, having among other things cleaned everything up and set the table before the cooks were called.

So went the hours of the watch. They were happy times, especially those night watches during the trip home after the end of the fishing season when the hold was full of salt cod. Then we all knew we had accomplished a good season's work, with the prospect of spending the money when we reached port. Further, during the return portion we were "running our easting down," and this was most often with fair wind. The Pacific Ocean in the latitude where we were has prevailing westerlies. During the month of August there are more frequent northwest rather than southwest winds, the former having predominately clear skies and dry conditions, whereas the southwest tends to produce more fog and rain. This was the most pleasant time to be on the night watches, just to be there with those tall masts, especially on the *Sophie Christenson* with her topmasts and topsails, those four tall poles with all that canvas up there, all in a straight line of masts and sails as they swayed back and forth across the sky. The clouds were the backdrop, with the tips of the masts and sails sweeping across the sky. Sails full and only the creaking sound from the blocks and rigging being strained; this was nature at its finest. No painting could ever capture the beauty, and many are the people who have paid good money to spend time on a sailing vessel for a vacation.

All this time, night after night, the crew spent the hours in quiet conversation, one with the other, enjoying the beauty and camaraderie. Many of the fishermen were from the Scandinavian countries and had literally grown up on the water. They had a weakness, however, and that was for the white lightning. This one item was the downfall for most of them when ashore. They could not resist it, with the result that very few could find steady work. Probably this one fact accounted for their following the sea and fishing. Here they were away from the alcohol for months and could enjoy life, hard as it was at times. On shore there was only the one lifestyle – that of consuming more alcohol than they could handle. They knew this and accordingly sought work away from it. Many of the men also found work in the logging camps during the winter. Here the same conditions prevailed – no liquor on the job – but every so often they would take a trip to the big city, where all savings were spent within a few days, then back to the camps. Many logging camps shut down during the summer season because of the fire hazard, and that was when we fished codfish. Therefore, by logging during the winter and fishing in the summer they had steady work and a steady place to live and eat under well-regulated conditions set by others.

⇒•◇•⇐

All the codfish schooners that I was ever aware of were originally constructed as lumber carriers to transport lumber and logs or piling from the mills of the northern states to the markets of San Francisco and Southern California. They were not built for speed, but were generally broad of beam and capable of hauling an enormous cargo of lumber, with the entire hold filled and lumber stacked on the deck up to ten feet high. The officers, consisting of captain and two mates, lived in the after cabin in what might be called "state rooms."

The remaining crew members or sailors lived above deck in the forward deckhouse, which generally had three separate sections. The forward end was the crew foc's'le, with opening or entrance from the forward end. Inside were six to eight bunks, and the entire length was six to eight feet. (Many of the lumber schooners operated with a total crew of eight or nine, which came down to six men in the foc's'le.) Next aft was the galley, where the cook prepared the food. There was a small pass-through to the foc's'le so the cook could pass the prepared food to the crew. The captain and mates ate in the after cabin, and the food was carried back to them.

Just aft of the galley was the donkey room, where the steam donkey engine was located. This machine was only operated during loading and unloading or when the sails were hoisted for the first time after the ship was towed to the ocean.

When each of these schooners was placed in the codfish trade, changes had to be made to accommodate the larger crews – from 20 on the small vessels to 45 on the larger *Sophie Christenson*. The former crew quarters were not adequate in any way. A new foc's'le was constructed in the forward end of the below deck hold. There was already a partition at the very forward end to separate the chain locker, but now a new partition was constructed possibly 25 to 30 feet farther aft to separate the new foc's'le from the fish hold.

Bunks were constructed against the inside planking of the vessel, three high. Each was sufficiently wide that there was a space of about two feet from the hull planking to the mattress, thus providing space for each man to store some of his clothes. There were lockers under the bunks and a long bench in front of the row of bunks. There were also bunks thwartship against the after bulkhead. There were several skylights, and a small coal stove in the center of the room for heat. On this stove was a three-gallon coffee pot filled with fresh hot water for washing. We used a coffee pot that had a large bottom and tapered to a small top. This was ideal because the vessel could roll heavily at times and the water would not spill out. The pot was securely lashed to the stove to prevent it moving. A common water bucket or pot was not satisfactory as it would occasionally spill on a heavy roll and the water would put out the fire in the stove, making steam and a general mess.

There was a dipper hanging on the wall behind the stove for dipping out the water. Each man had his own porcelain wash basin. He would dip out about a pint of water, set the basin on a bench or table, and wash his hands and face. Then he'd dump the dirty water in a five-gallon paint bucket and return the wash basin to its proper place, usually a nail on the bulkhead. His towel was placed on a higher nail or on a clothes line so it would dry. The bucket of dirty water was dumped overboard when it became full enough.

There were slats between the overhead beams on which to hang boots and other clothing to dry, as well as hooks on the front of the bunks and the stanchions down the center of the vessel for clothes drying. In the early years the only illumination other than the skylights was provided by several kerosene lamps. There were no electric lights until about 1925, when a 32-volt system was installed, which included a dynamo or generator on deck that was driven by a one-cylinder gasoline engine

101

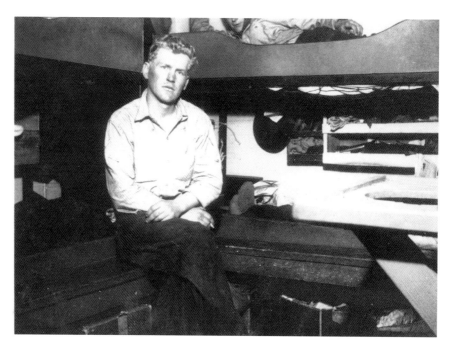

John "Whitey" Hill, second splitter, in the after cabin.

and a bank of batteries. The engine was operated possibly six hours per day, and the batteries served the remainder of the time. The *Sophie Christenson* had two plants, one forward and the other aft, serving their respective portions of the vessel.

There were additional bunks installed in the after cabin of each vessel, in the former first and second mates' rooms, to accommodate the splitters and salters, key people for successful processing of the cod that the fishermen delivered on board. There was a coal stove in the after cabin with another coffee pot filled with hot fresh water for washing. On the codfishing voyages everyone, including captain and mates, took their meals in the forward galley and mess hall. Everything served its intended purpose, and the crew suffered no ill effects.

———⟫◆⟪———

The galley was one of the focal points on every codfish vessel and included the mess hall, with a large pass-through opening from the galley. There was a large stove and, in some schooners, two ovens, a work area to prepare the food, and two sinks for washing the dishes. Under all of the work tables were storage bins for flour and other large items, and there were cupboards above for dishes, spices, and small objects. There was a hand pump connected to the freshwater tanks, and a 2° gallon bucket with water. Everything in the galley was secured so that as the vessel rolled, nothing moved or fell on the deck to break.

The mess hall table was on the starboard side of the room and long enough to seat at least eight men on each side. It was just aft of the galley. The *Sophie Christenson* had a second shorter table to accommodate at least eight more men at one setting. Over the table there was a hanging table about 18 inches wide and suspended from the overhead beams so it would swing as the vessel rolled. On the lower side were hooks for the coffee cups. In the various topside compartments were ketchup, salt and pepper, soup bowls, and cutlery. The main table had a raised edge of about one inch on each side, and two other raised boards about 15 inches apart ran down the length of the table. These were to keep the plates and dishes of food from sliding off the table. A wet red-and-white checkered tablecloth was spread to help keep the dishes from sliding as the vessel rolled.

On some days the tablecloth and the wood slats were not enough. In very rough weather the vessel would occasionally take two or three or more extra large rolls in succession. If this were during meal time, each man picked up his plate with one hand and his mug of coffee with the other and held them until the vessel finished those excessive rolls. He also had to balance

Four loaves of fresh baked bread are being removed from the oven.

himself during this time, swaying back and forth. His body was nearly vertical at times. Those men sitting on the bench on the middle of the room side did not have much to balance on and no back to lean against. Accordingly, when they leaned back as the vessel rolled they found themselves practically standing on the steep slope of the deck, with both hands full. Several times I have seen a man slip on his feet and slide under the table while his plate and coffee spilled on top of him. The men on the other side of the table were on the low side. The swinging overhead rack was literally in their faces. Then when the vessel rolled the other way, the men with their backs to the wall could not lean back as the wall was restraining them. If they slipped, they fell on top of the table. Meanwhile, the platters of food on the table might slip or the food on them could slide right off, over the table edge, and into the man's lap. The cook had his hands full with the same problem. This did not occur very often, but when it did there was always an awful mess. Generally on the days when the weather was this severe, the cook did not attempt to serve a regular meal but limited it to what could be handled. Some days there was only soup and bread and butter.

There were three main meals served every day, storm or calm: breakfast, dinner, and supper. With a crew of 30 to 45 men, food preparation was in itself an enormous task. We carried two men in the galley, the cook and his assistant, or as we called him, the "flunky."

Breakfast was the beginning of the day when the vessel was at anchor on the fishing grounds. At this time there were no watches; only the night watchman was up all night. The crew were called or awakened just in time so they could grab their pants and shirts before the breakfast bell rang. When sailing to and from the fishing grounds, of course, the watch on deck was up well before the bell rang.

The cook would be up at least 1° hours before breakfast. When he was called by the night watchman, the galley had been cleaned up, and a large pot of water was boiling on the stove and ready to make coffee or whatever else was needed. If corned beef was on the menu for the day, it would have been simmering all night. The soup for the day would be started. Very often this was pea soup, and it was put to boiling as soon as possible. The odor of the peas and ham cooking was glory to the nostrils, while that from the corned beef was not as pleasant. The odor of boiling beef fat or tallow has an unpleasant odor whether fresh or salt.

Then there was the setting of the bread. The timing depended on who was cook and when he desired to bake off the loaves. Many of the cooks set the dough, which is the mixing of the flour, eggs, yeast, salt, and water, the day before, and the pan full had been resting in a warm location over the stove all night, allowing the dough to rise. If that were the case, the

John "Whitey" Hill (left) and Captain Ed Shields take a sight on the sun to determine the position of the vessel *C A Thayer* in 1949.

cook had to knead the dough before breakfast for its last rising. Meanwhile, the flunky cleared off the table, took off the dirty tablecloth, opened out a clean one, and set the table.

The bacon would have been sliced up the night before. We carried slab bacon and this required nearly half an hour to slice for the crew of 45 men. The hotcake batter was mixed. It was made from basic ingredients and was not a prepared mix as today. There were hashbrown potatoes every day. These were cut up in the morning, or by the night watchman, from spuds that had been boiled the day before. In the morning they were placed in roasting pans in the oven, a generous amount of bacon drippings was poured over the top, and occasionally they were stirred. Fried eggs were also served, these being cooked in individual two-egg pans. Generally the cook first cooked half enough eggs for the number of places at the table and slid the two-egg servings onto a platter on the heating shelf over the grill. Next came the hotcakes on the grill or stove top. More egg pans were filled, cooked, and slid to the side. By the time the bell was rung the cook had the platters filled with eggs, hashbrown potatoes, hotcakes, and bacon.

The plates were set with the edge strip and the center strip holding them from sliding. The platters of food were set in the center of the table, usually three platters of each food on the long table and two of each on the shorter one. The coffee pots were also placed on the table, and each man reached for a cup from the overhead swinging table.

At all times when the ship was underway, day or night, storm or calm, there was a man at the wheel to steer the vessel.

No one was allowed in the galley or mess hall during the preparation period before the breakfast bell was rung – at 4:00 a.m. when we were on the fishing grounds, and at 7:30 when sailing. Then the mob descended on the table of hot food. A place was held at the forward end of the table for the captain and two mates. Talking was allowed, no rules to the contrary, but the transfer of food from the platters to mouths was of greater urgency. When each man had finished, he picked up his dirty dishes and brought them to the door between the galley and mess room. Here the flunky stood to take them after each man had scraped the leftovers into the slop bucket or garbage can. The dishes then went directly into the sink for washing. I have seen all the dishes washed and ready to set for the second setting in 12 minutes after the first bell was rung.

The sink had two compartments and an attached metal drain board. Each sink was about 15 to 18 inches high, roughly 18 inches deep and 18 inches long, with a pipe drain from the bottom to overboard. However, the sides were not straight; they tapered, so each compartment was less than 6 inches wide at the bottom. This meant that considerably less fresh water was required. Fresh water was most precious. We had only so much on board, and to stop fishing and sail close to shore to replenish the supply cost several days of fishing, so it was not to be wasted or used to excess.

There was no shortage of salt water, as we were floating in it and could have all we wanted. We just had to draw it over the side in a bucket or dip it from the barrels that were filled every morning by the deck crew. This salt water was used for some of the dirtier tasks. Coffee was made in a large pot by dumping the required amount of ground coffee into boiling water. When it came time to clean this pot, it was first rinsed out in salt water to remove the old grounds. Fresh water could not be spared for that, although the pot was next rinsed with about a cup of fresh water to remove all the salt before reuse.

When the cook needed fresh water he pumped it from the storage tanks into a bucket in the galley, using the hand pump. There was a metal dipper for dispensing water. This dipper was also used by the vessel's crew to obtain a drink of water when they were thirsty. This would not comply with good health requirements today, but it was the system then. (Water from this pump was also in the pots on the stoves in the after cabin and foc's'le.)

After breakfast was over, the cook had to turn to the task of noon dinner and baking the bread, weather permitting of course. We baked all of the bread when at sea, and this called for between a half and a whole loaf for each man daily. Fifty loaves every other day was normal on the *Sophie*. During the time I was on a codfish schooner, I was with two different cooks who were wonders at bread and pastry and kept a generous supply of cookies, cakes, pies, donuts, cinnamon rolls, butter horns, turnovers, and the like. (I heard of other voyages when the cook could not make bread worth eating. Fortunately I was not on one of those trips.) This may appear expensive, but it is cheaper than meat, and a happy crew is most important.

We had very little meat that had to be prepared in the ovens. Baked ham was one of those, along with sweet pickled picnics (pork shoulders). Meat like corned beef, pigs feet, and salt black cod or salmon was cooked on top of the stove. Thus the ovens were available for baking breads and pastries. The galley stove had two ovens and was principally fired with coal, except for the last years on the *C A Thayer* when we had an oil stove. Even then we required coal to supplement the oil at times.

Noon dinner when sailing to and from the grounds was at 11:30 and noon. It was served less formally on the fishing grounds, as a rule, although this was the heaviest meal of the day. If the dories had gone out that day, there was only the dress gang men on deck. Dinner was at 9 a.m. for those on deck and whenever they came on board for the fishermen, who would return sometime between 8 and 11 a.m. to unload the morning catch. Then they washed, removed their oilskins, and entered the mess room for dinner, which the cook or flunky dished up on a plate for them.

After noon dinner, the cook took time off for rest, spending several hours in his bunk. In midafternoon he would start the necessary preparations for supper. While sailing and standing watches, supper was at 5:30 and 6:00. In the Bering Sea it was 4:00 for those on board and whenever they came back for the fishermen.

Supper, the lighter of the two main meals, was often corned beef hash, sliced cold meat like beef tongue, canned lunch meat, or many times either boiled or fried codfish. While this was the fish we were seeking, it was also one of the finest fish to grace a person's table. Naturally, when we had 50,000 pounds of fresh caught-that-day fish on deck, the ones that went to the galley could be counted on to be nothing short of perfect. On other days, if there were a surplus of fresh halibut for the dory fishermen's bait, the cook was allowed to have one. Bait came first with the halibut, but there was usually a surplus at least twice per week. Many times I have taken a 40- or 50-pound halibut that the fishermen had just caught and sliced it so the cook could serve it for dinner. While halibut ranks behind fresh codfish with me, a fresh-caught halibut could easily displace any meat we had to put on the table.

It seemed we always had some men making their first voyage on a codfish schooner who stated at the beginning of the voyage, "They are not going to feed me fish every day, and maybe not at all." That thought soon left their minds after they tasted fresh-caught fish. What turned them off previously was the poor or old fish they had purchased at the market. Many times this so-called fresh fish of the market had already seen better days and was up to two weeks old.

After each meal was cleared from the table and the "joint" cleaned up, the table was set again, this time for mug up. This is a custom common to most seafaring men, especially fishermen. The coffee is always on the stove, and I do mean always. Except when the cook is in the process of putting food on the table, any member of the crew can come into the mess room, take a cup off the rack, go to the stove to fill it with coffee, then sit down with others at the mess table, where he can tell all kinds of tall tales. Naturally coffee alone is not enough, so the center of the table has bread and butter, jam, and any cookies, pie, or other pastry that the cook has made. Hard tack was also welcome at this time. Whatever the time, a man could always get a cup of coffee and something else. After his mug up, each man had to wash whatever dishes he soiled.

The schooner *Wawona* at sunset on the Pacific Ocean.

Four days after we left Seattle we shook out the reefs in the sails and set them full size. Seven days out the weather improved overnight and morning found us roughly 500 miles west of Cape Flattery with a light to fair northeast wind. We were sailing along at about 5 to 6 knots. The sky was clear but with a heavy overcast, typical of the stormy North Pacific in April. The head seas of the several preceding days had subsided and the vessel now had a dry deck.

Three days later the log book reads: "This day came in with very strong west wind and swells. The night was rough and the vessel experienced considerable laboring." Immediately after breakfast I called all hands on deck and we proceeded to reef the main and foresails. The spanker had been taken in the previous night, along with the outer jib. The first mate took charge on deck. With this large crew, and given the fact that all of the dory men had made several codfishing voyages and knew the "ropes" well, the work went smoothly. It would have been difficult to find more experienced seamen anywhere on the Pacific Coast. The after crew, consisting of the two mates, splitter, and salter, had an average of 20 years' codfishing experience. The remaining 12 dory fishermen had over 12 years' experience. They all knew what to do.

We lowered the mainsail first. There was one man at each of the halyards, and several more were taking in the slack rope on the downhauler, which was attached to the outer end of the gaff to prevent it from swinging excessively during lowering. When down, the slack canvas had blown out over the lee rail, falling on the dories in the davits on the lee side, so it all had to be gathered along the boom. Then the reef points, or short lengths of rope, were threaded through the reef holes in the sail and secured around the boom. In this fashion the sail, when raised again, would be only about 60% of its former height. The foresail was likewise lowered, the reef points set, and hoisted again. For the hoisting we had a gasoline engine to power the winch drums or gypsy heads. Thus the sails were hoisted by mechanical power rather than by man power as in former days.

On the westward crossing there were many days with rough weather. Here *Sophie Christenson* bucks a head sea.

I set a course as close as possible to the wind to avoid making headway against the high seas – we were "hove to," headed in a west-northwest direction. We remained in this condition for the next two days, until the wind had calmed down somewhat and shifted more to the south. When hove to, the action of the vessel is fairly slow, and living conditions are much more tolerable than when driving against a head sea. Sun sights are not easily obtained if at all, but the ocean is large, so there is no need to worry about the position. We were not going anywhere.

During this time the normal watches were maintained. The men on deck had to wear oilskins in order to keep dry, and they often came into the mess room for mug up. Those not on watch were reading, sleeping, or playing cards. Pinochle and cribbage were favorites. The stakes might be a pair of gloves for the best of three games with two people – never high enough to result in one person gaining a material amount of loot from the cards. In the foc's'le there was often a game of poker with higher stakes. There was no money on board and no credit, so the loser had to pay up with goods from the slop chest – a wool shirt, a pair of jeans, socks, gloves, or the like. The winner had to accept these. Someone would have brought a stack of chips on board. A blanket was spread over the table. There were no large losers, and the captain took great care to make sure the

The *Sophie Christenson*, with the lower sails set. The topsails are clewed up.

game did not become more important than fishing. The splitter on the *Sophie Christenson*, Ernest Carrigan, who lived in the after cabin, had a weakness for the cards. He would come to Father and draw an item from the slop chest, then go forward to play. Nothing was returnable. On his return aft several hours later, Carrigan was checked up by the aft crew to see his winnings. Never did we catch him bringing anything back. There was, on the other hand, a good amount of guffawing from the other aft gang concerning how he had been cleaned out. Still, this was entertainment and pleasure to him.

Two days later, the 12th day out, the wind died down and was now in the northeast. We shook out the reefs and stood on course, west by south, heading for Unimak Pass. During the storm we lost 47 miles, which was of no special concern. We continued thus with the full fore and mainsail, which was enough for the present as there was still a heavy swell running from the blow. By 4 a.m. on the 13th day out, the head swell had laid down sufficiently that we set the spanker and both jibs. Now we were sailing at 7 knots in the proper direction.

In the North Pacific, the wind blows from all points of the compass. The prominent direction is from the west, which was directly ahead for us, but seldom is the wind from this single point. Most often it is from some point west of the north-

south line, with an occasional southeast breeze, and the captain of a sailing vessel selects the tack that allows a course closest to that desired. On some days our course was south-southwest, and at other times north-northwest. These generally canceled each other out, and we made our desired course in the long run. It is 1800 miles by the Great Circle route from Cape Flattery to Unimak Pass, but as we were not able to sail Great Circle, we logged over 2200 miles in making the crossing.

The weather continued with heavy overcast and occasional rain. On the evening of the 19th day out we were sailing with a fair fresh wind abaft the beam from the northeast, a most favorable direction, and we had made considerable distance to the west. By the 20th day we were about 300 miles east of Unimak Pass, the entrance to the Bering Sea.

On the morning of the 21st day the wind shifted to the south and southwest. We could stand on our course but were close-hauled. Fog and haze set in, and I was not able to get a noon latitude sight on the sun. I was reminded of Captain Charlie Foss in the three-mast schooner *Joseph Russ* in 1912. He was far to the north of the course, and on April 21 the vessel grounded on Chirikof Island, a total loss. The first mate lost his life. Several of the crew members took off in dories and several days later landed at Chignik, just before the mail steamer *Dora* arrived. The *Dora* immediately took off for the location of the wrecked schooner. The crew had no shelter and only what food they could salvage from the wreck. Without the assistance of the *Dora*, most of the crew of 29 would have died. I had no intention of repeating this mishap.

On the 1949 *Thayer* voyage I had a good position from the day before and trusted my dead reckoning. We continued on, making nearly 7 knots, a good speed for this vessel. Sometime during the night we would pass south of Sanak Island, which has a very rocky shore, and the offshore Sanak Reef.

I had a portable radio direction finder, and the signal from Scotch Cap Lighthouse indicated I was to the north of my dead reckoning position. I gave the mate on watch instructions to call me if there was any break in the mist so I could get a sight on the moon. At about 11:30 he called me and I got a fair sight, which confirmed my dead reckoning that we would clear Sanak Reef well to the south. One sight is not sufficient, and an hour later I got another sight. Both agreed and we continued on.

On the morning of the 22nd day the wind died down, then shifted to a very light breeze from the northeast, a fair wind for us. We proceeded on, taking soundings regularly with the lead line that indicated the approach to land on Davidson Banks. The fog cleared enough to give about five miles visibility. Sharp lookouts were maintained as we proceeded. Just after noon dinner I took the binoculars and joined the lookout on the bow. Shortly thereafter I spotted breakers on the starboard bow and recognized the headland as Scotch Cap, with the lighthouse. We were heading directly into Unimak Pass, our immediate destination. Such a relief!

The approach of a sailing vessel to Unimak Pass has always been a nightmare for the captain. Fog prevails much of the time in the spring and fall, and since the Pass is a breach in the near-continuous mountain range on the Alaska Peninsula and Aleutian Islands, the wind blows through either from the north or south almost continuously. My father spent nearly a week making his approach in the four-mast schooner *Sophie Christenson* in 1933. As the wind was from the north, he had to stand forth and back south of the entrance, sailing east of Scotch Cap and west of Ugamak Island, attempting to hold his position until more favorable conditions arrived. He was too far offshore to anchor.

The journey to the Bering Sea in 1949 was my first experience as captain, and on the outward portion of the journey there were several snide remarks about whether I could find Unimak Pass. After the approach described above, I never again heard any doubts about my ability to navigate.

———⬥◈⬥———

When the Pacific Coast Codfish Co. was first founded, the *John A* never entered the Bering Sea. Rather, Captain Grotle fished on the south side of the peninsula, south of Unimak Island and near Sanak Island. Dory fishing was conducted also to the south and east of Siminof Island, called Siminofski by the fishermen, and from there west to the bight between the

Captain J.E. Shields taking a sight on the sun from the schooner *Sophie Christenson* in 1934.

Shumagin Islands and Sanak Island (though this order of notation was not necessarily the order of progression). Hans Olson, known among fishermen as Sourdough Hans, often told stories of fishing off Cape Lutke and Cape Lazaref.

In the years that followed, the vessel captains decided to migrate into the Bering Sea in the later portion of the season. By 1915, all of the fishing was conducted in the Bering Sea, with no stops south of the peninsula. It was considered far more dangerous to fish around the Shumagin Islands than in the Bering Sea, especially with the advent of larger schooners, including the *John A*, which did not feel as safe in these restricted quarters.

It is 20 miles distance from the Pacific Ocean to the Bering Sea at the north end of Unimak Pass. The south entrance to the Pass is 14 miles wide, with Scotch Cap on the starboard side and Ugamak Island to port. Scotch Cap is named for its resemblance, when seen from the north side, to a tam worn by Scotsmen. Ugamak Island, known to codfishermen as The Mug, is a large solid rock island in the middle of the Pass between Unimak Island on the east and Akun Island on the west. There are three distinct pinnacles that make it recognizable.

Once past Ugamak Island, the Pass becomes over 20 miles wide. There are strong tidal currents of up to 5 knots at times, and these can present difficult sailing for a codfish schooner.

With clear sky and a fresh southerly wind, we made the transit between Scotch Cap and Cape Sarichef on the Bering Sea end in five hours. The snow was down almost to the surf line, with Mount Pogrami standing clear on the starboard side. This is a sight seldom experienced, as this area is well known for its foggy conditions. Partway through the Pass, on the beach of Unimak Island, was the wreck of the Alaska Steamship Co. vessel *Mount McKinley*, lost in a snow squall during World War II when there was radio silence and no operating lighthouses.

On the Bering Sea side of the Pass, the western headland is Billings Head on Akun Island. In the spring of 1928 the square-rigged ship *Star Of Falkland*, of the Alaska Packers fleet from San Francisco, stranded there with the loss of one life. There was a head wind in the Pass, so several codfish sailing vessels, including the *Charles R Wilson*, *Wawona*, and *Louise*, as well as the larger square-rigger were anchored just off the Unimak Island shore, awaiting more favorable conditions. With a turn of the tide, several of the fore-and-aft rigged schooners hove anchor and set sail for the Bering Sea. The captain of the *Star Of Falkland*, not wanting to be outdone by the smaller vessels, followed. Because it was square-rigged, this large vessel could not be maneuvered as easily as the smaller schooners, and it did not clear Billings Head. However, this is the only known sailing vessel casualty in these dangerous waters.

———————————◆———————————

After sailing across the North Pacific, most of the codfish schooners entered Lost Harbor, a sheltered cove on the west side of Akun Island, before beginning to fish. Sometime around World War I a mine was opened here to produce copper ore. The mine operators constructed a wharf and erected several buildings as well as a pipe system to bring fresh water to the wharf. The mine was not successful, but the remnants of the plant and the wharf remained for many years.

The codfish schooner captains would bring their vessels either to the abandoned wharf or to anchor adjacent to the wharf. Here the vessel was prepared for fishing. The dories were all brought out and made ready. The crew set up splitting tables and the system of checker boards that contained the fish on deck as they were brought on board by the dory fisherman. Some years the dories were launched and the fishermen went out of the harbor on the Bering Sea side to try the fishing there.

All of the codfish schooners from San Francisco and Puget Sound – except the *Sophie Christenson*, the *Charles R Wilson* after 1937, and the *C A Thayer* after 1946 – required more fresh water for the trip than the tanks would hold when they left Seattle, so the captains seized the opportunity to take on more water while they were in Lost Harbor. Several dories were launched and loaded with clean empty barrels that were taken ashore to the stream unless the water was running on the wharf. The men filled the barrels and brought them back to the schooner, where they emptied the barrels into the freshwater tanks. This meant that at the start of fishing, all the freshwater tanks were full.

Oscar Franson, the head salter on the *Sophie Christenson*, related a story of being in Lost Harbor once on a vessel from San Francisco. The captain had taken a small wood barrel of moonshine on board before departing San Francisco and had made much use of the contents on the crossing of the North Pacific, being for the most part inebriated every day, The mate had all of the responsibility for the navigation and operation of the vessel. After a long day of work by the fishermen and deck crew in Lost Harbor, the mate suggested it might be well to give each man a cup from the barrel. This procedure was referred to on ships as "splicing the main brace." The men went to the galley and obtained a mug, then lined up at the entrance to the after cabin for the ration. The first mate operated the spigot on the keg. After each man had consumed his ration, he returned to the end of the line. After all of the men had made several trips to the keg, the captain inquired of the mate, "Is there no end to the line?" By this time the mate had accomplished his intended purpose and drained the barrel dry so the captain could sober up and direct activities on the schooner.

The codfish schooners sailed into and out of the harbor without assistance as there were no towboats available. From there each sailed past Akun Head and Billings Head, across the Bering Sea entrance to Unimak Pass, and continued northeast past Cape Sarichef to wherever the captain desired to begin fishing. The stop in Lost Harbor required about three days. There is no record of any vessel experiencing difficulty or striking any of the rocky shores.

At the end of the 1947 season the *Wawona* and the *C A Thayer* were heading for Unimak Pass, homeward bound. The *Wawona* required more water before making the crossing of the North Pacific and sailed into Lost Harbor to replenish the supply. The *Thayer* was able to sail out of the Bering Sea before the wind shifted, but it took the *Wawona* over three weeks to clear Unimak Pass. This illustrates the need for care to preserve what water you had.

⟫◆⟪

After passing Cape Sarichef, we proceeded northeast along the north shore of the Alaska Peninsula. Immediately east of the Cape is a bight in the shoreline known among the codfishermen as Dublin Bay. In past years this location produced many cod in the spring of the year and was often the first anchorage for the codfish vessels. The bottom is very rocky, and many times the vessel's anchor had become lodged and could not be retrieved. In 1937, when I was on the three-mast schooner *Charles R Wilson*, owned by my father and under the command of Captain Knute "Dempsey" Pearson, we anchored here, somewhat to the east near Billy's Bluff, as the fishermen called it, and shown on the chart as Cave Point. The weather being fine, the dories were launched in the morning, and the fishermen returned with only a few fish. Several fishermen lost their dory anchors to the rocky bottom. We hove anchor and carried on to the northeast.

Dublin Bay had the reputation among codfishermen as a nasty location, with unpredictable weather and strong currents from Unimak Pass. Oscar Franson related that about 1908 he was there in the schooner *Vega*, under the command of Captain Pete Nelson. At that time the schooner had rope for anchoring rather than chain. This rope was made from manila fiber, had the appearance of four ropes being twisted together, and was known as "cable laid." It would be at least 12-inch size (rope is always measured by circumference) and at least 3 inches in diameter. The weather had been somewhat stormy at Dublin Bay, and the captain, fearing that the rope hawser might become frayed on the rocky bottom, had the crew hoist the anchor for inspection. All was well. However, a little over an hour later the hawser chafed through and the vessel was adrift. The crew had to make sail, and they also had to haul in the anchor hawser again. The hawser was wrapped three times around the drum on the windlass, and half the crew was on the hand pumps to operate the windlass while the other half pulled on the slippery wet end to hold it tight on the drum. They sprinkled ashes from the stove on the hawser to gain friction with the drum. Once it was hauled up, they had to splice this exceedingly stiff, wet hawser to another spare anchor. Splicing rope of this size is quite a chore when it is dry and being done in a rigging loft. On the deck of the rolling vessel it was something different.

I also heard about the sad day of May 15, 1909, when the two-mast brig *Harriet G*, operated by the Matheson Fisheries Co. of Anacortes and under the command of Captain Robert "Bob" Firth, was in Dublin Bay. I summed this up in my book *Maritime Memories Concerning Captain J.E. Shields*:

> On this day in the spring, the weather was threatening and all of the vessels' captains except Bob Firth had held their dories on board for the morning. There was almost no wind and as the dories at that time were rowed

Three men are out on the jib boom of the *C A Thayer* (left), securing the sails. They used a downhauler attached to the top of the sail to haul it down after the halyard was loosened. The lowered sails were blown out over the lee side of the vessel and the sailors had to pull the slack canvas back on top of the jib boom, then secure each sail with the rope stops that were already secured to the edge of the jib boom. There was a steel wire cable on each side of the jib boom for the men to stand on. When all was secure, the sails would not blow out in the wind when the vessel was at anchor. Mending sails (right) was part of the daily routine.

by hand or sail, and the fish were on the inshore side of the vessel in more shallow water, they all went toward the shore or beach. On this morning, May 15, 1909, there was a sudden increase and shift in the wind, and instead of a very light air from the SE, there was soon a strong breeze from the SW. The dories were now mostly to leeward of the vessel and not capable of making it back on their own.

A few of the dories made it back to the *Harriet G*, but many of the men could not row the dories against the high wind and increasing seas. Some of the men anchored their dory in the hope the weather would moderate later in the day. However, the wind increased further, and shortly the anchor chain and cable on the vessel broke and the brig was now adrift. The rocky bottom had chafed the anchor cable. Captain Firth made what sail he could while the anchor cable was hauled back in. He sailed the little vessel toward the beach, then along the shore, just outside the line of breakers, picking up those dories and men that he could.

The mountains of Unimak Island as seen over the stern of the schooner.

The *Harriet G* was a smart sailer and could be counted on to tack when necessary, unlike most of the other fore-and-aft schooners. Further, Captain Firth was a tough bluenoser from Nova Scotia and was well schooled in picking up dories when under sail. He had sailed the Grand Banks and Davis Strait in his youth. His seamanship was superb, but in the end he had to give up with 9 of his 20 dories unaccounted for. Further sailing along the shoreline could result in the loss of the vessel itself in the heavy surf. One dory fisherman made it to the *City of Papeete* and was taken on board. Eight dories drifted ashore through heavy surf, with only two of the fishermen surviving. These two walked many miles to the Cape Sarichef Lighthouse for shelter. The next day Captain Firth brought the vessel close to the beach and sent a dory with four men ashore to look for the lost fishermen. They found eight dories smashed to kindling and the body of the first mate. The *Harriet G* continued fishing for the remainder of the season and returned to Anacortes in the fall with a small cargo of salt cod.

In the years I was in the Bering Sea, I have seen a repeat of the "widow wind" several times, but I had the benefit of hindsight on my side. One day when I was captain of the *Nordic Maid*, a 148-foot trawler fishing for king crab, a similar weather phenomenon occurred. In the afternoon the weather suddenly turned warm and the air became so clear we could see all the mountains. We were about to go back to the cannery at False Pass for oil and water anyway, so when the day turned nice I directed the crew to take the net on board as we were heading for the cannery. The crew was irate, to say the least, as this was the first time that year we had a "nice" day. However, we headed back to False Pass (we had been fishing on the west side of Amak Island) and proceeded through Unimak Pass, then northeast up the south side of Unimak Island. By midnight the wind was a genuine howling gale. Next morning at about 7, I called the *Deep Sea*, another American trawler, to see where he was. He had just anchored under the lee shore of Amak Island, with the wind well over 60 knots. He spent the next three days at anchor and then had to go to port for oil, while I spent the storm period tied to the cannery dock, where the crew did net repairs and other necessary tasks. When the storm was over, my crew was rested and ready to go back to fishing, whereas the *Deep Sea* had to leave the fishing grounds for oil, losing some fishing time because the captain did not recognize the widow wind.

From Dublin Bay, the codfish schooners would continue east along the north side of Unimak Island to the next landmark, Cape Mordvinof, known among codfishermen as The Watering Point. There was a nice clear stream on the point, and in the middle of the fishing season the vessels would sail close to shore, anchor, and send the dories to the mouth of the river to fill clean barrels with fresh water.

The *Sophie Christenson* as seen from a returning dory. The schooner is at anchor possibly 40 miles offshore. The one sail shown is the riding sail, which is set to help the schooner head into the wind and seas.

CHAPTER 7

ON THE FISHING GROUNDS

On my first trip to the Bering Sea in 1934 with my father on the *Sophie Christenson*, he selected the southwest corner of Slime Bank as the first place to try fishing. As we proceeded northeast, well offshore from Unimak Island after passing Cape Sarichef, we cast the sounding lead line frequently to check the depth and the condition of the bottom. The vessel would be brought somewhat up into the wind to reduce the headway. Then one man took the lead forward on the windward side of the vessel and cast it as far ahead as he could throw it. The lead plunged downward, and as the vessel still had some headway, the line was well aft before the lead struck bottom. The lead itself was a cylinder about 2 inches in diameter and 8 inches long. It was fastened to a coil of heavy new tarred fish line with a succession of knots which identified the depth of the water. The bottom end was hollow and filled with butter, so when it struck the sea bottom, some of the material would adhere and could be examined by the captain. Fine sand was a good bottom. Mud was not acceptable as there would be no cod there.

Of course this was long before the days of electronic navigation, and the codfish vessels did not have echo sounders. We calculated our position by taking bearings from the mountains or other landmarks when the weather was sufficiently clear. Sun observations were possible at times, but a captain seldom bothered to take them after anchoring on good fishing grounds, so the good positions shown in previous years' log books were not that accurate.

After several soundings, we would obtain a satisfactory one for fishing in 27 fathoms of water on coarse sand bottom. The steering wheel was "brought down," a term that refers to bringing the vessel up into the wind, and the four large sails were lowered quickly. Next we dropped the anchor and let out sufficient chain so that the vessel would not drag anchor. In 27 fathoms, usually about 100 to 125 fathoms was sufficient. The jib sails were lowered and secured. Each boom on the lower edge or side of the large sails was landed in a crotch and chains secured each way to hold it as the vessel rolled. The spanker sail was removed, and the much smaller riding sail was put in its place and hoisted so as to make the schooner head into the wind.

When the ship was at anchor, regular watches ended. One man in the crew was the night watchman, and his duty time was from about 6 p.m. to 5 a.m. At other times there were always enough men up to note anything out of order. As well, there was a man from the dressing crew assigned to be the day man or engine man. This relieved him of many of the duties performed by other members of the dress gang. However, he had to wash the vessel down fore and aft every morning, make sure the bilges were pumped out morning and night, run the light plant to charge the batteries, and start the winch engine so the fishermen had power to launch the dories. He provided wash-down water for the dress gang periodically, possibly every hour, and he tallied fish as the fishermen delivered their catch. He was the captain's right-hand man and also served the splitter when needed.

On the fishing grounds the meal schedule was changed, with breakfast at 4 a.m., dinner at about 9 a.m., and supper at 4 p.m. The dress gang was always at the second seating for breakfast if they wanted to eat at that time. Should any man

Berger Jensen returning to *Charles R Wilson* in 1938. The two dories in the foreground are on the long painter.

remain in his bunk for several hours, especially if the crew had worked late the night before, he would get a mug up, and this would hold him until dinner.

The fishermen all took their fish lines, leads, etc., to their dories. We had on board several barrels of salted herring, and each man took some for bait. Also, each fisherman placed his engine in the dory well and started it to be sure it would run the next day when the dories were launched for the first time.

The deck crew, or as we called them, the dress gang, completed fixing up the splitting tables and the checkers on the deck. Now was the moment we were all waiting for. Some of the dress gang cast their fish lines over the side of the vessel and began jigging to attract fish to take the hook. Almost immediately several large cod were brought on deck. More dressers cast a line over, and soon there were many fish on deck. Night came on. The cook had turned in for the night and now the galley was free, so several of the fish were dressed and brought to the galley where the night watchman proceeded to cook them in large frying pans. This was the first taste of fresh cod for the trip. Many of the crew came in for this pleasure.

On the first day of fishing, May 12, 1949, the dories brought in 8000 fish. The deck crew had its hands full and had to work under lights into the night. Later in the season, when everyone had become more familiar with the tasks, or were, as we called it, "broken in," the dressing went considerably faster. The dress gang was divided into two sections, the port and starboard sides. Likewise in the hold, there were two salters, each handling the fish from his respective splitter.

The next day the catch was 6000 large cod, and on May 14 there were again 6000 large cod. This amounted to 20,000 fish in three days, counting those caught from the deck. Three hard days at the start of the season took a toll on the fishermen. There were sore hands everywhere and tired muscles that had not worked for many months. These problems would pass as everyone became hardened to the work.

The dories were taken on board every night and secured. The 22 dories on
Sophie Christenson could all be hoisted on board and secured in 15 minutes.

Whether the first day of fishing was in Dublin Bay, Slime Bank, or farther northeast, there was no telling if the cod would be present on the day the schooner was there. As a result, there was much moving from one place to another in search of better fishing. If the dories came back to the vessel by 9 a.m. or earlier with an average of 50 fish or less each, the fishermen would be held in until all had returned. The captain would "set the jib," which was a signal for everyone to return immediately. The dories were hoisted on board, the anchor was hoisted, sail made, and the vessel moved to another location. This was called "making a berth." If the wind was from the wrong direction, they could not make the desired move and might have to wait until later in the day, when the wind changed.

A schooner seldom remained on the same location for more than three days. It appeared that the offal thrown overboard during several days of fishing caused the fish to move elsewhere. Small moves or berths were made as the conditions warranted. At times only three to five miles were enough to find clean bottom. Sometimes, during good weather, the captain would heave anchor after the dories were hoisted on board for the night and drift with the tide. The tidal current ran at a rate of several knots during the days of extreme high tide each month, and under these conditions it was possible to drift five miles.

John Markie standing in his dory on deck.

Slime Bank was a favorite fishing location for many years, and I do not know why we gave up there in the late 1930s. It is a shallow area in the Bering Sea north of Unimak Island, perhaps 50 miles long in a northeast to southwest direction, 10 to 15 miles wide in the other direction, and 25 miles offshore. The depths where we fished were from 20 to 27 fathoms. The fishermen did not like to fish in water over that depth as the lines would tangle and it was farther to pull the line to get the fish to the surface.

Slime Bank got its name from the many large jellyfish living there. They are brown in color and up to 18 or 20 inches in diameter, with trailing tentacles of 10 feet or more. They entangled themselves on everything and were a real problem for the fishermen. The jellyfish would become attached to the fish line and make it exceedingly slippery and most difficult to hold. Their slime would be all over the fishermen's hands and even came into contact with his eyes. This was most painful and caused sores on the men's hands.

The most prominent landmark when fishing on Slime Bank was Amak Island, an offshore island about half a mile by one and a quarter miles and 1800 feet high.

Fishing on Slime Bank started on the southwest quarter and progressed in a general northeast direction. In the 1930s there were the schooners *Sophie Christenson*, *Wawona*, and *Azalea* from Puget Sound, plus the *Wm H Smith* and *Louise* from the San Francisco Bay area. They would all be fishing near each other, with the captains keeping a close watch on the other vessels. It was normal to move the vessel a few miles every two or three days. Each captain had to maintain a distance of up to five miles from other vessels so as not to have the dories of two vessels competing on the same area. Therefore, the

A view of the starboard side deck with all the dories secured and no fish on deck.

movement of the other vessels was of prime importance to each captain. A short move of two to five miles indicated the fish were still there and the move was just to get fresh bottom. A long move indicated the fish had departed.

Father always wanted to be at the head of the line moving to the northeast. After working Slime Bank, the next normal stop was off the Black Hill, so marked on the charts. This was at least 35 miles past Amak Island. Once we arrived off the Black Hill, the question was "Where are the fish today?" Most often the cod were at a particular location because some form of feed was there. This might be spawning flounders or traveling herring. We could not tell from the vessel what was occurring below the surface. During the 1990s, a large fleet of mid-water trawlers were catching enormous quantities of hake and pollack. At times we found these fish in the stomachs of the cod, but we were not otherwise aware of their presence as they did not take our hooks. Sometimes there were good catches at Black Hill and at other times very little. The Bering Sea is a large area and it is easy to miss a former good location. If we'd had the modern depth finders and fish finders it would have been a different story. They can spot single fish. We operated on a hit-or-miss basis.

Normally there were no more than three or four days of fishing weather before a storm came up and prevented the launching of the dories. At times these storms were quite violent, with huge seas crashing over the vessel's rail and smashing things on deck. These storm days, which we called "blowing days," were a respite for the crew from the long days when there were many fish. Rest came first on these days, and very few men were to be seen on deck other than at meal times or for mug up.

121

When the fishing at one location diminished, it was usually necessary to set the sails in order to make a move. Here the men are hoisting one of the sails with the power winch in the small deckhouse – Billy Lund, the mate, is on the winch drum (right), and Hugh McCaffrey is coiling the line on deck (left), while Otto Andreason looks on. At other times it was possible to hoist the anchor and drift with the tidal current for several miles without hoisting any sail. On *Sophie Christenson*, Father installed the standing yard with a square sail. This sail could be set by just pulling the sail out on the yard because it was already secured to wire stays on the forward side of the mast. Thus two men could set this sail and the vessel could go to leeward or before the wind several miles at night without needing to involve the large fishing crew. They had already performed a full day's work and needed the rest.

Each morning after breakfast, weather permitting, the fishermen returned to the foc's'le and put on their oilskins. The captain and mates went aft to their quarters and the captain would decide whether they should launch the dories that day. Some days were too rough; on other days the captain decided to set several sails and move to what he hoped was a better location. If they were to fish, he gave the chief mate the word, and the mate went forward and called down to the foc's'le, "Throw them out." The fisherman then came on deck to launch the dories.

On the *Sophie Christenson* there were 16 dories in davits, while the *C A Thayer* and *Charles R Wilson* had 12 in davits. Each fisherman took the painter of his dory – that was the line attached to the bow – and tied the end on the schooner just

Two fishermen passing the time on deck. Fred Stuckey is standing in his dory
that is secured on deck (left), and John McIntosh is at right.

forward of where the dory hung, so when the dory hit the water it would not float away. The fishermen then began lowering the dories in the davits, starting first with the farthest aft one and working forward. First they loosened the belly gripe or securing strap that hung from the top of each davit and wrapped around a central point under the dory. Then the dory could swing freely and was lowered using the tackles on each davit.

After all those in the davits were down, those on deck were hoisted over the side using the gas engine winch. These were lashed on top of the checkers so that the lower unit of the engine, which projected below the bottom of the dory, was not damaged. On the *C A Thayer*, it took seven minutes to launch all its 14 dories.

When all the dories were in the water, floating free but held in place by the painter or bow line, each fisherman climbed down the Jacob's ladder and into his dory, started the engine, and ran possibly four miles from the vessel to fish. There was a considerable roar from the many exhaust openings as the fishermen started off. They always went to windward, never to leeward, so that in the event the engine failed, they could drift back toward the vessel. If there was no wind they all streaked for the shore. The fishermen claimed it was faster to haul the fish to the surface and into the dory in the shallower water. (There was also some correlation between the depth of water and the size of the fish caught. More often than not, those men in the dress gang who fished from the vessel landed larger fish than the dory fishermen who ran toward shallow water. The dress gang wanted larger fish, as there was more product from the same number of cod, but in the shallow water the fisherman often found more fish, and this made up for the reduction in size. It was the total weight of fish landed in Poulsbo that counted in the end.)

Each dory was fitted with a 15- to 25-pound stock type anchor and a hand-crank gurdy or windless with the necessary anchor rope. Once at his selected fishing spot, the fisherman would drop the anchor and cast one fish line with baited hooks over each side of the dory. Bait was anything he could catch, even a small codfish. Halibut was excellent bait as it was sufficiently tough that several fish could be caught before the bait was too ragged and required replacement. Small flounders were also good.

The water was from 22 to 26 fathoms deep, or 130 to 160 feet. The fisherman jigged the lines slowly to attract the fish to bite. He stood in the central portion of the dory with a kit board or partition just aft of him and a similar partition forward. There was a seat on the aft side of the forward partition so he could sit at times. With good fishing he would have two fish on a line before hauling it in, sometimes three. He hauled the fish lines in by hand. Each fisherman had cotton gloves and most also used rubber nippers to grip the fish line. The slack line fell at his feet and did not snarl as long as he did not move his feet. As he brought the fish in, the fisherman swung them into the after section of the dory, unhooked them, checked the bait, and then threw the lead and hooks over the side.

There would now be a fish or two on the other line, and he repeated the hauling-in procedure. After several fish were in the dory, the fisherman took his bait knife and cut the throat of each cod to allow it to bleed. When 50 or more fish were in the after section of the dory, the fisherman would transfer some to the bow section to balance the load.

Meanwhile, back at the schooner, after the dories were gone the captain and day man went to each davit and dory fall and secured them so the davits would not swing with the rolling of the vessel. Each fall also had to be coiled so it would not be lying on the deck and getting caught up in the fish when they came on board. We could not allow a mess of tangled ropes to trip on. Everything had to be kept neat at all times.

The deck crew fished over the side of the vessel. There might be 10 or 12 of them, and this many fish lines with baited hooks was a great attraction to the cod in the area. This is why the dory fisherman had to go a few miles from the ship. If the dory fishermen were only several hundred yards away, the the baited hooks of the deck crew would attract the fish away from them. After two days there would be enough offal on the bottom close around the schooner that the fish would not take the hooks anymore. On the days at a new berth, the dressers had to haul in their lines when the first dory came back and be ready to handle the dory fish.

When the fishing was good, a dory man might have 250 to 300 fish in his dory by 8:30 or 9 a.m. At that point he would hoist the anchor, start the engine, and return to the schooner to unload. He would bring his dory alongside the vessel and toss his bow and stern lines to the day man, who would secure the lines to other fixed lines or ropes so he could pull the dory fore or aft to keep it opposite the open fish port. The fisherman then pewed the fish from the dory through the open port and onto the deck. Each fish was counted and recorded on the tally board to the fisherman's credit. (His pay was based on the number of cod he delivered to the vessel.)

While the dory was alongside the vessel it was always subject to the motion of the sea. In calm weather the dory would move up and down about two feet with each wave. Under other conditions it could move five or six feet up and down, and the day man on the rail had to hold the bow and stern lines so the dory was always opposite the open port. Under these conditions the fisherman had to be very careful in his timing so that he pitched each fish to correspond with the dory being at the top of the swing.

Once it was unloaded, the dory was slacked aft so another fisherman could unload while the first rinsed out the dory, came on board, then washed his hands and face before entering the mess room for noon dinner.

In the afternoon he would go out again for another catch. When he returned, after he unloaded the fish, the dory would be hoisted up for the night. In the bottom of each dory was a plug, about 1° inches in diameter, with a short length of rope

The dories were hung in the davits and secured every night, ready for lowering the following morning. Here Olaf Kittle, one of Captain J.E. Shields' crack fishermen and sailors, is standing in his dory, checking that everything is in readiness for tomorrow.

Dempsey Pearson's dory #14 is held in place, ready for unloading, on the starboard side of *Sophie Christenson.* Behind his dory is one that was already unloaded and waiting for the fisherman to return from dinner.

threaded through it. The fisherman pulled this rope, popping the plug out of the hole after the dory was hoisted out of the water at night. This allowed any water in the dory to drain out. The rope extended some 18 inches below the bottom of the dory, and there was a loop spliced into it so that in the event a dory should capsize, the fisherman could place his arm through the loop and hang on until someone came to his rescue.

＝＞•◇•＜＝

It was the job of the fishermen to deliver the fresh cod to the deck of the schooner. From there on it was up to the dressing crew or "dress gang" to preserve the fish. One man would pew the fish into the heading box, where the header slit the belly open, cut the throat, and broke the head off. The next man took the fish from the box, removed the entrails, and placed each fish on the splitting table in the proper position for the splitter, who split the fish from neck to tail so it lay flat. With the

Mike Tomko waiting to unload. He has tossed both the bow and stern lines and is ready for the day man to give him the fish pew, though first the dory will be pulled tight alongside the vessel. There are possibly 250 cod in the fish pens.

Facing page, clockwise from top left – Dan McEchern, a tough bluenoser from Nova Scotia; Ray Press, a high-line dory fisherman; Oscar Franson, a Swede and head salter; and Eddie Ostberg, fisherman.

Waiting for the dories to return are, left to right, Captain J.E. Shields,
Andrew "Bozo" Jorgenson, Tom Pointer, Clyde Bovee, and Scott Goodfellow (standing).

Facing page, clockwise from top left – Two fish dressers each with a small halibut caught over the rail; Ben Shanahan with a 40-pound halibut; Hans "Sourdough" Olson splicing a rope; Fabian "Pjoiken" Johanson and Captain J.E. Shields working on a dory engine.

Martin Meisingseth and Ed Ostberg.

return stroke of the knife, the splitter removed the backbone behind the belly cavity and cast it overboard. The split fish was dropped into a tank of water, where most of the blood soaked out. Then the "dressed" fish was removed from the tank, placed in a drain box, and forked into the hold for curing and preservation.

The salter stacked the fish in the hold of the vessel, laid each one open, and applied a handful or scoop of salt to each. He used about one pound of salt for four pounds of fresh fish. The salt converted the water in the flesh of the fish to salt brine, which dripped out of the fish and into the bilge of the vessel. Within two weeks the fish was cured and preserved. During this time the fish lost half its weight. In the Bering Sea, even during the summer, the temperature was never above 40°F, thus preventing the fish from spoiling before the salt preservation was complete.

The kenches or stacks of salted fish were about 10 feet long fore and aft of the vessel and extended from the side of the ship to a water tank. Some of the kenches were eight feet high.

We saved and preserved all of the fish that was marketable. In the fish head is the cod tongue – a boneless fillet that is removed from the lower jaw and is a great delicacy when fried fresh. We had a tongue cutter who was paid by the pound for the salted tongues. These were sold to steamship companies and served as creamed cod tongues over toast for breakfast. (In the Atlantic both the tongue and the sound, a membrane separating the belly cavity from the backbone, were removed and preserved with salt.)

Facing page, top – The *Sophie Christenson*'s 1935 port side dressing crew in oilskins, dressing the cod (left) and setting up checkers on deck (right). Below, two fishermen – Knute Anderson (left) and Andrew Larson.

Sam Allen, left, is removing the head and slitting the belly open while Scott Goodfellow (right)
removes the entrails and places the fish ready for the splitter to perform his operation.

To cut the tongue, the man straddled a bench that had a sharp prong sticking up at the end in front of him. He picked up the fish head in his left hand and speared it on the spike with the mouth away from him and the head upside down. The spear caught the head on the belly side where the gills were. With a motion of the left hand to open the mouth, the tongue cutter thrust his double-bladed knife through the flesh of the lower jaw and away from him. Next he grabbed this flap of flesh with his left fingers, and with a second knife cut he severed it from the head. It was a slow process, and it took the man nearly an hour to cut a five-gallon bucket of tongues. Still, it was worth the effort.

After World War II there was a high price for vitamins, and I developed a process for preserving the cod livers using a mixture of salt. We added one man to the dress gang and arranged the dressing set-up so that as the gutter removed the entrails, they were dumped into a chute and slid down to a man who sat behind the splitter. He removed the liver and tossed the remainder of the entrails overboard. The livers were dropped into a bucket and then carried to a place where they were mixed with salt in the proportion of about five pounds of salt to five gallons of livers. This mixture was then put in five-gallon cans with friction top lids and stored in the hold. A cod has a relatively large liver – my guess is it makes up 8 to 10% of the fish's total weight – and 15 to 20% of this is oil.

We unloaded the salted livers in Poulsbo at the end of the voyage and shipped them to Seattle, where the oil was rendered out, yielding pure cod liver oil. We should have saved the livers during the war years, but we did not know then that the vitamin strength of those from the Bering Sea was several times more potent than the livers of cod caught off Cape Flattery or in Hecate Strait. The U.S. Bureau of Fisheries had the information all the time in a man's desk, but did not bother to make it known to the fishing industry. Once the information was out, we still had difficulty selling the cod liver oil as the

John "Whitey" Hill, left, the second splitter, with Ed Shields, second salter, on the deck of the *Sophie Christenson*, 1935.

Salting the cod in the hold of the schooner.

vitamin strength was so much higher than the cod liver oil from the Atlantic Ocean, the buyers said it would cost too much to purchase the other oil to use to dilute our oil down to the drugstore strength. At this time, my wife and I were purchasing a special potent vitamin product that we gave to our children at the rate of three drops per day. We paid five dollars for a bottle from the drugstore. When I examined the label, I found the vitamin strength of the cod liver oil that we produced had the exact strength for equal volume as the super product in the drugstore. The cod liver oil that we produced on our vessel in the Bering Sea brought us less than five cents for an amount equal to the contents of the five-dollar bottle.

There is a lot of talk these days about ecology. Nature is to be preserved, and the damage done by man is to be held to the minimum. The codfishing practiced on the sailing vessels operating in the Bering Sea far exceeded modern conservation efforts. The hook-and-line method of catching fish resulted in few other species being taken. In fact, it was normally a problem to catch enough fish of other species to provide the required amount of bait. Further, the hook and line did no damage to the bottom. Today, by contrast, the large trawlers towing their heavy nets with cables and otter doors literally

The port side fish hold on the schooner *C A Thayer*, showing three kenches of salted cod, each at a different level. The kenches or stacks of salted fish were about 10 feet long fore and aft of the vessel and extended from the side of the ship, on the right, to the enclosure of a water tank on the left. There are two half-bushel measures or buckets on the left, and the salter kept one of these between his knees, filled with salt, when he was stacking the fish. At the end of the season the salted fish would extend from one end of the hold to the other. Some of the kenches were eight feet high.

plow up the bottom, causing considerable ecological damage. We bled the fish shortly after they were caught and produced fish free of the bruises that are found on trawl-caught fish. We saved the body flesh, tongues, and livers. The remaining portions of carcass were returned to the ocean the same day. Those bits that floated were quickly consumed by the many gulls and other birds, while the backbone and entrails that sank became food for crabs and other bottom-dwelling species, returning to the food chain in the same waters where the cod were caught.

A large sea slamming over the port side rail of *Sophie Christenson* when at anchor in Bering Sea.

As mentioned earlier, Dublin Bay was the first place in the Bering Sea where the old-time captains considered it worthwhile lowering the dories to make a fishing effort. While I have seen some fish caught there, it was more a case of not passing up any potential fishing place than of expecting to have great success.

From there we proceeded northeast along the coast towards Bristol Bay. (Fishermen referred to the movement of going northeast as going "north." The opposite direction was called "south.") All the way from Dublin Bay to about 35 miles southwest of Amak Island was at some time productive for catching cod. Slime Bank produced good yields before the 1940s. One year Father caught 80,000 cod there on the *Sophie Christenson*. During the years when I was there, the first location where good fishing occurred was on the southwest corner of Slime Bank, offshore from Cape Mordvinof.

Then we made a long jump from the south to north side of Amak Island. There is shallow water and mud bottom all around this island, and no codfish were caught within 20 miles of it. Cod like sandy bottom. We needed a strong wind to make the move in one day, and as we passed the island, the wind would often veer to another direction or corner of the compass. We might start off from Slime Bank with a good southwesterly and have it die out entirely when we were off the island, or it could become a head wind. The winds were very unpredictable.

The last year we sent vessels to the Bering Sea, there were few if any cod south of the island. For reasons unknown to us, the abundance of fish in different locations would change. The same thing happened to the cod around the shore stations in the Shumagin Islands and on the island of Sanak. These were very profitable for many years, but then the supply of fish

Washing clothes on the vessel.

Fred Stuckey cuts Andrew "Bozo" Jorgenson's
hair while Oscar Franson watches.

diminished drastically. The decline did not all occur in one year, but over many seasons between 1915 and 1925. Similar conditions occurred on Slime Bank, although not as drastic. There were always some fish to be caught.

There were sometimes good catches at the Black Hill, Nelson Lagoon, Port Moller, Bear River, Cape Seniavin (Cape Savin), Hillocks, Preacher's Rock, Port Heiden, and some years as far as halfway to Ugashik. From there the general progression was offshore to where you could see Cape Constantine. Next the vessels moved to a location off Hagemeister Island, and from there in a southwest direction to the Middle Grounds, a shoal on the north side of the gully that extends southwest from Bristol Bay. These locations were not always productive, but over the many years that codfishing was conducted in the Bering Sea, all of them had yielded good daily catches at one time.

The old-time fishermen always remembered some place where they had experienced good fishing in the past and suggested to the captain that they could do better there. Seldom would a vessel backtrack after going up the coast; they always moved in the direction indicated above. Why? I do not know. That was the rule and rules made many years before were adhered to for no other reason than the precedent had been established and there was to be no variation.

Father had good catches on the so-called Middle Grounds. This is where he set an all-time record for one day's catch: over 16,850 fish on July 24, 1933. The previous and following days were almost as good. That year, 1933, there were many days when over 10,000 fish were caught. Dan McEchern set a record on July 24 when he delivered 1051 fish. At an average estimated weight of 14 pounds, this amounted to about 14,000 pounds of fish. He had to make three trips with his dory to bring them all in. The 16,850 fish of July 24, would have weighed about 235,000 pounds.

Every year was not as good as 1933. That season there were five schooners on the grounds, the *Azalea, Wawona, Wm H Smith*, and *Louise* as well as the *Sophie Christenson*. Five vessels can do a better job of locating the main body of fish than a single vessel can. The cod have fins and tails, so they can and do swim from place to place as the feed moves or shows itself. After 1947, when only the *C A Thayer* was fishing, it was far more difficult to locate these concentrations of fish.

After about 1932, most of the schooners had some form of radio communication. At first this was wireless, using dots and dashes, but later there was radio. Many times the reports from one vessel to the others were not entirely truthful. However, a captain could detect from voice inflection what was good or bad. Secrets could not be kept long, especially if the vessels were within sight. At other times a fisherman would visit another vessel and then the word was out.

Sometimes we could tell why cod were at a particular location. For example, in early June there were large numbers of small flounder on the Port Moller banks, and these filled the stomachs of the cod. At Bear River, on the north side of the entrance to Port Moller, and somewhat inshore from the usual fishing depths, there were large numbers of eulachon (oolichan), a smelt-like fish that was spawning in the ocean surf. On the Middle Grounds in August there was a prevalence of a small creature we called Sea Mice. They were about two inches long and very watery. This creature lived in the sand, but at certain times of the year they came out of the sand in search of a partner for the breeding season. Any self-respecting cod would immediately recognize the prospects of a good mug up and scoff off as many as he could hold. The stomachs of the cod were gorged with these creatures, but that did not stop the cod from taking the baited hook of the fisherman. Evidently, the more food in the cod's stomach, the more anxious he was to take more. It was common to catch a cod with the tail of another fish protruding from his mouth. The cod were so hungry that they took the baited hook even when they had several pieces of food in their mouth that they had not swallowed. Apparently it was the practice of the cod to hold this food in the mouth until they could swallow it.

We had special names for some of the locations. There is a large volcanic crater northeast from Port Moller named Venidminof Crater. On the Bering Sea side there are several ridges extending from near the crater to near the beach, with deep canyons between. The canyons are normally full of snow or ice during the summer season, while the ridges are bare. We called this Five Finger Mountain, for the five white valleys that showed. Farther on to the northeast was Black Peak. There was one large outcropping about two-thirds of the distance up the mountain, and perhaps a dozen other smaller outcroppings below, near the foot of the slope. We called this Preacher's Rock, because the large outcropping resembled the preacher in his pulpit and the lower ones were the congregation. At least this designation made it easy to identify, and it was an important point from which to take bearings. A good bearing could assist the captain in finding the same location another year. Since the tops of the mountains could often not be seen because of the cloud cover, it was practical to watch for landmarks on the lower slopes, which were usually visible. We often could not observe the sun because of haze or fog.

⸺⸺⸺◈⸺⸺⸺

The Bering Sea has the reputation for dishing out bad weather. The mountains down the center of the Alaska Peninsula caused severe weather conditions where we were fishing – on the north side of the peninsula and, most of the time, over 20 miles offshore. The low pressure centers of storms all came from the west with great gusto. There was no appreciable advance notice available through the weather service, even in the last days when I was there fishing for king crab in the late 1950s, and on the schooners we did not have the radio to listen for weather.

The most common storms came from the southeast, and there were two distinct types: the dry southeaster and the wet one. The first was clear and the mountains were visible, while during the second there were many rainy periods, but more of the time it was just heavy overcast with heavy mist. There was seldom enough rain for us to catch fresh water. This would have been good for washing our clothes, as rain water was much softer than that in our tanks.

We all remembered the story of the *Harriet G* under Captain Bob Firth. Occasionally when the dories were out fishing, the weather would clear off and be calm. This was a signal that something drastic was about to occur. The wind would suddenly come from the southeast with gale force. If the dories were out, they had a hard scramble to return before the full fury was upon them. This was probably the most dangerous condition for the dory fishermen. What appeared to be a wonderful calm day was suddenly a raging storm. The old-timers called it the widow wind, and for good cause.

Other storms were from the northeast, southwest, northwest, always on the quarter points of the compass. The northwest storms, especially before the middle of June, could be most severe. That was the storm that the old-timers had the most respect for, due partially to the severity and also the fact that land was directly astern of us. Should the anchor chain break during a storm, it would be necessary to set sail immediately. In a northwest storm with the vessel near the Black Hill on the northeast side of Amak Island, it might not be possible to clear land on either tack. The idea of sailing behind the island was not considered worthy of another thought. It was too dangerous, although I have sailed through that passage under favorable conditions. There is ample room, but with a sailing vessel in a storm and poor visibility, this is out of the question.

A further danger in northwest storms was that if the chain broke, the vessel would swing broadside to the seas, creating havoc on deck. The seas would come over the rail, and with all the gear we had on deck, it might not be possible for the men to go there to set the sails, A half-set sail under those conditions may rip itself apart before it can be fully hoisted. In the spring of 1928 the *Charles R Wilson* under Captain J.J. Kelly experienced such a problem, and my cousin Andy Shields reported to me that the vessel was nearly lost before sail was made. Naturally the sails must be reefed to withstand the fierce gale. If this were not done before the storm gained full force, it required considerable additional time and effort. Meanwhile, the vessel would be drifting toward the lee shore and shipping one sea after another across the deck. On the *Wilson* in 1928, they finally made sail and were able to stand to the northeast.

Should the vessel fall off on the wrong tack when the chain parted, the captain might not be able to get her on the proper tack. In this case it would be necessary to "wear ship" or "jibe ship," or in lay terms, make the maneuver of going to leeward until the sails filled on the other tack; and then come further around and up into the wind. With the *Sophie Christenson* this was always the case. I never saw that vessel tack; it was always jibe ship and you hoped there would be room.

Normally all that was necessary in a storm was to give the vessel more anchor chain to ensure she did not drag. This required that we open the windlass. That is, we disengaged the locks on the main shaft so the wildcat drum could be released, allowing more chain to go out. This was fine, except it also meant the windlass brake had to stop the wildcat and hold until the locks were again engaged and the devil claw attached for additional retention. Sometimes it was touch-and-go if we could get all secured again.

One time on the *Sophie Christenson* we gave her all the chain we could, and as soon as the drum was stopped, we slipped the devil claw on. This was held by several turns of heavy rope leading to a massive beam on the vessel. It also had a turnbuckle in it so it could be set up tight. The vessel took all the chain and before she had drifted back to tighten it up, the devil claw had been placed. Before we could lock the windlass, the vessel surged back on the extra chain and broke the rope to the devil claw, slipping the windlass drum. She took about two fathoms of chain on that surge. We managed to get the locks engaged before the next heave, and all held. We retrieved the devil claw from where it had stopped in the hawse pipe and, working fast, we got it back to where it belonged and tied a new rope to the beam, as well as attaching additional rope preventers. It all held. At the time the schooner was dipping her bow under the seas while at anchor, which is a tough condition for the anchor gear to perform under.

On this occasion, Father ordered all three large sails reefed and again secured, in readiness so that should the anchor chain break, we could set the sails without delay. We drifted several miles that day, but as the wind was from the northeast we had ample sea room to leeward without fear of going ashore. The *Sophie Christenson* carried nearly 200 fathoms of 1 $^{5/8}$ inch stud link chain on the port anchor, and the anchor itself weighed 3000 pounds. When a vessel drags anchor with that amount of chain, the conditions had to be very severe. Several days later, when we hove anchor again, we found that much of the chain was shining like a new silver dollar. Dragging it over the bottom removed all of the rust.

One morning on the *Sophie Christenson*, someplace between Black Hill and Nelson Lagoon, Father had the fishermen remove their engines from the dories for fear we might lose some from the davits. One dory had already been smashed before breakfast. He was worried about the vessel dragging and took compass bearings on the mountains every few minutes. In one period between checks, he found the bearings had changed over a point (i.e., 11° degrees). I never saw this amount of concern from him. After about an hour, I discovered that one of the fishermen had lashed his engine to the binnacle stand. Each engine has a fixed magnet in the flywheel to make the magneto or spark. This magnet was pulling the compass card. When I removed the engine to a more remote location, the vessel recovered all the ground lost by dragging. Father was relieved no end. This was the only time I saw a sailing vessel recover a distance to windward in a storm, even though it was caused by the engine magnets pulling the compass card and thus giving a wrong reading of the vessel's heading.

The severity of the storms lessened as the season wore on, until by the last of June we could anticipate three or more days of fishing before another storm came through with enough violence to prevent launching of the dories. However, during the period of the summer solstice around June 21, we could always anticipate a more severe storm than others before or after that date. After the middle of July, the approach of fall was on us. The days did not shorten immediately, but there was no doubt the season was drawing to a close. By August 21 it was difficult to find half the days calm enough to fish, so a vessel seldom remained after that date.

On stormy days, the dories remained on board. If there had been three or more days of good fishing, then after breakfast on the stormy day the fishermen were not to be seen. They were a tired bunch of men. There was little activity all day unless the captain decided to make a berth. This usually occurred only when the previous day's fishing had been poor. Meals were always on time, though the cooks on those days had a most difficult task to provide good hot food with the ship rolling heavily. Generally, after noon dinner some of the men would break out a deck of cards and the games began – cribbage and pinochle in the aft cabin; poker in the foc's'le.

We had one fisherman who was a jewel, Alfred Todnem by official name, though few in the crew knew it. He came from the town of Stavanger, Norway, and as nearly all fishermen had a nickname, his was Stavanger. Well, when tempers started to rise in the foc's'le, for whatever reason, Stavanger would break out his accordion and strike up some tune. There was no other source for music, so his notes were most welcome. He enjoyed Norwegian music like the polkas or schottische. Whatever argument there had been soon faded into the past, while most of the men in the foc's'le sat and listened. In other years there was a crewman who had a guitar.

At times I have seen the bad weather continue for days, seemingly with no end. Time was slow with little to do, though there were always a few tasks. This was the time for clothes washing. If there was a good wet southeaster, we would collect the water that drained off the top of the house after it had rained enough to wash the deck clean. Another place to collect fresh water was where it dripped off the masts or booms – good for clothes but not for drinking. If there was no rain water, we would sometimes wash clothes in salt water. There was no fresh water available for clothes washing except for the cook's use. His clothes, the tablecloths, and the dish towels had to be kept clean.

Once a month or more often, the tank of mixed gas had to be refilled. We had a hand pump and the men took turns operating this to draw gasoline from the tanks below deck to fill the one on deck. We would add the lubricating oil to this by pouring it from the 55-gallon steel drums. We used a mixture of one part lube oil to eight or ten parts gasoline. Eight hundred gallons of gasoline was a good quantity to pump on one day and then add two barrels of lube oil. The rolling of the vessel had it mixed before the drum was empty. The vessel never quit rolling.

The *Sophie Christenson* was the largest vessel in the Bering Sea codfish fleet, and as such was looked on by Father as the most comfortable one to live on. The smaller ones like the *C A Thayer* and *Charles R Wilson* could lay like a duck, while the larger *Sophie* was doing her stuff at rolling. I think now this was partially due to improper loading. Being the largest, she was not so burdened with salt at the start of the trip or with fish at the end of the season. The result was that she had the highest G.M. This is a measure of the vertical distance between the metacentric center, or center of buoyancy, and the center of gravity. The larger this figure, the quicker the vessel would right herself after a roll. It is good to be nice and stable, but too much makes life very uncomfortable. In other words she was too stiff. When she was in the lumber trade and loaded with lumber 15 feet high on deck, she behaved like a duck. The rolling was slow, both the displacement by the seas and the recovery or return roll, though not so slow as to cause any fear of tipping over.

Sophie Christenson was also the lightest construction of our fleet. Hall Brothers, the builder, constructed fine vessels intended for freighting lumber. When well stowed, this commodity is one solid mass and acts with the hull as a unit. The case is different when you're codfishing, as neither the salt nor the cured fish are rigid. Sometimes when the vessel was at anchor, I stood on the stern looking forward as the vessel rose in the bow and then in the stern as a large swell passed under. I was amazed at how much the hull would bend. I remember sighting on a mark on the mainmast and another on the extreme forward part of the foc's'le head. I stood still. The mark on the mainmast would go up and down over one foot from my line of sight. The movement was evident on the top of the bulwarks or rail amidships, too. The top timber was cut with a scarf at each end. The end of the adjacent timbers would open and close by at least one inch in movement. We always cautioned the crew not to sit on top of the rail in rough weather. Another place where the movement was noticeable was the water pipe from the freshwater tank in the forward hold to the galley pump. The pipe passed through the foc's'le on the underside of the beams, secured by straps. At times the pipe would slide forth and back in the straps several inches.

⟫◈⟪

With the size of crew on the codfish schooners, it was inevitable that occasionally someone would suffer injury or sickness. At the start of each voyage there were always several men suffering from sea sickness. The cure for this malady was generally fresh air and time. After several days the problem was solved and the man could perform normal duties.

I have previously mentioned the problem with withdrawal from alcohol. Some men had problems with the D.T.'s. After a week at sea and no additional alcohol, the men were O.K. for the season.

Many seasons someone came on board with some form of a cold or the flu. Often those germs were passed from one man to others, and at times it took up to two weeks before all were cured. One of the solutions we had was a prescription Father had acquired many years previously. One of its ingredients was quinine, which came in a powder form and was administered along with a good drink of hot whiskey and lemon juice. Then the patient went to sleep, and usually by the next day the man felt much better. After WW II, I obtained several shots of penicillin from my personal doctor. This worked wonders. After about two weeks there were no new cases of flu.

Injury was another thing. Men received many scratches and bruises, and these were treated with normal first aid. On the 1937 voyage of the *Charles R Wilson*, we were sailing under full canvas one morning when a huge sea came on board, possibly 50 tons of sea water in one crash. There was some damage on deck, and the after hatch broke, admitting much water into the hold. Dan McEchern had been on deck at the time, and after the wave passed he found himself in the hold, drenched with water. Also his left shoulder was out of joint. We contacted the Coast Guard doctor, who suggested we attempt to snap it back in the joint. This did not work. When we were entering the Bering Sea, the Coast Guard cutter met us and took Dan to Dutch Harbor, where there was a regular doctor. He was able to reset the joint, and Dan came back several weeks later on another trip of the cutter. No permanent damage was done.

Several times when I was on one of the vessels, one of the fishermen ran a fish hook into his hand. He had to hoist the dory anchor, start the engine, and return to the vessel by himself. Then we had to shove the hook fully through the hand so the point and barb protruded, take a hacksaw and cut the hook off, and then pull the smooth shank out of the hand. We would flush the wound with antiseptic and apply a salve, and the man rested for a week or more. The hand healed without further treatment other than daily new dressings. We made a salve on the schooner mixing carbolic acid, Vaseline, and powdered iodoform. The odor was foul but the results were almost fantastic.

Many of the men, especially the dory fishermen, developed open sores on their wrists where the oilskin sleeves chafed the skin. To lessen the problem, some of the men wore wool bands on their wrists. They washed these every night and hung them to dry. Other fishermen wore ladies silk or lisle stockings. This was before nylon stockings. It was much easier to keep these clean.

Another ailment suffered by a few was boils, which usually formed on the wrists but could appear at almost any location on the body. They were very sore, and a man with boils normally was unable to work. I was very successful at removing them. First I would apply a poultice for one or two days until the boil had a self-contained form. Then carefully, with tweezers, I removed the entire core as one self-contained sack. After the core was removed, the wound healed quickly.

Cuts were another common occurrence. When he removed the fish hook from the codfish, a man often just took hold of the shank of the hook with his hand and gave it a severe twisting motion and a shake. Sometimes the teeth of the cod would cut the fisherman's hand as he did this. Generally the wound would heal within a day or two. Sometimes a man would be cut by his bait knife or the splitter's knife. One day when I was splitting, I removed my gloves to sharpen the knife and accidentally let the knife slip from my grasp. There were about 1° pounds of lead on the handle, and this caused the extra-sharp blade to cut two of my fingers to the bone as it slipped. I had the cut cleaned, antiseptic and a bandage were applied, and I was back to the splitting table. The splitter often nicked a finger of his left hand that was holding the fish in place. As a precaution against deep cuts, each splitter had two canvas gloves on the left hand. When the glove was wet, the surface was very tough and the two layers of glove were enough to prevent a cut through the skin of the finger.

On the sailing vessel, we had to cope with these problems without outside assistance. Before 1931, when there was a serious injury the vessel had to heave anchor and sail to Dutch Harbor. After 1931, when there was a wireless set on board the schooners, we could call the Coast Guard to come to the vessel. During the 1930s the large Coast Guard cutters carried a doctor, who made at least one visit to each schooner during the season.

Another serious ailment was toothache. We had forceps on board to "treat" this. I have seen the Coast Guard doctor use our forceps rather then his own when removing an infected tooth.

The most serious problem that I experienced was on the 1947 voyage of the *C A Thayer*. Arthur Gillie suffered a stroke. He was confined to his bunk and could not get out. The Coast Guard removed him in a stretcher and transported him to the hospital in Dutch Harbor, where he died.

———⬦———

Father was not known for using caution when it came to sailing the *Sophie Christenson*. Several times when I was with him, I felt he was carrying considerably more canvas than good judgment would suggest, especially for a vessel of the age of his flagship. If the *Wawona* were ahead and Father thought he could beat her into Unimak Pass, then look out. One spring, Father was racing the *Wawona* with Captain Tom Haugen in command. The *Sophie* was considerably the larger of the two and by this measure alone could stand more driving in a given sea condition. Well, Father made it to the Pass without mishap, but the *Wawona* tore up several sails.

Sophie had a long history of throwing butts. That is, the vessel would work or twist in the seaway and finally one of the caulking seams on the end of a plank under the counter or stern would come out. To put it in lay terms, the vessel would develop a bad leak. The sea water would pour into the vessel.

In the spring of 1939, Father was cracking on to take advantage of a fair wind. However, the forestay on the vessel carried away. This was serious, but by quick action to reduce the sails and install other preventer wires, no other damage occurred on deck. However, the vessel was strained to the point that several seams opened up and she was making water. The pumps were put to work, and by almost steadily pumping the hold, she could be kept dry.

The passage through Unimak Pass that year was most difficult, and Father anchored the vessel several times while the wind blew with gale force from the Bering Sea. Finally they were able to proceed into the Bering Sea and tried fishing on the Slime Bank without much success. The vessel was moved north of the Island and then farther, to Nelson Lagoon. Here they found good fishing.

On May 28 they experienced a strong northwest gale. On this day the log entry showed Father had 35,000 fish; the *Wawona* under Captain Haugen had 10,000; while the *Azalea* under Captain John Grotle had not launched the dories for the first time. The next day the dories caught 3800 good fish, but the log also notes the *Sophie* was now leaking about three inches per hour. On May 30, Father called the Coast Guard and requested a tow into Port Moller, where the damage could possibly be repaired. The Coast Guard ship *Hermes* came to the schooner's aid and towed the vessel to an anchorage in the channel at Port Moller, then departed.

On June 1, 14 dories towed *Sophie* toward the cannery wharf, where Father intended to set her on the beach at high tide so that the underbody could be examined and repaired. The outgoing tidal current caught the vessel and set her on the beach near the end of the sand spit, not where Father desired. At low tide the crew did the necessary caulking work on the starboard side of the hull, and the schooner floated off on the high tide the same day. All was well so far. There was not sufficient depth of water in the channel northeast of the cannery wharf for the vessel to proceed there, so they anchored southwest of the wharf, still in the channel, with one line to the wharf and another straight in to the shore. The night of June 1 was calm, with the vessel just touching the beach on the after end of the keel.

June 2 came in with a gale out of the southeast. The vessel could not be turned around so that the port side would be exposed and repairs made there. June 3 the weather was even worse; by now the wind had reached full gale proportions, still from the southeast where there is a sweep across the mountain range and then across the bay. By noon Father estimated the wind strength at 55 knots, probably based on a wind gauge at the cannery. The seas were breaking clear across the *Sophie*, and she drifted ashore. During the low tide that day the wind moderated somewhat, and even though there was still three feet of water around the schooner, the men were able to complete the last of the repairs.

At the tip of the high tide that night, 11:30 p.m., a severe squall came out of the southeast and the mooring line to the wharf parted. The bow of the schooner was forced high up on the beach. She was now in a position from which the combined force of the crew and the cannery workers with their small tender could not extract her. Outside assistance was required and soon. The log entries for the next few days show the efforts Father made to obtain help from the Coast Guard and commercial tugs. Part of the shoe, that timber on the lower side of the keel, was torn off by the storm and came floating up alongside.

Both Father and the crew members had considerable doubt that the *Sophie Christenson* could be refloated. If she were not, she would soon become a total loss. Accordingly, Father decided that the fish should be removed before the vessel filled with water, as this would damage the salt cod by removing the salt and allowing decay to set in. Father agreed to pay the men for the time they spent removing the cargo, and the crew was put to work removing the salt cod from the hold and placing it in burlap sacks that were obtained from the cannery. The fish was then shipped to Seattle on the Alaska Steamship Co. vessel *Latouche*.

On June 10 the log book notes that the tug *Mathilda Foss* had left Sand Point in the Shumagin Islands on the Pacific side, bound for their assistance. On June 12 at 6 a.m., the *Mathilda Foss* arrived. She tied up alongside and began the task of dredging a channel from the *Sophie Christenson* to deep water in the channel The towboat, being much smaller than the schooner, could float while the larger vessel was aground. The tug worked her engine so as to move the light volcanic sand with the current from the propeller. She moved the sand first in one direction and then in another, but always away from the schooner, where the storms had built a large ridge of sand alongside the vessel. At low tide the tug had to move over to the cannery wharf to avoid going aground. Then the tug captain changed his position so as to thrust the propeller wash under the schooner. Soon the muddy water was seen to be coming up on the port side, which was next to the beach. This was a good sign and indicated that a hole had been excavated under the keel. The tug was moved slightly alongside the schooner so as to widen the opening under the keel, until by 6 a.m. on June 14, when they had to stop on account of the tide, there was an opening 50 feet wide from below the foremast to the main hatch. The tug returned at 2 p.m., and by 5 p.m. had the vessel afloat and then moored her to the cannery wharf.

The schooner remained at the cannery wharf the next day while preparations were made to return to fishing. The vessel was now tight and not making any water. Father managed to talk the cannery superintendent into giving him 2000 gallons of fresh water. Under normal conditions no water was available from the cannery at this early date in the season as the water line from the ponds, nearly a mile away, was not yet connected. The water line was opened up every fall and drained to prevent freezing, and it was not until mid-June that the area was sufficiently safe from night freezing to allow the line to remain full of water without danger.

At 5:30 p.m. on June 16, with everything back in seagoing condition, the *Mathilda Foss* took the schooner in tow out through the narrow entrance and northeast to an anchorage on the fishing ground off Cape Seniavin. The tug then returned to Sand Point and had a considerable amount of sand to remove from her piping systems. Fortunately the engine cooling water pipes did not become clogged during the operation.

From then on the *Sophie Christenson* experienced very good fishing and returned in August with a total catch for the summer of nearly 360,000 fish. The log entry on August 8 states that the dories were launched at the usual 4:30 a.m. time, but the wind sprang up from the north and by 7 a.m. all the dories were aboard with 2000 fish. Then the entry states: "hove up, sailing SWxS everything set G O I N G   H O M E." Evidently Father was happy to see the end of that season, as that is the only log entry in capital letters.

This was not the *Sophie Christenson's* first episode of leaking during the time Father owned her. The first occurrence was in 1927 on a voyage from Vancouver, B.C., to Suva in the Fiji Islands under Captain Hans Anderson. That story is included in the account by Andy Shields, who made the voyage as a seaman. Captain John Grotle took the vessel to the Bering Sea in 1932, and on the return portion of the trip, when they were still several hundred miles west of Vancouver Island, a severe storm "started the caulking" (loosened the caulking in a seam), with the result that she began making an excessive amount of water. Captain Grotle requested assistance from the Coast Guard, and the USCGC *Snohomish* was dispatched from Port Angeles to tow the schooner into safe harbor at Neah Bay, where a commercial tug took over and continued the towing to Poulsbo. Once more, this time in 1941, good old faithful that she was, *Sophie* threw a butt under the port counter or stern. The crew could see water in the store room in the stern, running down to the bilge. The leak was under the skin, and repairs could not be made from the inside of the vessel. The leaking began near the end of the fishing time in the Bering Sea, and near-continuous pumping was required from then until after the vessel had been unloaded. At that point, the lightening of the vessel raised the leaking seam above the waterline.

The leaking seam was always in the same location – under the port counter on the end of one of the planks. I have since learned that this was a common fault with some vessels, as the ship builder did not properly space the ends of the planks in the region where they were tapering. As the planks went aft and were narrowed down, at some point the two planks finally became the width of one plank. The builder cut the after plank so that one of those forward would butt the end, and the other plank would be butted several frames farther aft. At times the ship builders spaced the butts only two frames apart. When the vessel was working in a seaway, it caused movement of the joints and the result was that one or more caulking butts would loosen until the caulking fell out. From then on the vessel had a severe leak. This appears to have been the problem with the *Sophie Christenson*.

———————⟾⬦⟸———————

By the Fourth of July, most of the codfish schooners had been on the banks for two months and the supply of fresh water was running low. The *Sophie Christenson* and, after World War II, the *C A Thayer* carried sufficient fresh water for the entire season. However, for most codfish schooners there were not enough tanks to last out the entire season. By mid July of 1940, the *Charles R Wilson* was fishing on the Middle Grounds, about 125 miles from shore. One day a northeast breeze made the sea too rough to fish, so Captain Dempsey Pearson ordered the anchor hove in and set sail southeast by east for the Hillocks. They sailed all day and by 9:30 p.m. were off the Hillocks, where they anchored for the night. Next morning at first light, around 3 a.m., they again hove the anchor and set all sail heading to the east and closer to shore, cruising along the beach all day, just far enough offshore to feel safe, looking for the mouth of the river. Finally they found it at dusk, slightly to the southwest of where it had been the previous year. This is normal as the river shifts back and forth along the shore. The schooner was anchored for the night only three miles offshore, and due to the closeness, a more careful watch was maintained all night. Should the wind switch to the northwest and blow hard, they would have been in a dangerous position.

The next morning breakfast was at 4 a.m. as usual. Immediately after, the dories were launched and filled with empty barrels. These were taken ashore and above high tide line, where the men dug a hole in the bed of the small river so they could bail the water out of the shallow stream and pour it into the barrels, using a funnel and strainer to remove feathers or other objects. As soon as the first few barrels were full, the crew began the task of rolling each barrel down the beach and into the dories, then headed back to the schooner. The barrels were hoisted on deck and the contents dumped into the freshwater tanks. The weather held favorable, and at the end of the day all of the tanks were full.

As soon as everyone was back on board, they hove anchor and set sails just before sunset. There was still a gentle northeast breeze, and the schooner proceeded back to the Middle Grounds. The return trip took one day and two nights, so

The dories being launched from the schooner *Wawona* to collect fresh water, circa 1920.

A Japanese trawler, 1938.

the whole operation required four days. However, the first day was too rough to fish anyway, so only three fishing days were lost. This provided sufficient fresh water for the rest of the trip without another filling.

The Japanese started their offshore fishing of the eastern portions of the Bering Sea sometime in the late 1920s. Andy Shields reported that when he was a crew member of the *Charles R Wilson* in 1928, he was alongside a couple of Japanese trawlers. They were operating as a two-boat team. One boat launched the net and payed out one of the tow lines. The other vessel came alongside and attached its cable to the other side of the net. When the net was taken in, the second boat would release the other's tow line. Then the lead boat took all of the fish on board. Should that vessel become full, the other vessel would take all of the fish. Andy reported there were many codfish and flounder and very little else. The fish were delivered to a mother ship on the grounds that day.

The Japanese mother ship, 1938.

Sometime later the Japanese brought to the Bering Sea a mother ship fitted out with six or eight 35-foot fishing boats with bottom tangle nets for catching king crab. The first season I was in the Bering Sea, 1934, the Japanese were there with both trawlers and king crab mother ships. They would set the nets around every codfish schooner, as the offal dumped over the side of the schooners attracted the crabs, which then became enmeshed in the tangle nets. The mother ship would have from 40 to 50 miles of tangle nets in the sea at all times.

These were somewhat troublesome to us. When the trawlers approached a fishing dory, the noise from their engines had an adverse effect on the codfish, who stopped taking the baited hooks. The mile-long strings of tangle nets were a constant problem as the dory anchor would become fouled in these nets and then the fisherman could not retrieve his anchor. Sometimes he was able to get the anchor back with a portion of the tangle net, from which he removed all the king crabs he could reach, but more often the dory anchors were lost. Father did not appreciate this.

One day in 1934, Father had the *Sophie Christenson* anchored off Cape Seniavin, and the dory fishermen were out in their dories, fishing. A Japanese Navy vessel with many cadets came alongside and launched a small boat, which came over with two officers decked out in gold braid from head to toe and three or four cadets. Father was out in one of the dories testing a repaired engine, so the Japanese group came on board without requesting permission. Father was soon back and demanded that they "Get the hell off of my ship." They wanted to bring 31 other cadets with cameras and note pads to "inspect the manufacture." Again Father said, "Hell no!" and "Get the hell off of my ship." Eventually they left.

Father was adamant that he was not about to give these visitors a lesson in how to dress cod. Their desire was to sell salt codfish on the Pacific Northwest in competition with him, cutting the price with their cheap labor, but up to that time the Japanese had not put up a successful pack of salt codfish. One or two years previously the Union Fish Co. of San Francisco had purchased a full cargo of fish from the Japanese, but it was not properly cured and not suitable for the American market.

Father wrote to congressmen about Japanese encroachment on the fisheries along the American shores, but received little satisfaction. The State Department under Secretary of State Cordell Hull did not consider the Japanese invasion of our coasts important enough to do anything about it. Father also reported this visit to the U.S. Coast Guard, which indicated it could handle the situation. The Coast Guard also told Father that the Japanese were making a survey of the Alaska coast, and warned him that in the future he should be very cautious with foreigners.

Father had his own ideas about the Japanese and didn't think the Coast Guard was taking it seriously. After all, Father was attempting to earn a living by fishing, while the Coast Guard was paid out of moneys collected from Father and other fishermen regardless of whether the fishermen could make a living. This running battle continued for many years, Father remaining polite only to the point that the Coast Guard would bring mail and a doctor when needed. Little did Father realize that without the fishermen, there would be no need for the Coast Guard in the Bering Sea. If the American fishermen disappeared, those officers would lose their jobs and become unemployed. He attempted to gain the assistance of the salmon canners, especially those with canneries in the Bristol Bay area of the Bering Sea, but most took the attitude they were not being personally affected.

The Japanese were back a year or two later with a fleet of catcher boats operating from a mother ship. They were engaged in a test fishing operation in the eastern portion of the Bering Sea, where the red salmon school up before heading for the rivers. The Japanese had many miles of surface gill nets to trap the salmon before they could reach the limited area where American fishermen could fish. The Americans were prohibited from fishing on the high seas and limited to the mouths of the rivers of Bristol Bay because this was the only method by which the government agencies such as the U.S. Bureau of Fisheries could limit the catch and maintain an adequate escapement to the spawning beds upriver. What they didn't seem to realize was that non-Americans fishing outside the three-mile territorial limit could affect the spawning numbers. Years later the canners were wishing their ears had been better tuned to what Father was trying to tell them, for after World War II the Japanese mounted an enormous salmon fishing effort on the high seas and nearly decimated the Bristol Bay fishery. It is always necessary to provide for escapement to the spawning beds, and when the Japanese took huge numbers of salmon after the war, there were barely enough returning to the rivers to provide for the spawning stock. The American fishermen and canners suffered severely.

I was back in the Bering Sea during the 1937 season, this time on the *Charles R Wilson* under Captain Dempsey Pearson. We were fishing outside Port Moller in the later part of May. The Japanese were all around us and they had a large cannery ship anchored somewhat offshore from us. I remember one incident especially. It was a day we considered too rough to fish with dories, although the Japanese mother ship had launched the 35-footers that pick up the tangle nets. Sometime after our supper at 4 p.m., one of the Japanese boats came alongside and its occupants, using hand signs, began begging for food. Their hands went first to the stomach, then to the mouth, with a finger pointing inside, then were outstretched in a begging motion. The sequence was repeated several times. We gave them a pie and several loaves of bread, and this brought happy smiles to their faces. Apparently they were also cold, as their boat had been out since early in the morning and there was no cabin or heat. They had a small charcoal burner on the stern where they cooked some flounders and small crabs that had become tangled in their nets. There was no indication that they had any other food.

In 1938, Father had two schooners on the Bering Sea banks, the *Sophie Christenson* and the *Charles R Wilson*. The Japanese showed up in larger numbers than before with their salmon nets, and on May 24, 1938, Father sent his most famous telegram,

The square sail is set here, along with the mainsail on *Sophie Christenson*, 1936.

The fife rail at the base of the foremast with all of the halyards, buntlines, ropes, and lines to control the square sail.

ordering rifles. "BERING SEA COVERED WITH JAPANESE FISHING BOATS AND NETS NORTH OF BLACK HILL. NO CUTTER AROUND. WE HAVE GOD GIVEN INSTINCTS TO SHOOT STRAIGHT. PLEASE SEND DOZEN HIGH POWERED RIFLES, PLENTY OF AMMUNITION. DUPLICATE FOR WILSON." The message went from the *Sophie Christenson* to the shore cannery in Bristol Bay by voice radiotelephone, and no one knows how many were listening in. It went from the cannery to the Alaska communication network the next morning, and then to Father's office in Seattle, where George Shields was holding the fort. Naturally everyone with a radiotelephone intercepted the message, and those of us on the *Wilson* heard the boats repeating the message down the coast. We had no explanation from Father, so needless to say we were very disturbed and concerned. Next morning a Coast Guard airplane came from somewhere and flew over us to take a look-see. They flew around for perhaps half an hour and then left. We were uneasy for a while, but that wore off with time. The only communication between the two vessels belonging to Father was by voice radio, and he did not want to go on the air and tell us what he was up to because that would tip his hand to anyone listening in.

The word reached Seattle via ship-to-shore radiotelephone within minutes and spread up and down the coast of Washington, Oregon, and California, to say nothing of all of Alaska. This was the effect Father desired. He wanted action and he got it.

It was not long before the Coast Guard was informed and paid a visit to George. Captain Dempwolf, the district commander for the 13th Coast Guard District in Seattle, was red with fury. This was a declaration of war and no small two-bit fisherman could do that. This was up to Congress, etc., etc., etc. George Shields knew very well what was desired – namely, the most publicity possible – and there never was any thought of shipping any rifles. Naturally the Seattle newspapers got the word from the grapevine. Reporters have good ears for a story, and some person who had illegally intercepted the radio message passed it to the *Seattle Times* and *Post-Intelligencer*. They came to see George and find out the scoop. There was no use hiding anything, so George showed them the message and it made the front page of the Seattle papers and also the national news services. The May 25, 1938, issue of the *New York Tribune* carried the story. Now the U.S. State Department could not help but see.

Naturally the Coast Guard was against the shipment of guns to fishing vessels that could start an international shooting spree into which the Coast Guard would be drawn. A literal embargo was laid down on the Seattle waterfront to prevent any guns going on the steamers sailing to Alaska with cannery supplies. Still the fire had to be fed fuel. George was the referee between the news media and the Coast Guard and also the cannery tenders. He was an expert at doubletalk. The newspapers carried stories for several days and all he had to do was say, "The tender *Umpety Ump* is sailing for the Bering Sea tomorrow morning," and there would be a flurry of activity. There was no mention that the tender had any supplies for Father. However, Father did want some small items and these were sent on a friendly cannery tender and the news allowed to leak out. The vessel would be inspected and the newspaper story would state that no guns were found, but the inspection had not required all the cargo to be unloaded, implying there might be something hidden in the hold. The fires continued to flare.

George received at least two letters from men who wanted to join in the "One Man War." One said he was good with a machine gun and the other offered his services as an expert rifleman. George showed these letters to the newspapers, which printed the story, each day with more flavor and in more detail. The Alaska Fishermen's Union officers vocally supported Father's position: "Get rid of the Japs." Father gained the national attention he desired, and the upshot was that the Japanese were receiving more adverse publicity all over the country than they could stand. At this time the Japanese were expanding their empire on the coast of China and had taken Korea by force. The papers were full of the atrocities being committed on the poor Chinese and Koreans. The Japanese were also forcing their way into China proper. A U.S. gunboat had been sunk, and the American crew, all U.S. Navy men, were either killed or wounded. Hence it did not take too much additional anti-Japanese propaganda from Father before sales of Japanese products on the American market were suffering from the anti-Japanese feelings. In the end the Japanese withdrew from the Bering Sea. Not a shot was fired.

After the end of hostilities with Japan in World War II there were several treaties drawn up and signed by both parties. Our generous State Department gave away what the Japanese could not get in 1935–38 by fishing efforts and exploration or by the 1941–45 war efforts. The pen is mightier than the sword. Needless to say the politicians who did the giveaway were not concerned financially with the effect on the American fisheries industry.

Thus began the incursion of foreign fishing fleets off the shores of Alaska. Immediately after the war, Father attempted to gather the West Coast fishing industry behind him to stop the foreigners before they attained a foothold. The fishermen said that the foreigners would never be seen on the coasts of Washington and Oregon, and they were not going to fight Shields' war. How little did they know the size of the foreign fleets that would appear on our local shores and completely decimate the fishery until Congress enacted the 200-mile fishing limit. The State Department is still willing to give the foreigners the lion's share.

I believe this episode was the high point in Father's career. He was the hero of the "One-man war with Japan." Even today there are many men on the waterfront who remember the incident and remind me of it when we meet. Just imagine, the story is over 60 years old.

In the various voyages on the codfish schooners, I was fortunate to see many whales at different times. On the trip from Cape Flattery to Unimak Pass in the spring, there were often groups of whales around the vessel. This was the normal time for their annual migration from the southern California coast to the Arctic regions. One time we came across three whales that appeared to be sleeping as we passed. The two large ones, each about 70 feet or longer, were on either side of the smaller one, possibly 30 to 35 feet long, and seemed to be looking after it. We passed within about 100 feet and they did not seem to care.

Another time, in the Bering Sea, a large whale that we estimated at 85 feet long was jumping clear out of the water like a salmon. There did not appear to be anything chasing it. We were glad when he departed. Our worry was that in jumping he might fall on the schooner and do great damage. He weighed many tons.

On another occasion we were sailing on the *Sophie Christenson* in the Bering Sea on a near calm afternoon. One whale was swimming along with the vessel and then surfaced and blew within about 25 feet. Whew! The odor was out of this world. At first we thought one of the fishermen was cleaning out his bucket of rotted fish bait. That did have an awful odor if the bait had been there for several days. The whale was far worse and he did it several times.

On the return voyage of *C A Thayer* in 1949, we were becalmed about 75 miles out from Cape Flattery on the LaParuse Bank, with water depths of less than 100 fathoms. A pod of large whales were there and apparently feeding near the bottom. They would sound and lift their flukes out of the water. What a sight. This continued for nearly an hour.

In the Bering Sea we fished many years on the Slime Bank with Amak Island to the southeast. Just offshore on the northern corner of the island is Sea Lion Rock where the sea lions have breeding areas. In the spring the female animals come ashore to have their pups and to breed with the large dominant males. The smaller males are not allowed ashore by the large bulls, and we found them bothersome. A sea lion would come close to the vessel, and as the deck fisherman was hauling in a cod, the sea lion would bite at the fish and most often take it off the hook, or at least take half the fish, leaving the fisherman with only the head of the cod. At times the sea lions got caught on the hook and took all of the fisherman's line until he cut it loose. I have seen a sea lion jump out of the water to grab a cod as it was being hauled from the water's surface to the top of the rail. At least in these instances no real harm was done, other than losing a fish line.

The case of the dory fisherman was much different. The sea lion would take many fish off the hooks, and at other times he would raise his head far out of the water and look in the dory, as if he were thinking of coming into the dory in search of fish. If this happened, the sea lion would probably swamp the boat, and the fisherman would likely drown. I never heard of this occurring, but it was a great worry. These juvenile males weighed about 200 to 300 pounds. Later in the season there were all sizes of the animals out in the water. The large males weighed at least 1000 pounds and could easily kill a man in his dory. Oftentimes the fisherman would hoist his anchor, start the engine, and move away. Some of the dory fishermen had revolvers to shoot sea lions. We also shot any animal that came close to the schooner, just for good measure. Today this would not be legal.

<hr />

Father became captain of the *Sophie Christenson* in 1933. This was his first experience on the Bering Sea codfish grounds. He discovered through experience in both 1933 and 1934 that the vessel had to be moved many times on the codfishing grounds, preferably after all of the dories were hoisted on board for the night. It required most of the fishermen to set one or more of the large fore-and-aft sails, which were needed to make even a small move of three to five miles. Likewise a sizable crew, generally from the dress gang, was needed to lower the sails and make up the canvas in tight rolls over the booms and gaffs.

During the winter of 1934–35, Father decided to install a standing yard on the foremast. This had been the rig on some of the largest schooners in years before when they were engaged in the offshore lumber trade. Father already had all of the necessary iron work for slinging the yard; he had salvaged it from the Nieder and Marcus scrapyard in Seattle. This yard had scrapped many former sailing vessels. When all the salvageable materials were removed, the vessel was towed to

Richmond Beach and burned, after which the metal fastenings were collected from the ashes. Father had purchased rigging wire, blocks, sails, and other items and had them stored in the warehouse in Poulsbo. Thus all of the iron work was available.

Father sent a large log to the Spar Manufacturing Co. shop in Ballard, where it was turned down to the necessary size for the yard – 75 feet long. (The following year, 1936, the yard was shortened to 60 feet to reduce the top weight and strain on the rigging.) The new sails were made in our sail loft in Poulsbo, using canvas from other sails purchased from the ship breakers years before. This rig required two separate sails, each about 70 feet high and 35 feet wide. When rigged, the sail was lashed to a wire rope, one on each side of the foremast and extending from just above the top of the deckhouse to the underside of the yard. On the yard there were many steel hoops somewhat larger in diameter than the yard. The top of the sail was lashed to these hoops. The yard was slung about five feet below the crosstrees. There were braces so the yard could swing and still always be secured. Ropes from the lower edge of the sail secured it when set. There were also several brailing lines that went around the sail at various points up the sail; when secured, these bundled the sail tightly along the mast. And there was a series of ratlines between the two wires on the fore part of the mast so a man could climb up if necessary.

On the fishing grounds, the captain and the night watchman could set or furl this sail without additional help from the rest of the crew. This meant Father could make a berth of several miles, especially to leeward, and only needed help hoisting the anchor, which required the day man to run the engine and one man in the chain locker to stow the chain as it came on board. All in all, the standing yard was a fine addition. When the vessel was sailing to and from Alaska, the sail could be used to great advantage in fair wind. When all of the lower sails were set, only the windward side of the square sail was set. The other half was behind the foresail, where it would not fill with wind.

When the U.S. Army requisitioned the *Sophie Christenson* in the late fall of 1941, the agreement with the government allowed Father to remove the yard and associated hardware. It was then installed on the *Charles R Wilson*, the only codfishing vessel that was not taken by the army. The yard was far too heavy for the smaller vessel and had to be removed at the end of the season. All that weight aloft caused excessive strain on the hull and rigging.

The codfish schooners were often fitted with another type of square sail. This consisted of a short boom, about ten feet long, on the top or head of the sail, and it was hoisted by the same halyard as the forestaysail. Another boom was attached to the lower edge or bottom of the sail and was about 40 feet long. The sail stretched between these two booms with a height of sail such that the lower boom would be horizontal and about three feet above the top of the forward house when the sail was hoisted. The head was just under the forward side of the crosstrees. Tackles were attached to both ends of the lower boom, and the one on the lee side tightened to force the boom out to windward on the weather side. The end had tackles leading forward and aft as well as to hold it down in place. It sounds awkward, but in practice it was very useful. Such a sail (called "Jimmy Green") is shown on some of the pictures of the *C A Thayer*.

———⋘◆⋙———

On the codfish vessels, the anchor gear was of utmost importance to everyone's safety. As described earlier, the vessel's anchor gear had been converted from manila fiber cable to iron chain. The latter was easy to retrieve with the gas engine and wildcat on the windlass shaft. We did have some problems, however.

One day on the *Sophie Christenson* we were heaving anchor when Father was captain. My usual station was on the port bow to watch the chain as it came in and to count the shackles so we would know when the anchor broke out from the bottom. I had to watch that the chain was not going under the vessel, where it might do damage as the links were hauled across the stem or the bob stay chains. I had to let the man on the engine know when to throw the clutch out before the anchor was tight in the hawse pipe, as otherwise there was the danger of stripping some of the gears or twisting a shaft. We never hove the anchor home tight in the hawse pipe with the engine. Always the last foot or so was by hand. When we were in the Bering Sea, we just brought the anchor to that point where the stock was well entered into the hawse pipe and left it, as we would be dropping it again in a few hours. On this day I came down as usual to the engine when the anchor was

The 12-horsepower engine used to hoist the anchor and sails.

Knute "Dempsey" Pearson and Andrew Larson
working on a dory engine.

visible at the top of the water, and Oscar threw the clutch out. As was the custom, the clutch was then re-engaged to bring the anchor home for the last few feet. We watched from inside as the anchor stock entered the hawse pipe. On this day something was not right, for when the anchor shackle came in contact with the outer lip of the hawse pipe, the anchor dropped off. Either a shackle was open and ready to let go or it became stuck in the groove the chain had worn in the lip. At any rate, we lost the anchor and had to take another spare from on deck and shackle it on.

Another time, not the same season, I noticed a knot in the chain as it was coming on board. The anchor was "broke out," that is, the anchor was off the bottom, but because of the knot we could not take it through the hawse pipe. We had to stop the windlass and engage the deck winch so that the sails could be set, thus giving the vessel control. Then we threaded a heavy wire through the exposed links of chain and made it fast around a beam of the foc's'le head deck. The slack chain was hauled out of the chain locker by hand until we came to a shackle. These were at every 15 fathoms. We opened the shackle and carefully worked the slack chain out the hawse pipe, with the slack being taken on deck from the outside by two men in a bos'n's chair hung over the bow. The next operation was to untie the knot in the chain and thread all the slack. Threading the chain was not easy as 15 fathoms of chain weigh over one and a half tons. The task was eventually accomplished, we threaded the end in through the hawse pipe again, re-shackled it, and hove the anchor home. As near as we could figure out, the last time the vessel was anchored the chain must have been allowed to run out too fast, forming a mound on the bottom. When the vessel finally surged back to take out the slack, a loop was pulled under the anchor and the remainder of the chain tied the knot. It is difficult to recover from that position with the vessel under sail and all that chain dragging along.

Another accident occurred on the *C A Thayer* as the anchor was being hove in when the vessel was in Unimak Pass in the spring of the year. No one noticed that as the clutch was engaged to heave in the port anchor, the starboard side of the windlass was locked or also in gear to heave in that anchor. As the starboard anchor was already fully home, the main windlass shaft could not turn. Instead the shaft was twisted off. We had to heave the anchor in by hand using the pump-type hand gear. Then we sailed to Unalaska to get it fixed. This was in 1946, just after the end of the war. There were still some military people there, and they assisted Captain Dempsey Pearson. He had to cut off the broken shaft, which was about four inches in diameter, with a hand hacksaw so the coupling could be attached. Quite a task. However, with his perseverance, the repairs were accomplished and the vessel completed the season.

———≫◆≪———

Many of the crew members had superstitions about various things. For instance, no member of the crew could bring on board a black suitcase. This was a grave mistake and would result in some form of misfortune during the upcoming voyage. Both the man and black suitcase had to leave the vessel or disaster would follow. The vessel could not depart on a Friday. This would bring bad luck. There were also certain subjects or words and names that had to be avoided. One season the name of the principal work animal on the farms was considered verboten. Instead of using the forbidden word, the men referred to these animals as "trackdeers." For example, "The vessel had an engine of so many trackdeers' power."

Another omen all of the fishermen believed in was that of the overturned hatch cover. Each schooner had one or two hatches leading to the hold. They were generally about 10 feet wide and nearly 20 feet long (generally somewhat reduced in size from the days of hauling lumber). The sides or hatch coamings of the opening were raised 12 to 18 inches above the deck level so as to prevent water on deck running down into the hold. Each hatch cover was about five feet long in the thwartship direction and about four feet fore and aft. Each was fitted with two ring bolts in diagonally opposite corners, so two men could lift them out of the opening, leaving a space where a person could enter the hold or the crew could send the fish down. This was called "opening the hatch." When the hatch cover was removed, it was essential that it be placed on the side of the hatch. Under *no* condition was one to be inverted or placed with the lower side up. This was the worst omen that could occur. It was a foreteller of bad luck.

The *Sophie Christenson* had a ghost on board all the years Father owned her, or at least some of the crew so claimed. Early in 1921 the vessel cleared Grays Harbor with a full cargo of lumber for Callao, Peru. When the ship was 20 degrees south of the equator, the Japanese cook killed Captain L.W. McCarron by stabbing him with a long butcher knife as the captain slept in his quarters. This was followed by the mate, H.A. Friese, killing the cook. For his horrid deed the cook was imprisoned on the vessel in the form of a ghost. On dark and stormy nights, especially when the vessel was at anchor in the Bering Sea, some of the crewmen saw the ghost just forward of the windlass and under the foc's'le head or shelter deck. He never showed on a nice day. I never saw him, but then I did not live in the forward portion of the vessel. Much later, on a nice summer day in Poulsbo, a group of men from Korea came over to examine another vessel we owned. One of the Koreans told me as soon as he was on shore, "There is a ghost on the *Sophie Christenson*." The old derelict schooner was moored beside the boat we were looking at, and the man from Korea had taken the time to go on board and look her over. He was considerably shaken by the experience. (As for the rest of that 1921 voyage, H.A. Friese chose not to enter a South American port with two murders on his boat. Instead he went in to San Francisco, 107 days out of Grays Harbor, and was signed on as the formal captain. The vessel then resumed her interrupted voyage. Captain Friese delivered the cargo of lumber in Callao and returned to Puget Sound in ballast in the record time of 54 days. The captain claimed that he lost at least 8 days off Cape Flattery in a gale of wind when he was not able to enter the Strait of Juan de Fuca.)

———≫◆≪———

As the season wore on, we moved up the line towards the northeast. In a good weather year the vessel would launch the dories up to 70 days. In other years the captain was hard-pressed to launch dories on 55 days. During May, the first month we fished, there would be one or two days of good weather in a row and then several days of storm when the dories could not be launched. Some years we fished up to 20 days in May, while other years there might be only 10 days.

The weather would start to improve, and during the month of June we generally experienced the best weather. We could look for many days of calm, and the dories launched almost daily. The storms were less frequent in June and of less severity or duration. There was often poor weather during the first week of July, or it would be so stormy that we could launch dories only twice a week. This was almost the beginning of fall season. If we didn't produce fish in June, there would not be a trip worth recording. The end of June had to see at least 50% or more of the anticipated catch. Several years we had 65% on the first of July. June was the month that paid off best.

By midseason, most of the vessels had to take time off from fishing and go for fresh water. After that we continued along the coast in the general northeast direction towards Bristol Bay and usually found fish. However, after World War II and with only one vessel it became more risky to continue north, as there were no other vessels to help. When I was captain in 1949 and 1950 I did not go past Cape Seniavin, but remained primarily on the grounds off Port Moller. The catches were not as spectacular, but I had to be satisfied with fair to good daily catches. I could not risk exploring alone for a week or more without good catches.

When Father was in the *Sophie Christenson*, the largest codfisher, he was willing to proceed farther north and then west, finally arriving on the Middle Grounds, where he made spectacular catches some years. Other years the catch was far less on these isolated grounds. Possibly the fish were always there, but if you were several miles off the location, or if the spawning time of the sea mice was early or late, you would miss this super fishery. Other times the cod were feeding on migrating small fish and moved considerable distances from day to day. We had to move with them, and if we moved in a wrong direction, all was lost.

July was a month of searching for productive grounds. We could count on the weather to be generally good, giving us 22 to 28 days when the dories could be launched. Some of these were only half a day of fishing, as it could be too rough to launch at 4:30 a.m., but by 9 it was better. Other days the wind blew up by afternoon and it was too choppy. The season was already turning, the days were shorter, and the total calm periods were fewer. But we did manage to continue fishing. That was why we were there in the first place.

If we experienced continued good weather and fishing in August, it was a gift. If the captain was able to find fish in quantity, the vessel might remain on the banks until August 10, but this was the exception. By now the men were becoming tired of the long grind. Many of them were anxious to get back to port, especially those who did not have a family but spent all of their pay immediately. The captain, however, wanted to bring home the largest catch possible, so we continued to fish. By now the bills were all paid and what we caught became the profit for the season. One year with Father on the *Sophie Christenson*, we remained until September 1.

In August the fish hold should be nearing the full mark, or at least that point to which we had hoped to fill it. On the larger schooners the hold was never actually completely full, as the vessel could not float that much fish. But the salt should be nearly all consumed. Only once in all the trips I made to the Bering Sea did we wet or use all of the salt and have to depart while the fishing was still good. This occurred in the *Charles R Wilson* in 1937 under Captain Dempsey Pearson. We had more than a load for the poor 49-year-old schooner, which did not have the same strength of timbers as when she slid down the builder's yard launchways. She was deep in the water, and as near as we could determine, the deck was less than twelve inches above sea level. As we were at sea and rolling all the time, an exact measure was not possible.

Many times we headed for home the first week of August. Several days of poor fishing combined with bad weather were enough to discourage us. A strong blow from the northeast, which was fair wind from the fishing grounds to Unimak Pass, was sufficient for the captain to call "Heave anchor and set the sails."

Sophie Christenson's standing yard and square sail.

CHAPTER 8

THE END OF THE SEASON

The trip from the last fishing location to Cape Sarichef at the western entrance to Unimak Pass normally required at least three days. The first day was spent clearing up the deck, taking down the checkers and splitting tables, cleaning the dories, and stowing them where they would be safe for the ocean crossing. Sea watches were again set: four hours on duty and eight hours off. On the *Sophie Christenson* the topsails were brought up from the lazarette or sail locker and bent and set to the wind.

It was a pleasure to be able to walk the full length of the deck again when it was cleared. All the time we were on the banks, the checkers prevented our walking from the poop deck to the foc's'le head. It was now another world.

Navigation was most important as we sailed from the last fishing location to the Pass. Fog was a common condition in August, especially when the weather became calm. It was under such conditions in 1928 that the three-mast schooner *Maweema*, under the command of Captain Bob Firth and with a full cargo of salt cod, struck a reef on the shores of St. George Island in the Pribilof Islands far to the north. They had drifted for ten days in fog without sight of land and without a chance to take a sight on the sun. No one had bothered to take soundings with the lead line. About 2 a.m. on a Sunday morning the vessel went ashore as a total loss.

Whitey Hill, later a splitter on the *Sophie Christenson*, related the story. After three bumps on the rocks, the backbone of the vessel was broken and water was entering the hold. Bob Firth ordered the dories launched. It was dark, so they had no idea where they were. The crew remained close to the vessel until daylight. They had jumped in the dories taking only what each was wearing. After daylight they went back to the schooner and collected what clothing they could. The vessel was resting on the bottom and the foc's'le was above water level and had not flooded. Next they went to the store room and took several hams, a few cases of eggs, a barrel of butter, and what little bread remained in the galley from the previous day. They rowed the dories along the south side of the island and found a village where the native people were just leaving church. The crew was welcomed and given a warehouse to live in until the Coast Guard cutter came several days later and took the men to Dutch Harbor.

I do not know if there was any insurance on the cargo of salt cod or on the vessel itself. My Father did not carry insurance on cargo or vessels. The insurance companies did not want to have anything to do with a sailing vessel at this time. There were so few in operation that there was no practical way to spread the risk or loss among them. Therefore, the insurance rates quoted were fantastically high and there was no insurance on Father's vessels and probably not on the *Maweema* either. This was the only codfish schooner lost in the Bering Sea, though there were several losses from the salmon fleet in their voyages to and from Bristol Bay.

Two old dory fishermen, John Markie (left) and Ben Shanahan, sitting
on the main hatch to pass the time. Both were formerly Gloucester men.

Sophie Christenson homeward bound loaded with salt codfish.

No codfisherman wanted a repetition of the problem on the *Maweema*, so we kept careful lookout during the fog. Because we were a considerable distance offshore and could not see the mountains unless it became very clear, we had to depend on dead reckoning and what sun sights I (or the captain) could obtain. We were generally too far offshore to anchor. We set the limit on anchoring at 35 fathoms with good weather and less when stormy. In the offshore gully the depth is 50 fathoms, and deeper in places.

You might think the best approach to Unimak Pass would be to remain close to shore and just slip around Cape Sarichef and then through the Pass. This approach is fine for a power vessel but does not work at all for a sailing vessel. We would have to be under a strong northwest wind to exit from the Bering Sea in this manner, and that occurs in August only during a full gale force storm, a condition we did not desire at all, as we were sailing under a lee shore.

As well, Unimak Pass has a unique tidal condition that greatly complicates the exit from the Bering Sea. We of the codfish fleet were not aware of it prior to 1948, when I was captain. We thought the tide – that is, the rise and fall of the water along the shore – and the strength of the tidal current were in phase, as is the case in most locations in the world. When I became captain of the *Thayer* in 1949, somehow I had the presence of mind to purchase both a tide table and a current table for these waters. Lo and behold, in Unimak Pass the current tables show that for three or four days each month the current runs from the Pacific Ocean to the Bering Sea for 22 hours without reversing direction. During this time the tide rises and falls on the shore. The current reaches maximum, slows somewhat, and reaches another maximum, all without reversing direction. High tide on the beach coincides with full strength of the current; at half tide the current is at the minimum or reversing; at low tide the current is at full strength again. Without the current tables, a person would not be aware that the current and the tide are out of phase. Many times in previous years a codfish schooner had a light fair wind from the Bering Sea towards the Pacific Ocean and was sailing at about 4 knots, but was not making any progress through the Pass even though the tide tables indicated a fair tidal current.

The last year I was captain on the *C A Thayer*, 1950, we were under near calm conditions as we approached Cape Sarichef, about 75 miles distance. One morning at 5 or 6, more in jest than otherwise, I said to Billy Lund the Finn mate,

Charles R Wilson sailing south through Unimak Pass in 1944.

"Launch the dories and tow the vessel." He did just that. Next thing I knew there were three dory engines purring beside the vessel. It was calm enough that the dories could be lashed alongside. We launched a couple more, making a total of five. With a little wind and the dories we were making 3 or 4 knots, 5 knots if there was a slight breath of air. The engines were lashed so they would not rotate, and no one was required to be in the dories. Each engine had a gas tank that held just over one gallon, which would last one hour. Every now and then an engine would run out of gas and someone jumped down to fill the tank and start the engine again. Along about twilight there was a little more breeze and the dories were taken on board. Surprisingly, we made about 70 miles that day. During the night the wind or light breeze continued, and by midnight we were well to the westward of Cape Sarichef.

We squared away and headed into the Pass. All was well for a few hours until fog set in. We were in the middle of Unimak Pass with a baffling wind for a while, then it hauled to the southeast. Fortunately we were far enough through and sufficiently to the east that we could clear the east end of Ugamak Island. From there on in we had continuous southeast winds and the crossing required 30 days before we had Cape Flattery in sight. It was the worst case of continuous head wind I ever saw.

The passage from the fishing grounds to and through Unimak Pass was not always as smooth as just described. The best approach was to sail well west of the Pass when the wind was in the southeast and hope for a change to the southwest. A northwest wind was not likely to occur. There were only two codfish schooners in the Bering Sea in 1947 when I was on the *C A Thayer* under Captain Dempsey Pearson. We were about 50 miles ahead of the *Wawona* out of Anacortes and had sufficient fresh water to last for the homeward trip. The *Wawona* was short of water, so Captain Tom Haugen sailed her into Lost Harbor to replenish their supply. They encountered adverse weather every day thereafter. We on the *Thayer* talked with them daily on the radio and heard of their difficulties. After we reached Poulsbo and started unloading, we heard that the Coast Guard cutter had finally towed *Wawona* through Unimak Pass. The cutter had to remain in the vicinity to render assistance should it be needed; rather than wait longer, the Coast Guard District Commander ordered the crew to tow the *Wawona* out so they could depart and perform other duties. This goes to show the difficulties of passage through Unimak Pass in a sailing vessel.

Once in the Pacific Ocean, the weather would often be much improved. The ocean temperature in the Bering Sea in August was about 33° to 34°F, while in the North Pacific it was in the lower 50s. The winds were generally from the west.

Fred Stuckey, left, and Axel Hakestad, mate, lower one of the sails. Note the inside of the bulwarks or rail with all of the belaying pins and the associated ropes or lines attached.

Practicing marlinspike seamanship to pass the time.

Southwest winds brought rain and mist, while winds from the northwest were usually accompanied by clear weather and sunshine, a great change from the Bering Sea. As we were sailing with fair winds, conditions were more comfortable on the schooner.

The crossing from Unimak Pass to Cape Flattery, a distance of about 1800 nautical miles, normally took from two to three weeks. At times the crossing was made in 10 days, but more often in 15 to 20 days. This was called "Running our easting down."

The watches continued day and night, but there was little to do other than steer the vessel. Most of the work on dories and fishing gear had been accomplished on the outward portion of the voyage, though each fisherman should now dismantle his engine and thoroughly clean everything, removing the salt that would corrode the metal. The sails on the schooners were old and had seen many years of hard use. Often they were made up of pieces from various sails that Father had bought from sailing vessels that were being scrapped. There were patches here and there, and places where the sewing threads had worn and been restitched, so a small tear or rip in a sail was a common occurrence and had to be repaired immediately.

Other than these small chores, there were card games but few other pastimes. We spent many hours in the galley and mess hall after the cook had retired for the night. The night watchman kept the galley in order during the night and had everything in readiness for the cook in the morning. Harry Oosterhuis performed this duty many years. One year when we were about halfway from Unimak Pass to Cape Flattery, he found a one-pound can of Hills Brothers coffee. This was something special. He immediately made a small pot with the new-found grounds, and all present enjoyed the brew. Shortly a second pot was required. Word of this very special find spread the length of the vessel. The next night there was

Walter Stockwell at the steering wheel of the *Charles R Wilson*, 1937.

Schooner *Sophie Christenson* homeward bound with all sails set.

a request for more of this brew. Harry fished out the one-pound can and proceeded to make another small pot. This did not satisfy all present and a second one followed. The happy fishermen drank it along with their mug up of pie and cookies. This continued until the vessel was at Cape Flattery. The one-pound can never seemed to run out. Somehow each night after all had retired, the can was refilled from the regular supply of standard bulk coffee that was used all season.

During the homeward portion of the trip there were many hours during night watch on deck for conversation with other crew members. This was quiet time even on deck, with no loud shouting any time and no work to be done. So we chatted, walking forth and back in pairs, swapping information about who was the best bootlegger and where we found the ladies, and telling tales of good times in port. There was a man in the dress gang named Andrew Jorgenson. He was called "Bozo." None of the crew knew his real name. He was good at removing the head of the cod in the dressing process so the fish would be ready for the splitter. Bozo lived during the bottom of the Depression in "Hooverville," a shack settlement on a portion of the Seattle waterfront. Many single men lived there for lack of better lodging. They scrounged lumber wherever they could find a board. The railroad tracks were a good place, as sometimes boards that had been used as dunnage or blocking

The *Sophie Christenson* was a beautiful vessel built in Port Blakely, Washington, by Hall Brothers in 1903. She was the largest vessel in the codfish fleet and the pride of Captain J.E. Shields. During the late 1930s the codfish schooners were the only sailing vessels remaining in operation on the Pacific Coast, so they attracted considerable attention from the local newspapers. This is why there are more good pictures of these vessels than any others. Often when the *Sophie Christenson* was approaching Cape Flattery, a commercial photographer would be on board the towboat to catch a last picture of these beautiful vessels under sail.

to secure the contents were left in the empty boxcars. Bozo lived as a beggar during the winter season. When he operated near the Seattle Public Market, the policeman on duty would give him a nod of the head in the direction of "Skid Road," and this indicated he was to depart from "The Market" or the wagon would be called. However, Bozo stated many times he had much better results begging on 5th Avenue, an upscale part of town, in the evenings, when the men were taking ladies to dinner or a show. The men did not want to appear cheap in front of the lady, so they would contribute more.

One day Bozo was picked up by the Seattle Police on some charge, possibly begging. Judge Gordon was about to give him 30 days in jail, but Bozo convinced the judge that he had a cat at his shack and if he were placed in jail for a long period of time, the cat would die from starvation. The good judge yielded, and this story was repeated many times.

Harry Oosterhuis.

The towboat brought newspapers.
Here three men catch up on the news.

Hjalmer Larson, one of the fishermen, had another story about Judge Gordon. Hjalmer had been picked up for being "drunk and disorderly" on the streets of Seattle. Judge Gordon gave him 10 days in jail to think it over and recover. Hjalmer told us that the judge could have given him 30 days just as well. It was the end of January and the streets were covered with snow and ice. The weather was cold. Thirty days in jail at that time would have provided a warm lodging and hot meals. This was much better than living on the freezing streets.

We had a tall skinny man on board who fished over the side of the schooner's rail. He was not competent to operate a dory and he stuttered terribly all the time. One day he was on the deck of the *C A Thayer* when the schooner was being towed from Lake Union to the Seattle waterfront. It was a Sunday afternoon, and as they passed through the government locks they saw a group of young ladies standing on the lock wall. The men on the schooner chatted with the women, and it developed they were from the University of Washington. The ladies asked our tall fisherman friend where he came from and he replied that he was "fr-fr-fresh out of c-c-college" and his name was "T-T-T B-B-Bone R-R-Red." From then on he was "T Bone." None of the crew knew his real name.

Then there was the story told many times about "Sven The Terrible Swede." He was one of the old-timers and had spent many summers on the cod banks of the Bering Sea. One spring Sven came on board after a winter enjoying the pleasures associated with the joy juice sold by the bootleggers. On departing from Seattle, he was immediately deprived of this pleasure. After about three days, Sven was suffering from withdrawal problems, more often called D.T.'s. One morning, Sven was in his bunk and talking to the Devil. It seems the Devil had Sven on the "Tipping Table." The Devil was talking to Sven in Norwegian, as Sven had come from that land of ancient fishermen. But the devil was having trouble communicating with Sven in Norwegian and decided to switch to American as he had much more experience with Americans. Anyhow, whenever Sven gave an answer the Devil did not like, he gave the table a tip and threatened to dump Sven in the hot fire.

166

The poop deck of the *Sophie Christenson*, showing many of the crew fishing over the stern with trolling spoons for salmon or other fish. On this vessel, the after or poop deck ran the full width of the hull, in contrast to the schooners built by Bendixsen in Eureka, California, which had trunk cabins with a half-deck walkway on both sides and at the stern.

This discussion continued periodically for several days until Sven had recovered from the D.T.'s. None of the other fishermen wanted to go through a visit with the Devil like Sven had.

One morning, just prior to first light, we were approaching Vancouver Island on the way home, though we were still at least a hundred miles offshore. Dempsey was captain and Harry Oosterhuis was on the poop deck at the time. Suddenly Harry sang out, "Light on the port bow." We all immediately glued our eyes to the light, as there was nothing else to do anyway. The light grew brighter very rapidly as the vessel closed in on us, until we became worried that it would run us down. A sailing vessel is quite helpless to get out of the way of a steamer and has to depend on the larger, higher-powered vessel to obey the rules of the road and give the sailing vessel the right of way. Well, this did not last more than possibly two minutes before it became evident that the large steamer was in fact the upper limb of the new moon as it was rising in the east. For a few minutes we had that helpless feeling, and then we got a good laugh. So goes life on the ocean.

Taking the tow line, offshore from Cape Flattery (overleaf).

Beginning in 1932, the codfish schooners had radio communication via Morse code. In 1937 this was upgraded to a voice radio. With these various radios the captains could communicate with other vessels and the home office. As they neared Cape Flattery, there was almost daily communication with the home office, and when they approached the west coast of Vancouver Island, the captain requested a towboat. The home office usually called on the Foss Launch and Tug Co. for this service, and the office also purchased a supply of fresh vegetables, milk, fresh meat, and newspapers to be given to the crew during the tow to Poulsbo, which usually took about 30 hours. The fresh food was greatly appreciated by the crew.

———————⊷◇⊶———————

When the schooner was under tow from Cape Flattery to Poulsbo, the crew had some end-of-the-voyage work. When we reached the north end of Bainbridge Island, one or more of the dories in davits were launched and from there were towed behind the schooner. This was so the towboat could come alongside the schooner to provide better control while proceeding through Agate Passage and the channel at Keyport, as well as to be able to set the schooner alongside the wharf at the Poulsbo plant. Just before landing at the wharf, all of the dories on the port side had to be launched. By the time we were secured at the plant, there were six or eight dories in the water from one schooner. The dories stowed on deck did not have to be removed before mooring. When we had two schooners returning, there was quite a fleet of dories in the water, possibly as many as 20. We did not want to take them on the wharf or dock at that time as there was not sufficient space to stow all of them in the open before final washing for the winter layup. Each dory was 20 feet long, and together they would have filled the open wharf deck, leaving no room for unloading.

With the vessel home again, the voyage had come to an end for the crew members. Their next concern was collecting the pay for the season of fishing. Some of the crew were now asking, "How soon can I get to Seattle where I can find a room for the winter and clean clothes that do not smell of the bilge and the salt cod?" Next they'd be looking to secure a bottle of booze. Before the repeal of prohibition this involved finding a bootlegger; later it simply meant a purchase from the liquor store. There was also a search for some female companionship for the next several weeks while the money held out. A few of the crew had families, and they were willing to work unloading the summer's catch, which started the next day.

This work would last for at least two weeks with the *Sophie Christenson*. When the *Charles R Wilson* was also back from the fishing grounds, this seasonal work lasted for a month. Andy Shields was plant foreman from about 1928 to 1932. He told me men were out of work everywhere, as this was the bottom of the Great Depression. Here was a prospect for at least two or three weeks of work. Many of those waiting were well known to him and needed the pay check, as there was no such thing as unemployment insurance or welfare then. Work meant they could purchase food and possibly some clothing. He said it was one of the most difficult days when he had to tell so many good men, whose families needed the money, that he did not have enough jobs for more than half of those waiting and seeking work.

Once an unloading crew was selected, the first task was to remove the sails. These were cut loose, tied in long rolls, and loaded on the company truck, then taken across the highway to a field behind a house we had rented. There they were unrolled and spread out on the pasture grass for the rain to wash out the salt spray and the sun to dry them.

Next we removed all loose material on deck that could not be left until later. After this we opened the hatches and began the actual unloading of the salted cod. We had a small electric-powered winch on the end of the wharf and a swinging boom. A table was set up on the wharf with 2 x 4 boards for the top, spaced 1° inches apart, so that when the sling load of fish was dumped on the table, the loose salt would fall through the cracks and thus be separated from the fish. The codfish companies purchased all of the fish at the end of the trip and were willing to pay the previously agreed-on price, but they did not want to pay for excess salt.

Joseph Russ homeward bound in 1911 with a strong fair wind.

171

The schooners *Sophie Christenson*, next to the wharf, and *Charles R Wilson* alongside in 1941.
Note the dories under the stern of the schooner.

The men working in the vessel's hold used single-tine fish pews to remove the fish from the kenches and place them in the rope slings for hoisting to the wharf. The filled slings were hoisted and dumped on the table, where three or four men sorted them for size and placed them in fish carts to be transported to the storage tanks in the various sheds. When each cart was full, a man wheeled it to the scale for weighing. At the scale was one man selected by the crew and paid by them to oversee that the weight was correct.

After this the man wheeled the cart into the sheds where, with a fish pew, he placed the salted cod in the storage tanks. Each tank held about 20 tons of fish. After it was filled, the tank was flooded with a salt brine solution of 100% saturation (checked with a salinometer). The salt brine kept the air from contacting the fish, and as this was during the winter, no further refrigeration was necessary. Different tanks held the various sizes of fish. This allowed us to select the size of fish for each particular order.

The unloading proceeded at the rate of 50 to 70 tons per day. The full unloading crew at this time was approximately 35 men. When all of the salted fish had been removed from the hold, the remaining salt, if any, was unloaded and we scraped up the salt that fell off the fish. It was all used to make salt brine for covering the fish in the tanks.

For many years after the codfish plant was constructed in 1911, there was no winch and crane on the end of the wharf for unloading. The fish were removed from the hold with a fish pew and landed on the deck. The winch greatly reduced this portion of the work. Another work-saving change involved the method of storing the fish in the tanks. Father told me that

The *Sophie Christenson* moored next to the wharf, with the *Charles R Wilson* on the outside. Both schooners have returned from the Bering Sea with full cargoes of salt cod after the 1941 season.

when the plant was first placed in operation, as the fish were pewed into the tanks, there was a man inside carefully placing each fish skin side down and sprinkling it with a little salt. In other words, the fish were kenched in the tanks. This allowed about 40% more fish in each tank than when they were roughly dumped in, as was done in later years. I did not see any advantage to kenching in the tanks other than space saving. It involved too much work.

Next all of the nonperishable groceries were off-loaded. We took the perishable groceries ashore shortly after the schooner was moored to the wharf and distributed them among the family members or crew members living in Poulsbo. Perishable groceries consisted of an open barrel of butter, bread, hams, bacon, and other items in the galley like flour, spices, loose cans of fruits and vegetables, etc. The full cases of cans, full sacks of flour, and other nonperishables were placed in a locked storage room with a metal lining to exclude rodents. The medicine chest and slop chest items were taken to Father's home in Seattle, where they were kept dry and accessible.

Finally, when all of the fish and salt had been removed, we washed the hull with sea water inside and out. Everything that was loose was removed to the warehouse. The running ropes like the halyards were all removed either to the foc's'le or the warehouse where they could remain dry. They had to be hung up so the air could circulate freely, and they could not be left in coils as the air would not circulate enough to keep them dry. At this time all the ropes were made of natural fibers and would rot quickly if left in a damp state. Today ropes made of synthetic fibers can remain wet and suffer no damage.

The *Sophie Christenson* just returned from the Bering Sea in 1937 with
600 tons of salt codfish. Note the sails have not yet been removed.

Some nice afternoon after all of the fish had been removed, the crew went to the field where the sails were out in the open, drying in the sun. The men rolled them in long bundles, tied them securely, and took them by truck to the sail loft adjacent to the wharf, where they were piled along both sides of the room. Each sail was marked with a stencil in each corner for identification purposes so the sail maker could select what sail to work on during the winter.

The dories were also removed from the water, thoroughly scrubbed, and placed in storage in the loft spaces over the fish storage tanks. The Poulsbo codfish plant had storage room for 1000 tons of salt cod, 50 dories, sails for four vessels, and all the other equipment required on all the vessels. This was in addition to space used for further processing and packing the cod for shipment.

Prior to 1946, after the schooners were unloaded and cleaned up, they were towed to Lake Union in Seattle for the winter. The departure of the schooners left the face of the Poulsbo wharf open for the freight boat to Seattle to land and

Unloading the salt cod.

The *Sophie Christenson* at the Standard Oil Co. dock at the north end of Lake Union,
taking on gasoline, stove oil, and lube oil for the outboard motors.

deliver supplies or ship out the finished packaged cod. At the end of World War II, the steamer service to Poulsbo was discontinued and a good auto freight service was in operation. We had our own truck, too, and used it many days to transport the packaged cod to Seattle for further shipment.

The moorage in Seattle was closer to Father's office, allowing him to daily supervise the winter activities. Before the Lake Washington Ship Canal and government locks were completed in 1917, the vessels remained at Poulsbo, moored between the end of the wharf and a pile dolphin. This was most difficult for the crew working on the vessels, as in stormy weather the bay was too rough for a small skiff to transport the men.

During the 1930s there were four schooners in the combined codfish fleet of the Pacific Coast Codfish Co. and Captain J.E. Shields. They were moored side by side, bow by stern, usually along with several other vessels that operated in the fishing industry. After a towboat brought a schooner and moored it alongside another vessel, the towboat would back under the bow, attach a line to one of the anchors, tow this out several hundred feet, then drop it. Next the tug returned for the other anchor. After both anchors were out, the tug departed and the vessel's captain and another man hove the anchor chain tight, taking care not to pull too hard as the anchor would drag through the mud of the lake bottom. Thus the vessels were secure.

The schooners at anchor in Lake Union in spring 1935. Left is the stern of the *K V Kruse*, a large 5-mast schooner constructed in 1920 and scrapped in 1935. Next to it are the codfish schooners *C A Thayer*, *Charles R Wilson*, and *Sophie Christenson*. The wheelhouse over the steering wheel on the *Sophie Christenson* had just been constructed. Some of the sails have been "bent" or attached to the masts and booms. The mainsail gaff has been raised slightly as the sail is secured to the mast hoops. The vessels are at anchor in the middle of Lake Union and fleeted together so they will not swing with the wind. It was most desirable to keep the vessels in fresh water when they were not operating. In the salt water of Puget Sound or the Pacific Ocean, wood-boring creatures attack the underwater body of the vessel, causing great damage.

These were not the only vessels anchored in Lake Union. During World War I there were many wood vessels constructed for the government war service. After the Armistice, when these were no longer needed, they were moored in the lake. Also, several steamship companies experienced financial difficulties and had many of their vessels likewise moored at anchor in the lake.

During the layup season, security on the codfish schooners was a continuous problem. People were curious and would come out in a rowboat and go through the entire vessel. Stealing was a problem; nothing of value could be left on board. At one time someone entered the *John A*'s cabin. The door to the captain's clothes locker had become stuck because of the damp air. The person assumed something of value was inside and smashed the door with an axe. To try to prevent the worst of this, Father allowed one of the fishermen to live on each schooner in exchange for being the watchman. This worked well. The man had a place to live that he could heat, and the vessel's owner had some security.

During the winter, the men living on the vessels kept them pumped dry. As spring approached, Father hired several of the fishermen to paint the schooners that would be fishing that year, overhaul the machinery, and perform other necessary maintenance work on the rigging. The outside of the hull was painted green with a white stripe at the deck line. The deckhouses and inside of the bulwarks were painted white. The booms and gaffs were an off-yellow called "mast color." The galley and mess hall along with the foc's'le were likewise painted.

In the Federal Record Center in Seattle, I found an official 1908 log book for the schooner *Maid of Orleans*, under the command of Captain John Grotle. There were 21 men in the crew plus the captain. The agreement provided for compensation as follows: mate, $35.00 per thousand fish caught by him; second mate, $32.50 per thousand; and the other crew members either $25.00, $27.50, or $30.30 per thousand with no apparent reason for the different rate to fishermen other than the mates. Also, the rate for Andrew Slatstrom was $40 per thousand. The cook's pay was $80 per month; the splitter and salter received $85 per month; header, $35; and dress gang, $25. There was a provision that the fishermen were to receive an extra $2.50 per thousand for fish caught in the Pacific Ocean – referring to fish caught when the vessel was fishing south of Unimak Island and around the Shumagin Islands, as these fish were larger. The log book did not note it, but fish had to be 28 inches long to be a counter. After the new Pacific Coast Codfish Co. purchased the *Maid Of Orleans* in 1912, Andrew Slatstrom was the captain.

Thirty years later, the agreement for the *Charles R Wilson* and *Sophie Christenson* for the 1938 season was as follows: fishermen received $1\frac{7}{8}$ cents per pound of fish; the splitter and salter on the *Wilson* were paid $3.00 per ton, while the two men in each of the similar jobs on *Sophie* received $1.50 per ton. The mate had $\frac{5}{8}$ cents extra and the bos'n or second mate ° cent extra per ton. The tongue cutter's pay was $7.00 per 100 pounds. The dressers on *Sophie* were paid 50 cents per ton, while those on the *Wilson* received double this because of the single dress gang. When the cargo was discharged in Poulsbo in 1938, the fish weighed out at approximately 3° pounds each. This meant that the best fishermen, who caught 20,000 fish, had a pay day for the voyage of $1,160. This was during the last days of the Great Depression, and jobs were still scarce.

Over the years, the price paid to the fishermen and the others increased as times became better. In 1941 the scale rose to 2˜ cents per pound; in 1942 to 2 cents per pound; and in 1944 the government allowed a 30% increase over 1942. This was in consideration of supposed extra work the crew were to do. There was no fishing in 1943. In 1945 the scale was also 2 cents per pound plus a 30% bonus.

After the war the price slowly increased each year until by 1948, 1949, and 1950, the last year of fishing, the scale was 4° cents per pound. The rates for other jobs on the vessel were likewise increased.

The pay for a fisherman who caught 20,000 fish in 1934 would work out as follows: Average fish size was estimated at 3˜ pounds each when off-loaded at Poulsbo after dressing and salt curing. The agreement provided for a pay of $28 per ton, which works out to $44.68 per thousand fish (the agreement guaranteed the men at least $27.50 per ton after board). So for 20,000 fish, the man had a pay day of $893, rounded off. Only the highline fishermen caught this many cod in one season. There was a crew charge of $15 per month for groceries during the 1934 season, so the grocery bill for a five-month trip was $75. This meant the best fishermen earned a take-home pay of over $800. This was very near the bottom of the Depression, when jobs were few and far between and pay was lower than it is today.

By 1950, the fisherman with the same catch would be paid 4° cents per pound times 3˜ pounds per fish, or $146 per thousand fish, for a total of $2,920, again rounded out. From this would be subtracted his bills in the slop chest. After 1935 there was no charge to the crew for food.

Many of the fishermen made advance draws before leaving Seattle, and there was also a provision for the company to pay a monthly amount to some dependent – for example, a wife or girlfriend – during the trip. All of these advances were deducted when the crewman returned.

The agreement provided for the fish to be unloaded as soon as possible after the return to Poulsbo. The men could make draws against their estimated earnings while waiting for the unloading to be completed, after which they were to be paid in full within three days. Not all the men requested pay that early, and some left money with the company so they could draw it out over the winter instead of spending it all immediately.

About 1934, the codfishing men formed their own local in the Codfish Union and were able to negotiate for the summer's pay themselves. This proved very satisfactory for both company and crew. Many other seamen's unions made such exorbitant demands that the entire industry was shut down and never operated again.

Schooners *Charles R Wilson*, foreground, and *C A Thayer* at the Poulsbo plant in 1947. After 1945 the freight and passenger boat service from Poulsbo to Seattle had been terminated and there was no requirement for the face of the wharf to be open. Hence the vessels were moored there.

CHAPTER 9

WINTER

The Pacific Coast Codfish Co. and Captain J.E. Shields produced from 600 to 1000 tons of salt codfish on the Alaska banks each year and delivered the product to the Poulsbo, Washington, plant for further preparation for market. The salt cod were stored in 20-ton wood tanks at Poulsbo.

The first step in processing the fish into one-pound packages of boneless cod was to stack the cod, open side down, in kenches for several days to allow some of the moisture to drain out. Then the cod was scrubbed, placed in a fish cart, and taken to the skinning room, where men removed the outer skin, the skin lining the belly cavity, and remaining backbone. They pulled the skin from the fish by hand and placed the waste skin and bones in burlap sacks that were shipped to the Lepage's glue plant in San Francisco. There the waste was cooked and the glue rendered out.

The cod fillets, meanwhile, were trucked into the packing room where their rib bones and any blemishes were removed. Then a man cut them to fit the one-pound packages. The fish were placed in a form in a press, squeezed tight, and tied with string, then wrapped in parchment paper and overwrapped with moisture-proof cellophane before being placed in cardboard shipping cases.

This phase of the work continued from soon after the schooner was unloaded in September until May. It provided seasonal employment for nearly 20 people. This lengthy process of preparing cod for market differs from most other fisheries in which fish is caught and immediately delivered to a processing plant where it is either frozen or canned.

A considerable quantity of the salt cod was further dried for shipment to the market as "Baccala" or "Bacallo," depending on the nationality of the intended purchaser (one is Spanish and the other Italian). From May through September the fish would be placed on drying screens in the "flake yard" for drying in the sun. During the wet winter months the fish would be moved indoors to a steam-heated room. The cod were placed on wire screen racks, steam coils would heat the room, and a huge fan circulated the air. The fish remained here for up to 48 hours, until the desired dryness was attained. The fish on the upper racks dried faster, so it was necessary to remove dry fish from the top and replace them with less dry fish. These fish were packed into 100-pound wood boxes for shipment. Salted fish would keep for up to one year in cool storage and was therefore available for shipment to parts of Europe not subject to extreme temperatures. Some salted cod was further dried for shipment to southern Europe and North Africa.

We also processed lutefisk at the Poulsbo plant. This is a preparation method developed in Scandinavia and used particularly during the holiday season. The Scandinavians would freshen dried fish in water for several days so it reabsorbed

Schooners *C A Thayer*, foreground, and the hull of *Sophie Christenson* at the Poulsbo plant in 1947.

Steamships and sailing vessels in Lake Union for the winter.

Vessels moored in Lake Union are, left to right, *La Merced*, *K V Kruse*, *C A Thayer*, *Charles R Wilson*, and *Sophie Christenson*.

the water that had been lost during drying. Then the fish was placed in a vat filled with water and ashes collected from burning hard woods. (In the Americas, lye or sodium hydroxide was added.) This mixture was allowed to soak for several days. The lye or ash solution broke down the fiber structures and rendered the flesh somewhat like jelly. Then the fish was soaked in fresh water to remove the lye before it was ready for cooking. This method could only be used during the winter months when the weather was cold, or the fish would spoil during the process. The final product was called "lutefisk," or fish that has been treated with lye. This lutefisk was simmered in the family kitchen and served immediately with boiled potatoes and melted butter.

The Scandinavians brought the recipe for lutefisk with them when they came to the Americas, and it became a delicacy during the winter. This led to expanded markets for the Pacific Coast Codfish Co. We took several of the large wood storage tanks in the Poulsbo plant, soaked the cod and applied the lye solution, freshened out the lye, and shipped the product in wood barrels. This product had a very short shelf life unless it was frozen. By 1950, the last year we operated a codfish schooner in the Bering Sea, perhaps 100 tons of our catch was sold for lutefisk. Lutefisk was especially important to us after refrigeration became more widely available and made it possible for fresh fish to be preserved with ice or freezing. This greatly diminished the demand for salt cod.

———⟨◇⟩———

Several fishermen obtained off-season work in the Poulsbo sail loft. In 1930, Father purchased a used heavy-duty sewing machine because he thought it would be advantageous to perform all of the sail repair work with the fishing crew during the winter. Many of the crewmen were adept with palm and needle, so there was no problem obtaining skilled workmen. This also gave Father more control over this phase of the work.

The sail loft was on the upper story of one of the 100- by 40-foot warehouses at Poulsbo. Like all the others, this building was constructed of wood 2 x 6 studs, sheeted on the outside with wood siding, and supported by creosoted piles that allowed the tide to ebb and flood underneath. It was given one coat of red paint when first constructed. The inside of the building had not been finished at all; the exposed studs showed the back of the siding. The lower floor was devoted to the wood tanks in which salt cod was stored for the winter. The wash water and drainage from the storage tanks were discharged into Liberty Bay.

There were no posts or other obstructions in the floor of the loft except for the stairway from the lower level, and this was wide enough to drag dories or the large sails to the second floor. It was an ideal place to store and repair sails or empty wood fish boxes. There were ten double-hung windows on each side and three on each end, and most of the time these provided all the necessary light. During December and January it was occasionally too dark for work. The only other illumination was several dangling light globes suspended from the rafters. There was also no heat, which was no problem except during some of the winter days when it was too damned cold to work. On these days the sail makers were assigned other duties.

We had a row of rolled-up sails along each side of the floor. The accumulation of sails was extensive as it included full sets for four schooners plus many other sails Father had purchased from the ship breakers for a song when the vessel to which each had belonged was being scrapped. A new sail cost considerable money, so Father bought the used sails with the intention of using parts or all of them to fit his vessels. We also used a lot of canvas as hatch covers and to cover the cod in the hold of the vessel as it was being salted. These pieces were cut out of the sails purchased from the scrapped vessels.

Everything that could be salvaged from other vessels was reused where possible. There were huge stacks of wood blocks or, as land lubbers call then, "pulleys." Coils of wire or rope, new or used, hung from the walls every place that a spike could

The winter work crew at the Pacific Coast Codfish Co. Poulsbo processing plant, circa 1930 (overleaf).
The man near the right is holding a large salted cod.

The whole fish were removed from the storage tanks, scrubbed to remove the fish slime, then stacked to drain in piles called kenches before further drying.

be driven. Many of the sails were reinforced with wire rope along the edges, the foot, the head, the mast side, or the leach. This wire could be salvaged from one sail to be used on another. To use new rope cost money and was also a considerable task. You could not put bare wire next to the canvas, so each wire had to be tarred, covered with tar-soaked strips of burlap, then strips of canvas, and lastly some form of covering like being wound with twine or small rope. Further, the wire rope had to be spliced in the ends, and stiff wire was most difficult to handle. Both the labor and the materials for this covering were costly.

During the winter, each sail was taken out on the floor and opened up for inspection. We had one or two men assigned to sail making, but we needed more men to move the larger sails. The large fore-and-aft sails for the schooners, even when dry, weighed from 1000 pounds to nearly a ton. They were from 40 to 65 feet in height, up to 40 feet wide, and made up of canvas strips sewed together. These strips were 22 inches wide with 2-inch-wide marks along each edge to aid the sewing. When sewed together, the strips had a net width of 20 inches. Each edge was selvedged so it would not ravel. The strips of canvas ran the full height of each sail, so when the sail was assembled, the seams between the strips were of this length.

We had sails of different canvas weight or thickness. The heaviest was #00, then #0, #1, #2, and down to the lightest, #3. These were the designations used by the canvas factory that wove the canvas. #00 was 18 ounces per running yard length of bolt material 22 inches wide. Each number beyond was one ounce less per yard. #1, 16 ounces per yard, was the

The first step in the preparation of the salt cod for market as boneless fillets was to remove a daily supply from the storage tanks and wheel the cured fish to the skinning room, where men removed the outer skin, the skin lining the belly cavity, and the tail portion of the backbone that was not removed when the fish was split on the fishing grounds. In the foreground is John McIntosh, and behind is Chester Nelson. The skin was pulled from the fish by hand, and the waste placed in sacks to be rendered into glue at the Lepage's glue plant near San Francisco. This is a good view of the fish carts.

weight for our large sails. Hence for a sail over 60 feet in height and 40 feet wide, an enormous weight of canvas is required before all of the ropes and other fittings or hardware are added.

When the sail was laid out for inspection, the men would look for places where a rope had rubbed against the sail when it was set and worn out the stitches. All worn seams on the sails were resewn. For a small worn spot the sewing was done by hand with palm and needle. For longer seams, the canvas was pulled over to the sewing machine and the seam re-done. Sometimes one or more of the strips of canvas needed to be replaced, and the machine was also used for this. It was similar in construction to a home machine except larger and stronger.

Several men were required to handle the canvas as it ran through the machine. When sewing a center seam in a 40-foot-wide sail, for example, half of the total sail had to be rolled up under the machine arm. It was no small task to squeeze 20 feet of canvas into a roll under this machine arm of less than 12 inches diameter. As the sewing progressed, all of the full roll of this sail had to be fed through the space under the arm as the seam was made. Our machine would sew one seam at a

The one-pound packages of salt cod were first wrapped with parchment paper by Agnes Porter, and then overwrapped with moisture-proof cellophane by Anna Jacobson at left.

Chester Nelson removes the skin from the cod.

time, and the design of the sail required three rows of stitching for each seam, one on the edge of each strip and the third down the middle.

One man would operate the machine, one helped feed the canvas to the needle, and one or two pulled the canvas away from the needle. Often only three or four feet of seam could be stitched before the machine had to be stopped and the large mound of canvas pulled forward. Further, the canvas had to be turned over to sew the second edge seam. It could not be made from the first or top side because there was no canvas edge to guide the needle along.

Each rope that was on the edge of a sail was given special inspection and replaced if it was damaged or rotten, for if a rope on the edge of a sail parted, the sail would rip in the wind from end to end and across, rendering that sail beyond repair until the vessel returned to Poulsbo. If this happened, the crew would take a spare sail from the lazarette and store the torn one there as soon as it had dried somewhat. If it were put in the locker wet, the canvas would rot. These sails cost a lot of money, so their loss was to be avoided if possible.

When we had to make a new sail from bolt canvas, the sail maker laid out the full-size design on the floor with crayon. This is why such a large room was required. Then the bolt canvas was unrolled, starting with the after leach of the fore-and-aft sail. Each strip was then nailed to the floor so it would not move while the following strip was unrolled. When all the strips were unrolled, the canvas was tacked along the edges with palm and needle so the strips of canvas would not slip or creep as they were being sewn.

When the strips had been laid out and stitched together, the ropes had to be attached to each side. The work of sewing the rope to the sail was slow and very difficult A large needle was used with many strands of twine, and these were given a heavy rubbing of beeswax so all the strands would lie together and not fly all over the place. When working in the corner of a sail where there were six or more layers or doublings of canvas, the sail maker had to take a hand awl to make the hole for each thrust of the needle. To slow the work further, both the needle and the awl were sharp on the point but smooth on

After the skin was removed, the fillets were trucked into the packing room shown here. The three women seated – Genevieve Drummand, Catherine Kalstrom, and Trina Haugen – are removing some of the rib bones with tweezers. The man in the distance removes another layer of rib bones by cutting them off. The man in the center is carrying the boneless fillets to the cutting table, where he will cut them to fit the one-pound package.

the sides so as not to cut the threads of the canvas when forced through. The sail maker sat on a wood bench that had pockets for all of his supplies such as twine, wax, spare needles, awls, marlin, steel rings to reinforce the holes on the sails where some rope would pass through, and also possibly some pipe tobacco and an old pipe. The canvas that he was working on was draped over his knees. The importance of the sails was prime and the equal of the engine in a power vessel.

The smell in this room spoke of the sea, especially during the hot summer days when the pine tar gave off its wonderful aroma. The salt that had impregnated the canvas also added to the odor, while the beach under the building had its own smell of clams, mussels, and other sea life. On top of all this there was the pungent odor of Stockholm tar. The sail loft was a wonderful place to visit or to work.

The cellophane-wrapped fillets were placed in cardboard shipping cases that were sealed shut, ready for shipment to the grocery trade.

As mentioned earlier, all vessels operating in salt water are subject to the action of marine organisms – including barnacles, clams, mussels, and seaweed – growing on the underwater body of a vessel. Vessels with wood hulls are also attacked by wood-boring organisms. Accordingly, it was necessary to haul the vessel out of the water prior to the annual voyage so that the bottom could be cleaned. Following this, a heavy coat of anti-fouling paint was applied. The codfish schooners were treated with a liberal application of a copper-base compound called copper paint. It was very toxic and prevented regrowth of these organisms until it wore off. Environmentalists have found that copper anti-fouling paint is not good for the marine environment, so other compounds are now used which are much more expensive.

Prior to 1946, the schooners were moved from the winter anchorage in the middle of Lake Union to the plant of the Lake Union Dry Dock Co. We would employ a small tug for this job, or at other times use Father's 65-foot diesel-powered fishing vessel. At least once the fishermen working for Father ran a rope line from the schooner to the drydock plant and, after the anchor had been hove in, tied the line to the winch and pulled the schooner to the drydock.

Lake Union Dry Dock Co. had a floating drydock, somewhat like a large barge or scow except there were wing walls on each side that were about eight feet thick and hollow. The drydock was first prepared by installing a series of three-foot-square blocks down the centerline for the keel of the vessel to rest on. The top of the blocks was shimmed up to conform to the configuration of the keel. When these vessels were constructed, they were straight on the bottom, but with age the

The drying of the whole salted cod had to continue during the wet winter months. A room was constructed with steam coils in the center (right of photo) and a large rotating fan. The fish were placed on wire screen racks, as shown, and remained in this heated room for two to three days.

overhang of both the bow and the stern caused the ends to sag and the center to rise. This was called "hog" and measured in inches. In 1938 the *Sophie Christenson* had a hog of about 13 inches. The tops of the line of keel blocks were adjusted to fit this alignment.

Then the drydock was flooded with enough water to sink the deck and allow the vessel to float in. It was aligned so the keel would rest on the keel blocks when the drydock was raised. Next the vessel was secured both fore and aft so it would remain in the proper place, and the drydock was raised sufficiently that the keel was resting on the keel blocks. Some of the water was pumped out, and the drydock started lifting the vessel. On the floor of the drydock there were a series of so-called bilge blocks, which were mounted on sliding fasteners so they could individually be hauled toward the center or the edge of the drydock. As the drydock started lifting, these sliding blocks were pushed tightly against the vessel's sides. Now the drydock was pumped out until the vessel was in the air. The weight of the vessel rested on the keel blocks, while the side blocks held some weight and prevented the vessel from tipping over.

The shipyard crew went to work with high-pressure hoses and scrapers to clean off the underwater portion of the hull. If the vessel had been moored in salt water for over a year, the amount of sea growth was remarkable.

The air dried the surface of the hull within a few hours. We always tried to have the vessel raised out of the water on Friday so it could remain in the air until Monday, when the copper paint was applied. The largest of our schooners, the *Sophie Christenson*, required at least 50 gallons of paint to adequately protect the hull. We asked the shipyard to paint the hull

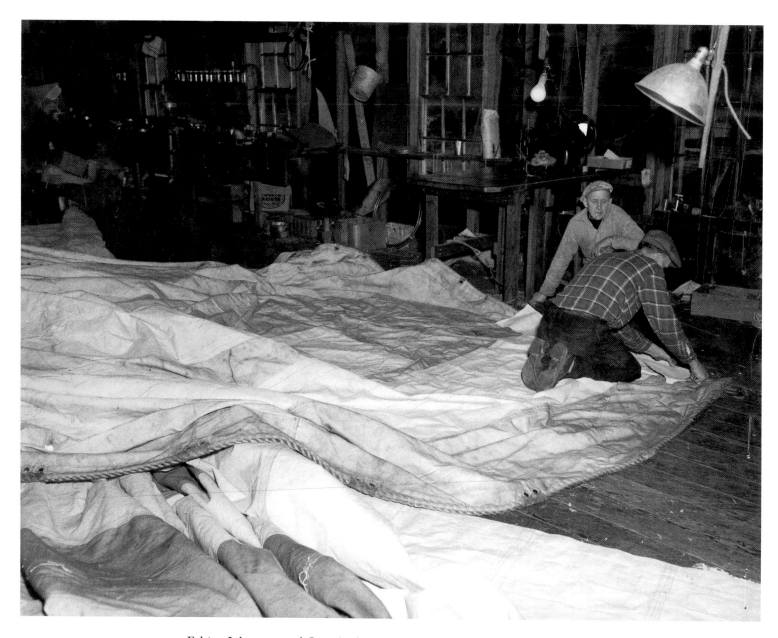

Fabian Johanson and Otto Andreason working on a corner of a large sail.

to about two feet above the waterline. Then we would refloat the vessel and work from floats to apply the paint ourselves to what would be two feet above the loaded waterline. This way we could paint a smooth line between copper paint and the green hull color, where the shipyard would have had to rig scaffolding to cut a smooth top line. Costs counted, and this was a place where we could save the expense in the shipyard.

Sometimes there was work required on the underbody. Occasionally one of the caulked seams needed extra oakum. There were times when the *Sophie Christenson* returned leaking considerably because one of the caulked seams at the end of a plank had worked loose and the oakum had fallen out. The vessel's pumps were always able to keep up with the leaking, and each time, after the cargo had been unloaded, the leak was above water. Then repair was postponed until the next annual drydock visit.

After World War II, the operations of the Poulsbo facilities changed considerably. Vessels were no longer allowed to moor in Lake Union, and since the Seattle freight boat no longer came out to the plant, the Poulsbo pier no longer had to

Schooners at Poulsbo.

be kept open. Accordingly, we kept all the vessels moored in Poulsbo, notwithstanding the effects of the marine organisms. For the annual cleaning, we found it practical to place the vessels one at a time on the beach just after high tide and allow then to rest on the sandy shores when the tide receded. We scraped the exposed side with spades, brushes, and a hose to remove the barnacles, working from a small scow as the tide receded until the men could stand on the beach. The hull dried quickly in the sun, and just before the returning tide reached the vessel, the men began applying the copper anti-fouling paint. We refloated the schooner that evening and turned it so the other side was exposed to the sun and wind. A similar procedure followed on the next day and all was painted except the bottom of the keel. This became expendable.

The *Sophie Christenson* in the Lake Union drydock.

When the *Sophie Christenson* returned from the Bering Sea in the fall of 1940, we knew that the spanker mast had considerable rot between the deck and the saddle where the jaws of the boom rested. When we examined the other masts, however, we found that both the foremast and the mainmast had extensive rot under the crosstrees and were not safe for another season. Three new masts were required. This was a major undertaking. The masts were made from Douglas fir logs and had to be 110 feet long, with a minimum diameter for two of 22 inches and 24 for the other.

The Spar Manufacturing Co., located on the Ballard side of the Ship Canal and just east of the Ballard Bridge, could turn the masts in their lathe. They knew of a logger at the south end of Hood Canal who might be able to furnish logs of the required dimension. We made the journey to see the logger on a cold and damp Saturday morning. He took us out to a deep gully where he was cutting fine Douglas fir trees. We spent two hours tramping over the hillside, looking at the tall trees. They appeared straight as an arrow until we stood next to the tree and cast our eyes upward. Then we could see the slight bend in each tree. Finally we had four marked, figuring a spare was good insurance.

When the logger felled the trees the next week, he cracked one of them. Still, we had the necessary three. The logger obtained a permit from the state patrol to haul the long logs on the following Saturday morning, and we hired a small fishing boat to tow them to the Spar Manufacturing Co. plant.

The first and second logs were placed in the huge lathe and turned while the cutters removed the excess material until perfect masts resulted, but when the third log was placed in the lathe, they found that it was not straight enough to make the mast. This firm could not make a mast with a curve, so we towed the crooked log to Poulsbo and hauled it up on the beach

The *C A Thayer* on drydock in Oakland, California.

C A Thayer on the beach in Poulsbo for bottom cleaning.

The *C A Thayer* on the beach in Poulsbo, circa 1950. The eight-inch hog in the keel line is visible here. Today the hog exceeds fifteen inches (the vessel is moored at Hyde Street Pier, San Francisco).

C A Thayer on the beach at the Poulsbo plant of the Pacific Coast Codfish Co., circa 1948. The men on the right are standing on the beach and scraping the sea growth off the underwater portion of the hull. The man on the left is standing on a small float or scow. This was used as the tide started to recede, until the men could stand on the sandy beach.

near the codfish plant. Some of the fishermen who were processing the salt cod were excellent craftsmen, so I hired three to hew out the mast.

The log was four feet in diameter at the lower end and 30 inches at the top. I ran a chalk line down the log and found it was 10 inches out of alignment for the 22-inch diameter required for the mast. After shifting the chalk line over 11 inches and adjusting it to a smooth curve, I established a new center line that we could use to make a mast out of this log. I chalked on cut lines 23 inches apart – that is 11½ inches on each side of the center line – and placed a similar pair of cut lines on the other side of the log. These measures were used from the bottom of the future mast up to within three feet of the crosstree level. The diameter was increased to 26 inches at the crosstree point, and from there the mast was marked for the square upper portion from crosstrees to the top. It was 20 inches at this level and tapering to 18 inches at the top, about ten feet higher. The mast is square above the crosstrees to hold the topmast and the square iron bands that secure them together.

We rolled the log a quarter turn and the workmen went to work with crosscut saws, making cuts down to the edge chalk lines every 15 or so inches along the length of the log. Then with wedge and maul they removed most of this surplus wood, first on one side and then the other. Now the log was two sided and flat. They made each side smooth and straight. On this smooth flat side I laid out the center line for the side with the offset curve, and the workmen followed the same procedure again.

Now the log was squared to 23 inches, and each side was planed smooth to remove any irregularities. I laid out another set of lines on the square timber and it was cut so as to have eight sides. Again the men used the crosscut saw, making cuts every 15 to 18 inches. The excess wood was removed first with wedge and maul, then axe, draw knife, and finally the carpenter's plane. The draw knife was applied to make 16 sides and finally the round mast. The final mast had to be true so the mast hoops would ride up and down without becoming stuck on some protuberance. As soon as the wood was dry, I applied several coats of boiled linseed oil, then rolled the mast back into the water.

The *Sophie Christenson* had been in Lake Union for the winter. After she had her cleaning in the Lake Union Dry Dock Co. drydock, the schooner and the two Spar Manufacturing Co. masts were towed in the water to the Port of Seattle Pier 91 at Smith's Cove, where there was a sheer leg crane capable of setting the masts. The Poulsbo mast was towed over by a small fish boat. The three masts were hoisted onto the wharf and our fishermen/seamen proceeded to install them.

First they had to remove the old foremast. The head stays were all slacked, as were the shrouds on each side. A pair of wires were attached to the masthead of the mainmast, the next aft mast, to steady it when the foremast was removed. These were secured one on each side of the vessel and acted as a forestay. Similar wires were attached to the head of the foremast, leading fore and aft on each side, to steady the mast once all the normal shrouds were removed. The vessel was moved so the foremast was opposite the sheer leg.

The hoisting sling was placed as low on the mast as possible. The crane did not have sufficient height to lift the mast out with the slings attached above the balance point, even at low tide. The mast needed to be raised 17 or 18 feet before the lower end, which was resting on the keelson (an extra large timber on top of the keel and a portion of the structural integrity of the vessel), could clear the forward deckhouse. Therefore the blocks on the crane had to allow this amount after all slings were tight. Further, the lower block of the crane was very large and required considerable distance between its hook and the place the sling surrounded the mast or it would create a twisting condition.

The rigging was finally let go and lashed to the base of the mast as it was hoisted. The crosstrees and rigging were still attached to the mast near the top, so we had to be careful that the mast did not up-end as soon as the lower end cleared the deckhouse. As the mast was hoisted we attached two 30-foot lengths of heavy anchor chain (about three tons) to act as a counterweight.

The mast finally cleared the deckhouse and was lowered onto the wharf. The new replacement mast had already been placed there. The iron work or bands at the top of the old mast were removed, then the head stays, and finally the shrouds were slipped over the head of the mast and the old crosstrees slipped off. They were not physically attached; only the weight held them in position. We stretched out the rigging wires and carefully examined them. Some excessively rusted stays were replaced with others that had been removed from vessels being scrapped. On the good wires we replaced the servings where they went around the mast and coated them with Stockholm tar.

The crosstrees were fitted to the new mast, and the shrouds were slipped over the masthead and down snugly on the crosstrees, first the starboard, next the port, then starboard and port again. The other iron bands and cleats for the peak

Knute Anderson preparing the crosstrees for the new mast.

halyard blocks, spring stay, the wire between the top of this mast and the next one aft, as well as the bands for the several forestays were all carefully placed and secured.

The two masts, old and new, were now alongside each other. Using the crosstrees as the control point, we made a cut in the heel or lower end of the new mast, about 12 inches wide and 18 inches long, so it would straddle the keelson. A heavy steel band was driven over the butt end to prevent the mast's splitting. This heel cut prevents the mast from rotating when under the strains of sailing. The new foremast was now hoisted into place using the reverse procedure of removal. The diameter of the hole in the vessel's deck through which the mast projects is probably 6 to 9 inches greater then the diameter of the mast, so we drove a series of wood wedges into this space to hold the mast secure at the deck. Then we placed a canvass boot around the mast and tacked it to both the mast and the deck to assure a watertight seal.

The main and spanker masts were replaced in like manner, and a silver coin was placed under each mast for good luck. The Poulsbo mast with the bend was used for the spanker, and the top of the mast was slightly forward of where it would have been with a straight mast. When it was in place, the bend could not be seen. I had brought rigging wires, as well as one crosstree, that had been in storage in Poulsbo.

With the three new masts in place, now came the task of reinstalling the topmasts. This is done with the vessel's own gear as the topmasts are far too high for the shore cranes. The procedure is very simple. There is a hole thwartships or crosswise in the lower end of the topmast. A line is run through this hole, with one end fastened to the top of the lower mast above the crosstrees, and the other end led through a block above the crosstrees and then down to the deck winch. The topmast rigging and various iron bands have been hoisted to the crosstrees and secured . A second line is attached to the top

The *Sophie* also needed a new bowsprit, and here the workmen install the necessary hardware.

of the topmast and led through the crosstrees to another block. The topmast is first hoisted to a vertical position; then the line through the butt is also tightened. Both are slowly hoisted, until the top of the topmast finally protrudes above the crosstrees on the forward side. Hoisting continues as the top of the topmast is threaded through the opening in the spring stay band at the top of the lower mast. Now the iron bands and rigging are put in place, after which the hoisting continues. When the topmast is finally at full height, a wood pin or fid is inserted through the butt and rests on the crosstrees. Finally the rigging is set up tight, and all is in readiness to do the same on the next mast.

Mast replacement was a very major expense for all wood vessels. A special vulnerable location where rot occurred was at the crosstrees. The crosstrees sat on the shoulder of the mast, and rain could run down between mast and crosstrees and remain there to rot the mast. (The crosstrees were made of oak and did not rot as easily.) Hence, the masts of the codfish schooners had a life of usually less than 20 years. During the days when Father ran the Pacific Coast Codfish Co. and his own fleet, there were many years when a new mast became necessary. In 1934 the *Charles R Wilson*, chartered to Washington Fish Co., was being towed north by the fish boat *Clipper*. One evening when the wind was fresh and fair, Captain John Hanson had set the large sails to assist in the tow. The schooner was overtaking the towing vessel, and *Clipper* hauled up into the wind and signaled to lower the sails or cast off the tow line. Before anything could be done, the vessel took a heavy roll and broke the mainmast in the crosstrees. Fortunately no other damage was done and the other masts stood, but the vessel required a new mast the next winter. This one was also made by the Spar Manufacturing Co. of Seattle and installed at the Port of Seattle Fisherman's Terminal south of the Ballard Bridge.

Charles R Wilson, foreground, and *C A Thayer* behind, with the motor ship *Nordic Maid* next to the wharf of the former Pacific Coast Codfish Co., later Captain J.E. Shields' Poulsbo Codfish Plant, circa 1952.

CHAPTER 10

THE FINAL MOORAGE

In December 1941, the U.S. was attacked by Japan and war was with us again. Within days the U.S. government requisitioned Father's schooners *Sophie Christenson*, *C A Thayer*, and *John A*; the *Wawona* and *Azalea* of the Robinson Fisheries; and Captain John Backland's *C S Holmes* for the war effort. Only Father's *Charles R Wilson* continued fishing during World War II, except in 1943 when the war regulations delayed the purchase of necessary food and other supplies until it was too late to sail for Alaska. Captain Dempsey Pearson was captain of the *Wilson* during these years.

The government used the former codfish schooners as barges. The *Sophie Christenson*'s topmasts were taken down, and cargo booms and winches were installed. She was loaded with materials, towed to the western Aleutian Islands, and anchored in harbor. A crew lived on board in the former foc's'le and mess/galley while the cargo was taken on shore. When it was empty, a steamer came to the harbor and off-loaded 600 to 800 tons more cargo onto the barge. When they had constructed sufficient shore facilities, the crew moved onshore and the schooner-barge was towed to another remote island to act as a floating warehouse and barracks. Thus the flagship of the codfish fleet served yeoman duty in her last years.

The *C A Thayer*, *Wawona*, *Azalea*, and *C S Holmes* were used in similar ways. The *Thayer*, which was in a tired state when requisitioned, was taken to the shipyard in Winslow where the masts were removed and a thorough caulking job done. The hull was found sufficiently sound to justify this extra work.

In late 1945 the government offered these vessels back to the former owners. Father purchased both the *Sophie Christenson* and *C A Thayer*. The *Sophie* had new masts from the spring of 1941 and other items remaining from codfish days, but her hull was in poor condition. The *C A Thayer* had no masts, as the government had removed them, but it had spent considerable monies in other repairs, including caulking the hull. My father decided to outfit the *Thayer* using three masts, rigging, oil and water tanks, and other equipment from the *Sophie*. This work was done at Poulsbo. The *C A Thayer* regained her former registered name and became a codfish vessel. Father intended to send both the *Wilson* and *Thayer* fishing in 1946, but there were not enough skilled dory codfishermen to provide a crew for both vessels. As the *Thayer* was in better condition, the *Charles R Wilson* was retired from the codfish trade, never to sail again. We did not know this at that time, as we contemplated sending her north in 1947, but this did not happen.

Robinson Fisheries, which had been out of business during the war years, purchased the *Wawona* and outfitted her for the codfishing trade. She sailed under the command of Captain Tom Haugen during the 1946 and 1947 seasons, her last voyage to the cod banks. The *Azalea* and *John A* were deteriorated to the point they were not worth operating again, and there were not enough fishermen to run them anyway. The *C S Holmes* was not returned to Captain Backland as his shipping/freighting operation was terminated in 1936 and he had no further use for the schooner.

Fishing for cod in the Bering Sea came to an end after the 1950 season of the *C A Thayer*. This was the last sailing vessel to make a commercial voyage on the Pacific Ocean. The *Charles R Wilson*'s last voyage was in 1945. The *Sophie Christenson* had made her last commercial codfishing voyage in 1941.

The days of the beautiful sailing vessels with their tall masts and huge spread of canvas are gone forever. Many fine wood sailing vessels, mostly two-, three- and four-mast schooners, were constructed by the ship builders of the Pacific Coast. The region's giant Douglas fir trees provided the massive timbers for their construction and also the cargo they were intended to carry from the saw mills of Washington, Oregon, and Northern California to satisfy the needs of the construction industry in Southern California. The design fit the need perfectly – they were vessels that could carry an enormous cargo of lumber south over the often troubled waters of these shores and then return north without need for ballast.

Other larger wood vessels were constructed for the offshore lumber trade to the South Sea islands, Australia, and South America. Many five-mast vessels were constructed during World War I, but by the time they were completed, the need for them was over. Many made only one or two voyages before being placed in layup. A few had their masts removed and were used as barges.

All of the former lumber schooners came to an end someplace. The rockbound shores of the Washington and Oregon coasts claimed their share. Old pictures show the wreckage of several once-proud vessels. A few were purchased by the motion picture industry and either sunk or set on fire for the benefit of moviegoers. Very few were lost at sea. During the 1920s and 1930s, ship breakers stripped many vessels of all salvageable items, then placed the hull on the beach and burned it to recover the metal fastenings. By the late 1930s the practice of burning vessels was stopped due to air pollution and the lack of enough salvage metal to pay the costs. Then how did the former beautiful codfish schooners end their lives? The San Francisco schooners *Galilee*, *Beulah*, and *City of Papeete* were towed to the mud flats of Sausalito, California, and allowed to rot.

The fates of the schooners owned by the Pacific Coast Codfish Co., Captain J.E. Shields, and the Robinson Fisheries are as follows:

The *C A Thayer* was employed as a codfish schooner from 1946 to 1950 and then laid up permanently. Charles McNeil purchased the schooner and placed her on the beach alongside the highway near Hoodsport, on Hoods Canal in Washington, as a tourist attraction. This did not prove profitable, and San Francisco interests purchased the vessel and, after considerable repair work, sailed her to the "City by the Golden Gate." The *Thayer* was further modified to return to the condition of a lumber freighting vessel and moored at San Francisco's Fisherman's Wharf, where she was opened to the public. Today she is used as a school ship for young people who spend a full day and night on board learning the tasks of sailing vessels.

The *Wawona* went through several owners. One, Captain Ralph Peterson, attempted to make her into a cruise ship for the south seas. Another owner was William Studdert, a Montana cattle rancher. In 1965–66, John Ross from the Boston area purchased the vessel, intending to turn it into a floating museum on the Seattle waterfront. This project failed. Some time later she was acquired by Northwest Seaport, moored at the south end of Lake Union, and opened to the public. Considerable work has been performed to restore many of the rotted timbers, but there is still an enormous amount of work needed to restore her to a condition where she could be permanently maintained. Visitors are allowed on board at times to learn of sailing and codfish vessels.

The *C A Thayer* and the *Wawona* are the only two remaining vessels of a once-mighty fleet of lumber carriers on this coast. Part of the reason these codfish schooners lasted so long was that the salt for preserving the cod filled the hold of the vessel and preserved the inner body, whereas other vessels developed rot and were no longer safe to sail in the oceans.

The *Sophie Christenson* and the *C S Holmes* were purchased as stripped-down hulks by the Gibson Brothers of British Columbia and operated as lumber and log barges for the Tahsis Logging Co, transporting logs and lumber from the outside ports on the west coast of Vancouver Island to Puget Sound. They both drifted onto the rocks of Vancouver Island and broke up.

The *Azalea* ended her life on the mud flats of Sausalito, moored stern to stern with the *Beulah* and left to rot. The *Charles R Wilson* was sold to Canadian intrests and placed as a breakwater at the saw mill in Powell River, B.C. The *John A*'s life also ended as part of a breakwater at the mouth of the Nisqually River, along with the hulk of the *William Nottingham*. Here the *John A* rotted away. A very sad end for such a beautiful three-mast schooner.

The stripped-down hull of the once famous and handsome schooner *Sophie Christenson*, with the masts of the *Charles R Wilson* showing in the background, circa 1946.

Appendix I

Captain J.E. Shields

There were many leaders or owners in the salt codfish industry and there is not sufficient space here to list them all, so I am concentrating on my father, Captain J.E. Shields. He became involved with the codfish industry in 1911 with the formation of the Pacific Coast Codfish Co. and continued producing salt cod until 1950, the end of dory fishing. Charles Cox and Chris Hale of the Union Fish Co., and Alfred Greenebaum of the Alaska Codfish Co. in the San Francisco Bay area were also producing salt cod, as were Captain J.A. Matheson on Puget Sound and J.E. Trafton of Anacortes.

John Edward Shields was born on September 25, 1881, on a farm in the Township of Mosa, County of Middlesex, Province of Ontario, Canada. He was the tenth child of Roland Hill and Euphemia Shields. There were six boys and four girls and they all lived to become adults, most of them living to be 70 to 80 years old. Farming provided a bare subsistence for the family, and five of the six boys left when they could earn a living elsewhere.

Father went to the local one-room school when the time came and then to high school in the nearby town of Glencoe. He spent four years of study there, and the last three he lived in a boarding room with a Glencoe family. The distance for commuting from home to school every day proved to be too much, especially during the winter when there were deep snows and severe freezing periods. There was no such thing as a car, there were none in the entire area, and his father did not have a horse to spare for daily riding to school. Father did tell me that at times he rode the train from Glencoe to a station near the farm along with two neighbor girls.

Father completed high school in Glencoe in the summer of 1899, then took his first outside job, that of teacher at a rural one-room school for the year of 1900. To prepare for this he attended Normal School for a few months. It appears from the letter I have stating completion of the contract that a schoolteacher took the contract for the calendar year of January 1 to December 31. He told me he received $225 for the year and had to pay for board and room out of this. Also, he said he was not paid anything until the year was complete, nothing each month for him to meet his own bills. In other words, the teacher had to finance himself for an entire year.

Teaching was not to Father's liking. He next went to Forest City Business College for six months, where he acquired skills in typing, shorthand, letter-writing, and business practices, including bookkeeping. Father found various office jobs for the next few years, but by 1902 he apparently thought life in Canada was passing him by without opportunity for gaining the better life, so he and his brother Roland moved to New York City and lived for a time with their older brother George and his family.

Stripped-down hull of the *Sophie Christenson* after the masts were removed to rebuild the *C A Thayer* (left).

Father obtained a job with the import/export firm of Ellis and Co. until the principals skipped the country, owing Father. During the time Father worked for Ellis and Co., he met Anice (Anna) Jones, and a courtship followed. She was working for the City of New York Public Library, first on Long Island and then in Queens. After Father and Mother were married on June 29, 1905, they took a trip to visit with all the relatives in Mosa on Father's side of the family. Mother's family lived in New York, her father being a carpenter. Father and Mother lived in a small apartment at 427 3rd Street, in Brooklyn.

The West Coast appealed to him, and in 1906 he came to Seattle in the employ of a food brokerage firm, the Kelly Clark Co. By 1911 he had set up his own office and business. One of his clients was the newly formed Pacific Coast Codfish Co., for which he was the salesman and office manager. He set up his office on the Colman dock.

Over the years he acquired stock in the company when someone desired to sell. The company prospered and Father, seeing the possibilities, expanded his endeavors, over the next few years purchasing several sailing vessels for his own account. These were engaged in offshore freighting of lumber and case oil from the West Coast to the South Sea Islands, Australia, New Zealand, and Alaska.

The business in Father's office soon increased beyond what he could handle by himself, and he wrote to his brother George, who was still in New York, with an offer to work in Seattle. George came west with his family in 1913. Father also made some sort of an offer asking Roland to come to Seattle, but I do not know when. However, at that time Roland was married and his wife Ann did not want to make the transition from New York to Seattle. She was a nurse and had some strong reservations about the move. Roland and Ann continued to live in New York for the remainder of their lives.

Sometime in the early 1910s, Father became the Seattle agent for the Oliver Salt Co. of San Francisco. This firm made salt from the waters of the bay, using large evaporation ponds at the south end of the bay. The salt crystallized in the fields as the sun evaporated the water. Well, Father became the major source of salt for the fishing industry of Alaska and British Columbia. He told me that one year he sold 17,000 tons of salt. He also was a broker for salt herring, salt salmon, and a little salt black cod.

Father developed a reputation as the best judge of salt herring in Seattle. The herring came from Alaska by steamer, and much of it was eventually destined for shipment to New York, where the Jewish trade consumed it. Father was called on to take samples and test or taste them. He would go down to the wharf where the barrels were stored, taking his set of coopers tools so he could open any barrel he might select. He would then reach down through several neat layers of herring and pull one out. The fish was torn open, exposing the flesh near the backbone. Father would take a bite of the flesh, chew it, and spit it out, all the while tasting and smelling it. He said he would exhale the air in his mouth through his nose and this gave the best results. Anyway, his word was final and accepted by the buyers in New York.

Father and Mother spent the summer of 1914 on the *Bender Brothers*, putting up a pack of mild cured salmon in the mouth of the Kuskokwim River. This was a most unpleasant summer for Mother. She was sea sick all the way from Seattle to the Kuskokwim River and likewise on the return. When the *Bender Brothers* returned, Father was informed that the Great War in Europe had started and as he was still a Canadian citizen, he was possibly subject to conscription in Canada. The U.S. government might deport him as a non-citizen of the U.S. so he could serve in the Canadian Army. Further, he was informed the Colman Dock, where his office was located, had burned. Such a fire would have destroyed all the office records. Father learned later that George had salvaged all the records and the fire had not consumed the entire wharf. As for being a non-U.S. citizen, this gave him many days and even years of worry.

The outbreak of war in Europe was accompanied in the U.S. by very hard times. The sale of salt codfish fell off drastically. Father decided extreme measures were required and he made a three-month trip all over the country to sell codfish wherever he could. He had good results in the Minneapolis–St. Paul area and some near Chicago. He went extensively through the southern states, with very little results, as the freight rates from Seattle were far more than from Gloucester, Massachusetts. However, he did hit a jackpot in Newark, New Jersey, in the firm of J.H. Beardsley and Co. This firm made a product called codfish cakes with shredded fish. Using only Atlantic cod did not produce the best product due to the coarse fiber texture of that fish. A better solution was to mix in a proportion of the fine-textured Pacific cod. Thus Father obtained an order for 3000 tons of salt codfish to be delivered at the rate of 600 tons per year.

With World War I raging in Europe he found this shipping very profitable, and during many winters he chartered the vessels of the Pacific Coast Codfish Co., as well as those of the Robinson Fisheries Co., for offshore voyages during the normal layup time. By 1918 he had three vessels of his own, two in partnership with Louis Knaflich (who was conducting freighting and trading in the Bering Sea), and three chartered codfishers all freighting wherever a cargo could be obtained. (In the purchase of these vessels, the ship's documents show the ownership as Anice J.Shields, half, and Louis Knaflich, half. At this time Father had not yet obtained American citizenship and therefore could not own any portion of an American vessel. However it was okay for him to own a portion of the stock of a corporation licensed under the laws of the State of Washington, and this corporation did, in fact, own vessels and Father acted as agent for the operation of those vessels when dealing with the U.S. Customs House.)

When the United States became involved in the war, there was a large demand for all kinds of vessels; anything that could carry a cargo from here to there was put to work. The government had instituted a massive shipbuilding program under the War Shipping Administration. Further, the government had requisitioned all the vessels it could lay its hands on, that is, all the vessels with engines. This left a considerable void in the normal shipping circles. There was a great demand for lumber in the various South Sea Islands, and the business of shipping to this area is described in an April 1918 article from Father's files.

Operating a fleet of sailing vessels, Seattle shipping men have developed an important trade with the South Sea Islands during the past winter as a direct result of the scarcity of carriers and as rearrangement of ocean lanes of commerce due to the European war according to J.E. Shields owner of the sailing schooners *Albert Meyer* and *A M Baxter* and secretary-treasurer of the Pacific Coast Codfish Co. "Instead of laying up the vessels of the codfish fleet during the winter months as in previous years, we have kept them in service carrying lumber to Hawaii and copra from the South Pacific to this coast," said Shields today.

COPRA INCREASES IN VALUE

Copra, which is coconut meat dried in the sun after being broken up, is a valuable commodity. One ton of copra will produce 1100 pounds of edible oil for oleomargarine or compound lard, 100 pounds of soap grease, and 800 pounds of cattle feed. The value of copra has increased as a result of the war and the advanced freights have made the transportation of this product a profitable business.

Shields said the schooner *Albert Meyer*, Captain H.J. Anderson, which sailed recently from Hawaii for the Philippine Islands, will load copra in Zamboanga, Mindanao, for Seattle. The vessel carried a cargo of 665,000 feet of lumber from Bellingham to Kahululi.

The schooner *A M Baxter* has arrived in San Francisco from Papeete, Tahiti, with a shipment of copra and a deck load of 98,000 coconuts. The *Baxter*, Capt. Harry Ashbury, will load case oil in San Francisco for Suva, Fiji, and in that port will take a cargo of copra for Seattle, coming from the South Seas to Seattle direct.

OUTFITTING FOR ANNUAL CRUISES

The schooner *Charles R Wilson* made a voyage to Levuka, Fiji, and delivered 400 tons of copra in San Francisco. The *Wilson* and the schooner *Maid of Orleans* are now in Poulsbo, outfitting for their annual cruises to the Bering Sea. The schooner *John A* of the same fleet is loading salt in San Francisco and upon her arrival here will outfit for her summer cruise in Northern waters. The *John A* of the same fleet carried a cargo of copra from Nukalofa, Tongatabu, South Seas, to San Francisco, arriving in the Golden State port on March 12.

Shields said that the vessels of the Pacific Coast Codfish Co. delivered 1000 tons of codfish in Seattle last fall and during the winter carried 1000 tons of copra from the South Seas to San Francisco.

During the years 1915 to 1920, when Father was 33 to 38 years old, he owned and operated the four-mast schooner *A M Baxter* and the three-mast schooners *Albert Meyer* and *Esther* in the South Pacific lumber and copra freighting trade. Together with Louis Knaflich he owned the auxiliary three-mast schooner *Ruby* and the auxiliary two-mast schooner *Bender Brothers* for freighting and trading to Alaska and the Canadian Arctic. He also chartered the *John A* and *Charles R Wilson* from the Pacific Coast Codfish Co. and the *Wawona* and *Azalea* from the Robinson Fisheries for lumber freighting to the South Pacific. Further, he chartered the *P J Abler*, an auxiliary three-mast schooner with gas engine, until that vessel was destroyed by fire near Juneau, Alaska. All this time he was also manager of the Pacific Coast Codfish Co., operating the *Charles R Wilson*, *John A*, and *Maid of Orleans* in the Alaska salt cod fishery. Additionally, he was the Seattle salesman for the Oliver Salt Co. of San Francisco. It was a far cry from the life where he grew up on the small farm in southern Ontario.

While business was prospering, Father and Mother were attempting to raise a family. Father had purchased a small house in the Ballard district where they lived for several years, about 1912 to 1915. They then moved to a house on the corner of 21st and East Cherry Street. The next residence was on the corner of 33rd and East Jefferson in the Madrona District. They lived there until about 1919, when Father purchased a large four-bedroom home, covering two full floors plus a basement and a full attic. This turned out to be the family home until his death in 1962. This home had a beautiful view of Lake Washington and the Cascade Mountains and was at 1703 39th Avenue.

Father and Mother had several children before me that did not live. My next older brother, John Edward Shields Jr., lived for three months. A baby girl lived only two days, so I never knew either of them. I arrived on the scene on January 1, 1916, and was followed by my sister Phyllis, who was born November 4, 1917. My other brother, John Riley Shields, did not appear on the scene until May 3, 1922. This completed the family.

Father was given to the old adage of "all work and no play makes Jack a dull boy." He loved the outdoors and hunting. He made several trips to Alaska for big game and bagged a large moose on one of those trips. He was a member of the Seattle Gun Club and spent most every Sunday morning trap shooting at the club site on Magnolia Bluff. The club house was on the south edge of the Fort Lawton reservation. He also joined a small gun club with club house at Dungeness. There he met a lifelong friend, Riley McCoy, with whom he had many enjoyable hunting trips and joint family recreation. I can even remember one summer the two families spent a week at a resort on the ocean beach at Mora on the north side of the Quillayute River.

Father was not the best sportsman. He played every game to win. There was never the thought of second place. It did not matter what the activity–duck hunting, fishing, upland birds, cards, or whatever–he played for first place. Second or, horribly, third place was utterly unacceptable. So when he did not get the largest fish or the most ducks, he was not the best of company and often became quite unhappy. However, this was his philosophy in all his activities of life. Never take second place. That was for the other fellow. For him it was always his goal to be first. This was the case in his business activities. He only took part in those projects or undertakings where he could excel. It was wonderful to live in a home where the head of the household held these thoughts so high. We could always look up to Father. He was the guiding light of our lives. He would always make a decision rather than parry a question. It was a wonderful environment.

Father's dream land was the waterfront. His office was always on the west side of the railroad tracks on the waterfront of Seattle, on one of the piers or wharfs. His office was on the Colman Dock for many years, but my first memories were after he moved to Pier 1. He had to be able to inhale the sweet odor of the seas, even though at many times the odor emanating from the bay along the shore and under the wharfs was enough to repel even those persons who were formerly associated with the Chicago stockyards. The dead fish that several fish houses had disposed of through the floor of their dock, coupled with the sewage outfalls along the bay, was more than enough to let you know when you were approaching that realm where the beautiful ships were moored.

Father was able to find profitable charters to haul lumber from the West Coast mills to those islands of romance in the South Seas until the early 1920s. Then the bottom literally fell out. There were many newly constructed wood sailing vessels, fresh off the builder's ways and with twice or more the size of Father's small schooners, that were willing to cut freight rates below the bone in order to get a charter. For those new vessels it was either operate at a loss or tie the vessel up and contemplate she would never make even one voyage before being burned to recover the metal fastenings. As it turned out, many vessels were scrapped before they made the first trip. Father was not to be left in the lurch. His eyesight had always been very keen and at this time he saw the writing on the wall and took precautions, though he continued making some trips to the South Seas until about 1927.

Another charter surfaced in 1927 when Father secured a contract to deliver a cargo of coal to Nome, Alaska, returning with a load of scrap iron. For this trip the *Sophie Christenson* was under the command of Captain Dan Martin, who had sailed for Father during the days of the previous war. The vessel's next voyage, also in 1927, was from the Hasting's Mill in Vancouver to Suva, Fiji, this time under the command of Captain Hans Anderson.

The summer of 1927 was also a time for a rest. Early that spring Father purchased a new Stutz automobile. This was the last word, a straight eight in a very high-class car. Father took us for several short day-trips that spring, essentially to get the new car broken in. Then right after the Fourth of July, all of us loaded ourselves and our clothing into that car and he drove across country to Ontario, Canada. It took ten full days to make the journey. We spent the remainder of the summer there, living in a house on one of the farms Archie McAlpine, his nephew, owned. That was a memorable time and he enjoyed the relaxation from the hard long hours of work that he had been driving himself to. We came home just before the start of school in September. Then it was back to the grind again for him.

By the late 1920s he had purchased all of the outstanding stock of the Pacific Coast Codfish Co. and was the sole owner, so the codfish operation was requiring closer attention and more efficient methods of procedure. He was also the Seattle agent for the Oliver Salt Co. of San Francisco. Through his close association with the fish packers of Alaska and British Columbia as well as Washington, he had become the largest dealer in salt for commercial use in this area. This was consuming much of his time. Still the days were most pleasant. One of the benefits was that he did not need to spend so much time in San Francisco, for during the feverish preceding years he was in that city nearly as many days per month as in Seattle. With travel by train requiring over two days each way, he was gone from home a considerable portion of the time.

The year of 1929 was the beginning of the horrible depression of the 1930s. In the fall the stock market crashed, and Father had more involved there than he could afford to lose. Additionally, and more disastrous to Father, were the losses from failure of his creditors. He was cutting a wide swath in the market supplying salt to the fishing industry. Most of this was on credit, with payment to be made after the packer had sold his season's production of fish. Many of those packers went into bankruptcy. This left Father holding the proverbial sack. He had to pay for the salt in full, and what little was received from the fish packer after the costs of bankruptcy were paid left the creditors on the short end. Father found he was $60,000 in debt at one time, so he told me. However, he did not default on his own creditors, and they were paid off in full in the end although this took some time.

Times were tough in the U.S. from 1930 to the middle years of the decade. The wages paid to the fishermen working in the preparation of the vessel for the upcoming codfishing voyage were two dollars per day. Pennies had to be counted and they were. However, when times are tough and jobs scarce, people must still eat. The food business does not suffer to the extent of other consumer goods lines. Automobile sales may dry up to nothing and home construction can be brought to a halt through lack of money, but there are still people to feed and they must eat every day. One of the most economical foods at that time was salt codfish with a white sauce or cream gravy. Hence the sales of the codfish did not suffer as much as most people might anticipate. Father even told me "The best business to be in is food, as people must always eat regardless of how hard the times are."

In the spring of 1933 Father decided that he would go to the codfish grounds as captain of the *Sophie Christenson*, though he had never previously held any position in a sailing vessel crew. This eliminated the cost of an outside captain. Father had a crackerjack crew and came home with a record cargo of 455,000 fish. He had lowered the minimum size of fish that the dory fishermen could deliver on board and this added to the catch. Because Father was the owner, he could exercise more options than other men hired for the job who had to follow the instructions laid down by the vessel's owners. The previous size limit was 25 inches and Father reduced this to 23 inches. He knew there was considerable demand for dried fish and for unprocessed fish that others would convert into lutefisk, both of which could easily use the smaller size fish. In fact, when the Pacific Coast Codfish Co. was founded and for many years thereafter, the fishermen were paid by the fish rather than the weight of fish delivered at the port of discharge. At that time the minimum size was 28 inches. This is quite a large fish, and as a consequence it was more difficult to produce a cargo. The fishermen complained that more than half the fish they caught in the dory had to be discarded because of being too small. The result in the early days was the schooner had to prospect far more to find a location where the larger fish were available. This size change was most welcome to the fishermen and made Father's reputation most highly prized.

On that 1933 trip, Captain J.E. Shields set several all-time records that have never been equalled. He caught a record season total of 455,000 cod and a one-day total of over 16,500 cod. Ray Press was high-line fisherman with 25,487 fish for the season, and Dan McEchern had a record one-day total of 1051 fish. As these fish weighed out at Poulsbo at 3˜ pounds each when cured, or 13 to 14 pounds each when fresh, the one-day total of 16,500 fish equalled over 225,000 pounds of fresh fish. It meant that Dan McEchern had caught on his hand lines approximately 14,000 pounds of fish—enough for three fully loaded dory trips that day.

While Father was gone, the office still had to function. George Shields was in charge in his absence, attending to the routine chores so essential every day—the orders, billings, collections, payroll, and other items. Esther Strahm was also there. During the winter when Father was home, he spent considerable time at the vessels moored in Lake Union, where he had a few men working. He considered it a necessity to make a daily visit to the schooners. (I use the term "Lake Union" somewhat loosely and include in it all the fresh water above the government locks in Ballard. The Port of Seattle operated a large fishing vessel moorage on the south side of the Lake Washington Ship Canal. It was called the Fisherman's Terminal, but we used the slang term "The Fisherman's Terminal in Ballard," even though the site was not on the Ballard side of the canal.)

In 1934 I had finished high school and was able to make the trip to the codfish banks with Father, and thus my education in the fishing business began in earnest. I continued with Father in the next several years, and each season he brought back a large catch, although not as large as the 1933 season.

For the summers of 1934 to 1936 Father chartered the *Charles R Wilson* to the Washington Fish and Oyster Co. to serve as a supply vessel for their cannery on Kodiak Island. In the spring of 1936 he sold the schooner *John A* to the Chatham Strait Fish Co. Otherwise, there were no major changes in his operation. The salt agency had long ago gone by the board as the Oliver Salt Co. had sold out to the Leslie Salt Co., and this firm, along with Arden Salt Co., maintained a company stock of their product on the wharfs in Seattle. This left no room for an independent operator.

The highlight of his fishing career occurred in the summer of 1938 when the Japanese were encroaching on the Bristol Bay salmon fishery. Father sent his famous telegram ordering a dozen high-power rifles for the two vessels on the fishing grounds. This became the start of the "One Man War Against Japan." No guns or ammunition were sent north, but the adverse publicity in the U.S. at the time of the Japanese invasion of Korea and the sinking of the U.S. frigate *Panay* resulted in the American people being unwilling to purchase Japanese goods. The result was the withdrawal of the Japanese fishing fleet from Bristol Bay, the result desired by Father.

The year 1939 saw only the *Sophie Christenson* on the cod banks with Father's operations. The *Charles R Wilson* was left in layup but in good condition. The *C A Thayer* had by this time deteriorated until the masts as well as most of the booms and gaffs were rotten. The decks leaked and generally she was considerably run down. I did not go fishing that season but remained in Seattle so I could complete my studies in the College of Engineering at the University of Washington. I received a degree of Bachelor of Science in Civil Engineering. During the season Father had a bad experience on the journey north when approaching Unimak Pass. This was when he drove the old schooner until the forestay carried away and she sprang a leak. This driving was all part of his character. He was never to be outdone. It seems he was racing the *Wawona* under the command of Captain Tom Haugen from Anacortes. No way could Father let the *Wawona* get ahead. If he could not come out on top in any competition, he would not want to take part. Father had to uphold his own image. There was no other choice as far as he was concerned. This was the drive that always put him on top and made him succeed where others failed.

In 1940 Father outfitted both the *Sophie Christenson* and the *Charles R Wilson* as in 1938, but I was not on the banks that season. I spent the winter of 1939–40 in Cambridge, Mass., attending graduate school at Harvard University, where I received a Masters of Science in Sanitary Engineering. I was back on the West Coast by the fall, when the fish from both schooners were delivered safely to the plant in Poulsbo, over 1000 tons again. With the return of the vessels, Father gave me the position of foreman in the Poulsbo plant. Also that fall, Louise Mangrum and I were married, making our residence in a small cabin on the beach alongside of the plant.

The year 1941 was a repetition of the preceding one. Two vessels were sent to the banks, the *Sophie Christenson* and the *Charles R Wilson*. Father took the larger four-master while Captain Knute Pearson had the *Wilson*. Again over 1000 tons of salt codfish was produced.

In the fall of 1941, after the vessels had been discharged and placed in winter moorage in Lake Union, the clouds of war continued to darken the skies of this country. War had broken out in Europe in the fall of 1939, two years earlier. France had been overrun by the German army and Britain was in dire straits. Freight rates were increasing and Father had one more attempt at offshore lumber freighting with a sailing vessel. He took a charter to carry a load of lumber with the *Sophie Christenson* from Vancouver to Suva, Fiji, with a cargo of copra on the return. Plans were made and steps were taken to prepare the vessel. I even constructed a brand new mainsail from new canvas for her. Then the days dragged on until there was not time to complete the offshore trip and return in time for the 1942 codfish season. Father became quite concerned and finally appealed to the U.S. government to prevent the trip by saying the vessel was needed in this country to produce fish.

All was soon settled. On December 7, 1941, the "Day Of Infamy" according to President Roosevelt, the Japanese military forces made a surprise attack on Pearl Harbor. The U.S. was now at war. A few days later the U.S. Army requisitioned the *Sophie Christenson* along with the *C A Thayer* and *John A.* (On December 11, 1941, Father had purchased the *John A* back from the Chatham Strait Fish Co. and I believe he intended to convert her to a tuna boat by installing an engine.) The U.S. entry into the war relieved Father of the charter but also relieved him of three vessels. He did not care so much about the *C A Thayer* due to her rundown condition, but otherwise his operations in the codfish trade were drastically reduced.

The *Charles R Wilson* was not taken, and Father outfitted her each season during the war. In 1943, however, he was not able to get permission from all the necessary governmental agencies to make the annual voyage, and that year no vessel went to the banks. That was the only year between the founding of the Pacific Coast Codfish Co. in 1911 and the last codfishing trip in 1950 when a vessel was not sent to the banks It was the War Ration Board that was so slow in approving the application for the priority items of groceries that the trip had to be cancelled. Father stated he had to have permission from 22 agencies. That year he only got 21. Sometimes government becomes too complicated.

The summer of 1943 apparently became a drag on time for Father. He was in Seattle during the summer, something he had not enjoyed since 1932, ten years before. He took a flyer and purchased the Rytak Co., with a baking plant at 1630 15th Avenue West in Seattle. Along with this came the Nordic Baking and Importing Co. He was now in the business of baking hard tack and toast. Further, the firms operated an importing business concentrating on Scandinavian specialty foods including cheeses and fish. This purchase came about because the former owners of the combined firms had run up a considerable account on the books of Father's office for the purchase of codfish that was being sold to the local grocery stores. Father figured the only way to recover the debt was to purchase the outfit. It was through this route that he entered the wholesale food trade in Seattle. He kept on the two salesmen, Floyd and Mel Peterson, who called on the grocery stores that were not associated with the large chains like Safeway. Because Father was well-qualified in the fish business and had excellent connections with the fish packers from many years' acquaintance, he was able to expand the business to include a wide line of fish products including canned salmon, tuna, anchovies, sardines, cod roe, fish cakes, and smoked salmon. This provided a wonderful outlet for codfish, as the salesmen covered many stores and were able to place salt codfish on the shelves of more stores in Washington and Oregon than before. The California trade suffered and was never fully recovered after the end of the war.

I took a position in the engineering department of the U.S. Navy Yard in Bremerton during World War II, while Riley, my brother, was in the U.S. Army. Father had no help from his two sons.

The years of the war passed slowly until, finally, the armistice with Japan was signed on August 14, 1945. Peace was with us again. Now Father could return to codfishing as before, though only the *C A Thayer* went to sea.

During the winter of 1945–46, Mother took sick and suffered a severe heart attack. Several subsequent attacks occurred and Father began to show the effects of Mother's illness. Mother continued to suffer from poor health as her heart was not up to the daily task of keeping the body going. Mrs. Maude McCoy was living with Father and Mother at this time in the

MANUFACTURERS OF
SALT CODFISH
SMOKED SALMON
KNÄCKEBRÖD
FINNISH TOAST
SWEDISH TOAST
SPISBRÖD
RYECRUNCH
OAT TACK
RYTAK

J. E. SHIELDS

SUCCESSOR TO

PACIFIC COAST CODFISH CO.

CANADIAN NATIONAL DOCK

SEATTLE

CABLE ADDRESS
SALTHOUSE

CODES { A B C 5TH
WESTERN UNION
PRIVATE

October 10, 1944

TO MY FRIENDS:

This is a letter from a young fellow just trying to get along, in the salt Codfish business. Thirty three years ago I started producing salt codfish - that was in 1911. Away back then I had about ten competitors, producing salt codfish of one quality and another. All of them every last one thought it wise to monkey around with JAP codfish, I was the only one who never handled a pound of JAP cofish, and every one of those companies have quit producing salt codfish. Short changing the buyers by running in Jap fish, under American brands had its reaction. I am the only producer left on the Pacific Coast.

I have fished every year since 1911 except 1943 when the War Labor Board pulled a boner and failed to make up its mind to either approve or refuse to approve the price agreed to by myself and the Codfish Union, for a bonus for the boys fishing on the battlefield in Bering Sea. My vessel fished on that battle field right off Dutch Harbor during the Battle of Dutch Harbor Alaska and Kiska Island Alaska in 1942. Not so nice but they stuck it out armed with fish hooks and produced the fish I sold you in 1942.

My vessel has just returned from Bering sea with 255 tons of first class salt codfish which I am offering to you and which you will be proud to offer to your customers. To get the right to fish I had to get the approval of

The War Labor Board	The U. S. Customs Service
The War Manpower Commission	The Federal Bureau of Communications
The U. S. Navy	The U. S. Employment Service
The U. S. Coast Guard	The War Production Board
The U. S. Department of the Interior	The Gasoline Ration Board
The Division of Fisheries Industries	The Office of Defense Transportation
The O. P. A.	The Navy Routing Office
The Department of Commerce	The Solid Fuel Control Board
The Immigration Service	The Selective Service Boards (Four of these)
The Maritime Commission	The War Risk Insurance Bureau
The Commissioner of Labor Statistics	The Food Distribution Administration
The War Shipping Administration	The Internal Revenue Office

Twenty four count them, but with their help ? ? ? ? ? I have scraped 255 tons of good fish off the bottom of the ocean when meat is rationed.

Captain J. E. SHIELDS
Order Snifflehound and codfish peddler.

Prices for Semi boneless (all large bones removed) FOB Seattle NET.

24/1# cartons White Flake	33 cents
20/2# packages " "	32 "
50 pound cases whole mediums	17 "
125 pound cases whole mediums	16 1/2 cents
125 pound cases whole extra large	17 1/2 "

No labor available for packing absolutely boneless.

214

Madrona residence at 1703 39th Avenue and was Mother's companion. As Mother became less capable of attending to the daily tasks of life, Mrs. McCoy took over preparing the daily meals and attending to Mother's other needs. Mother became more and more confined to her upstairs room. She had several subsequent heart attacks of a minor nature. Then near the middle of June she suffered another setback and was taken to Swedish Hospital. She seemed to improve rapidly, but the doctor suggested she remain confined there. After about two weeks she was doing fine and was scheduled to come home. On the morning of June 28, 1946, the nurse entered the room to rouse her prior to breakfast so she would be awake and washed. She had planned to come home later that morning. Then about one hour later the nurse returned to be sure Mother was prepared for breakfast. Alas. She had departed this world in the interim.

That day was the most difficult I have had to face in my life. First I had to inform Father, who was in Providence Hospital suffering from a nervous breakdown associated with Mother's failing health. Next, I had to arrange along with Riley for the undertakers and then select a cemetery and purchase two plots. One was for Mother and the other to be reserved for Father whenever needed so both of them would finally remain together. That was a most difficult task and one I would not wish on anyone. Earlier preparations would have made the task far less difficult. At any rate, Mother's body was laid to rest on the top of a hill in the Acacia Cemetery north of Seattle, in a place overlooking Lake Washington. The place I finally selected was close to her former neighbor, Mrs. R.W. Sprague.

At the end of the 1946 season, the vessel returned with only 98,775 fish, the poorest trip for a vessel of this size. The next year I decided I needed to return to the fishing grounds rather than spend the summer in Seattle when the codfish operation was at the seasonal low ebb of activity. I also decided it was necessary to find out what had occurred the previous year to reduce the catch so much, as the *Wawona* had far outfished the *C A Thayer*. Dempsey was captain and had produced good catches all during the war years when there was no other vessel on the Bering Sea banks. He remained as captain in 1947, and fishing was better than the 1946 season, with the catch reversed from the previous year; the *Wawona* under Captain Tom Haugen landing only 98,000 fish, while the *C A Thayer* had 140,000. This turned out to be the last season the Robinson Fisheries Co. sent a schooner to the Bering Sea.

By 1948 Father decided he was going north again to show the boys how it should be done. He came home with 210,000 fish, a very encouraging improvement from the two previous seasons.

One year was enough for Father, as he was not as spry and fit as before. I became the captain of the codfish schooner and took the *C A Thayer* to the banks in 1949 and 1950 As it turned out, 1950 was the last year for dory fishing in the Bering Sea, although no one knew at the time. This was the last commercial voyage for an American sailing vessel on the Pacific Coast.

From 1946 through 1950 the sale of codfish continued primarily through the sales outlets of the salesmen of the Nordic Maid Co., the name selected by Father for the grocery operation after he sold the Rytak Co. and Nordic Baking and Importing Co. Father continued to import selected foods and also handled a wide selection of preserved and canned seafoods. We manufactured over 100,000 pounds of lutefisk each year and marketed it through the Nordic Maid Co.

In 1947 Father purchased a 148-foot ex-U.S. Army motorship, intending to convert it into a trawler. We worked on the conversion for several winters before she was ready for the banks. In 1947 the U.S. Fish and Wildlife Service converted a Liberty Ship into a floating factory freezer ship for the offshore processing of fish. She went to Bering Sea in 1948 and had six small trawlers fishing for her. The majority of the catch was king crab, and when that season was over in June they switched to codfish. The latter were split and salted. The king crab operation appeared good, and we rigged the motorship for catching and freezing king crab. We decided to call the new vessel, which had no name when Father acquired her, *Nordic Maid*. She went to the Bering Sea in 1951 under my command, and we trawled for king crabs that summer. The catch was fair considering it was the first attempt at this type of operation by any of us. We returned to the Alaska Banks the following year also, but in 1953 the *Nordic Maid* remained idle. By 1954 we returned to a full-speed fishery, making two voyages to Bering Sea each year. We had installed canning equipment on the vessel and were able to operate the cannery under the

A letter from Captain Shields to his codfish customers (left).

most adverse conditions when the weather was rough. Otherwise, the crab fishery was a very long and tedious season. I departed from Poulsbo near the end of March, returning in the middle of June. The second trip departed right after the Fourth of July and lasted until mid-October, when the severe winter storms drove me out of the Bering Sea.

We continued king crab fishing until the spring of 1958, when just before departure time we decided to call it all off. Father was not in good health and not able to attend to all the activities in Seattle. My brother Riley had decided sometime before to seek his fortune as a medical doctor and was not with the family business. I could not operate the fishing side of the business and the marketing by myself. It was a sad event to terminate the family fishing business, but there was little else that could be done. The wholesale business of the Nordic Maid Co. was liquidated over a period of time. Father had sold the bakery building at 1630 15th Avenue West and purchased the building next door at 1634 15th Avenue West. We kept that building until all the merchandise had been disposed of and then sold it. Esther was still there to the end, faithful as ever. She married Percy Grange in 1946 but had remained working in Father's office. I fished the summer of 1958 along the Washington and Oregon coast with a 70-foot trawler, and then in the fall I went to work for the U.S. Coast Guard in the engineering department in the Seattle office.

Father's health had been declining for several years. He continued to live on at the old family home at 1703 39th Avenue in Seattle. He had a housekeeper, Miss Laurena Otis, living there and providing for his care. Much of his last year was spent in his bedroom on the second floor. The old heart had lost its former strength and his eyes had become extra sensitive to light. The curtains in the bedroom were pulled most of the time to protect his eyes from the pain caused by sunlight.

Then early on the morning of June 29, 1962, Captain J.E. Shields suffered a massive heart attack, collapsing to the floor in death. His body was buried alongside Mother in Acacia Cemetery, on the brow of a hill overlooking Lake Washington, that lake he had seen from the front windows of his family home for well over 40 years. His soul and spirit were carried across that distant bar and into that harbor reserved for seamen. There Father cast his anchor for the last time, in that peaceful harbor where the wicked cease from trouble and the weary are at rest. Then, to quote Longfellow, he met his maker, face to face.

Crossing the Bar

Sunset and evening star,
And one clear call for me,
And may there be no moaning of the bar,
When I put out to sea.

But such a tide as moving seems asleep,
Too full for sound and foam,
When that which drew from out the boundless deep
Turns again home.

Twilight and evening bell,
And after that the dark
And may there be no sadness of farewell,
When I embark.

For tho' from out our bourne of time and place
The flood may bear me far,
I hope to see my Pilot face to face
When I have crossed the bar.

APPENDIX II

LOG OF THE JOHN A

The following synopsis of Captain John Grotle's 1911 fishing trip on the *John A*, taken from the ship's log books, will give the reader some comprehension of the hardships and difficulties encountered by a codfish schooner.

The *John A* under the command of Captain John Grotle departed from the Seattle wharf at 10 p.m. on April 20 in tow of the tug *Mystic*. They passed Port Townsend at 5 a.m. on April 21, and at 6 a.m. the tug let go of the schooner with a light S W wind off Point Wilson. From there on the schooner had to sail on her own the full length of the Strait of Juan de Fuca, 90 miles before passing Cape Flattery. By 7 a.m. the flying jib had carried away.

April 21, 1911
At 5:00 P.M. anchored in Port Angeles

April 22, 1911
At 2:00 A.M. WSW wind and cloudy. Hove the anchor and left Port Angeles at 5:30 A.M. Very light WSW wind. At 10:00 A.M. drifting at Port Angeles in calm. At 3:00 P.M. sprung up a light WSW wind. Beating out. At 8:00 P.M. at Port Crescent. 10:00 P.M. calm.

April 23, 1911
1:00 A.M. calm and pt cloudy. Drifting in calm at Port Crescent all night. At 8:00 A.M. very light easterly wind. Noon at Clallam Bay. At 3:00 P.M. when at Seal Rock wind calmed down. At Neah Bay at 5:00 P.M., slatting about in calm and misty during the night.

April 24, 1911
Drifting around in calm and under very light wind between Cape Flattery and Vancouver Island. Light WxN wind. Fresh rain squalls. Passed Cape Flattery Light at 6:30 A.M. WxN winds and SWxS course. At 1:00 P.M. passed the schooner *Fearless* bound for Bristol Bay. At 5:00 P.M. blowing a fresh to strong W'ly wind with choppy seas and cold.

April 25, 1911
Course SW with wind WNW, fresh and squalls. At 2:00 A.M. blowing a fresh WNW wind and partly cloudy sky to 3:00 A.M. From then light and very light W'ly winds. Bent and set the flying jib at 9:00 A.M. Afternoon NWxW wind and course SWxW. Afternoon rain squalls. Obs Long W at 4:00 P.M. 129'12.

April 26, 1911
This day commences with a very light NWxW wind and rain squalls. Noon, rain squalls, very light NW'ly wind. Course WxS and WSW.

April 27, 1911
Very light NW'ly winds and calm in between with p'tly cloudy sky. Calm and rain squalls in morning. Obs Long W at 4:00 P.M. 132'27. Lat by Obs at noon 46'35. Calm and rain squalls in afternoon.

April 28, 1911
Very light airs of SW'ly and raining. Course W. Noon Obs 46'55N. D R Long at 2:00 P.M. 133'40W. At 10:00 P.M. fresh SE'ly wind and raining.

April 29, 1911
Blowing a fresh to strong SE wind with rain. At 5:00 A.M. took in the MT staysail. At 7:30 A.M. wind calmed down and left us to slat around in the rough sea and calm to 10:00 A.M., from then very light SSW wind. Noon Lat 47'4; Long 137'26. Obs Long at 4:00 P.M. 137'46. At 5:00 P.M. very light winds from south with rough seas. At 8:00 P.M. sighted MAID OF ORLEANS about 5 miles from us.

April 30, 1911
Very light SSE winds with slatting. At 5:00 A.M. set the fore MT Staysail. Noon Lat by Obs 48:30 N, Long 140"15 W. At noon on account of heavy slatting, lowered the MT staysail. Awful heavy rolling and slatting during the afternoon, evening, and night.

May 1, 1911

May commences with very light airs of SW'ly with choppy seas and slatting. Calm and rain. Set the MT staysail at 10:00 A.M. Course WNW, winds SW, SWxW, WSW, and SxW. Obs at noon 49'19N. Obs Long 141'58 at 3:30 142'13W. On account of slatting we lowered the MT staysail at 4:00 P.M, Light snow squalls in evening.

May 2, 1911

Took in the flying jib at 1:00 A.M. Blowing a fresh W'ly wind with snow squalls and cold, ugly weather. Noon Obs 50'06N, 143'10W. Obs Long at 4:00 P.M. 143'22W. Afternoon very light winds and heavy slatting. During evening and night, calm and heavy slatting.

May 3, 1911

This day commences with calm and rough seas and heavy slatting. By 9:00 A.M. blowing a fresh NNW wind and heavy snow from 10:00 A.M. Noon Obs 50'20 N & 144'00W. At 1:00 P.M. took in the flying jib.

May 4. 1911

Double reefed the spanker at 1:00 A.M. Blowing a strong NWxW wind with snow and rough seas. Set the whole spanker at 11:00 A.M. Noon Lat by Obs 50'18N Wind NWxN and course WxS. Set the flying jib at 1:00 P.M. Sighted the schooner MAID OF ORLEANS about 4 miles north from us at 1:00 P.M. Obs Long at 4:00 P.M. 147'46W. On account of calm and slatting we had to lower the spanker and jibs at 8:00 P.M.

May 5, 1911

Calm and rain squalls. Set the jibs at 7:00 A.M. and spanker at 8:00 A.M. Noon Lat by Obs 50'18. D R Long 148'30. Set the MT staysail at 3:00 P.M. Cloudy with very light ENE and NNE winds.

May 6. 1911

At 1:00 A.M. took in the MT staysail, head winds and misery. Various light winds from west and WSW, cloudy and cold. Noon Obs 50:33N & 150:15 W.

May 7, 1911

This day commences with very light SW'ly winds, mist and misery. Courses WNW & WxN. distance run 125 miles. Lat 52'06N, Long 152'06W. Afternoon, fresh south winds with mist and raining. Took in the flying jib at 7:00 P.M., blowing a strong S'ly wind with rain and mist.

May 8, 1911

Blowing a strong SxW wind with rain to 2:30 A.M. when the wind changed to SW and at 4:00 P.M. to WSW with rain squalls and cold. Obs Long at 7:16 A.M. 155'07W. Noon Obs 53'39N. Afternoon blowing a strong to fresh SWxW wind with ugly snow squalls. Obs Long at 3:45 P.M. 155'38W. Took in the outer jib at 7:00 P.M. Took in the spanker at 10:00 P.M. Blowing a west gale with heavy snow and rough seas.

May 9, 1911

Blowing a westerly gale with heavy snow and rough seas. Very ugly weather. At 10:00 A.M. jogging along under shortened sail in rough seas and ugly weather. Noon position: 52:56N, 156'35W. Fresh snow squalls. Set the spanker and outer jib at 1:00 P.M. Obs Long at 3:30 P.M. 156'39. At 5:00 P.M. light SWxS wind, course WxN.

May 10, 1911

Blowing a light SE wind, rain and bad cross seas causing very heavy slatting. Sighted a cannery ship at 8:00 A.M. headed for the pass. Noon Obs 53'26N, 159'58W. Afternoon, light NNW wind becoming fresh and later strong from NW with snow squalls.

May 11, 1911

Set in heavy snow and strong SE'ly wind and at 7:45 A.M. on that account we stood off land at 8:00 A.M., under foresail, mainsail, & forestay sail. Strong heavy snows. Noon position 53'32N, 163'11 W. Set the jibs at noon. Obs Long at 3:00 P.M. 163'43. Sighted Shishaldum Volcano at 5:00 P.M. Snow squalls. At 10:00 P.M. jogging along SW course with NWxN wind during the night. Thick and snow squalls.

12th May 1911

Jogging along to 3:00 A.M. when we started under way. Heavy clouds obscured the island [Unimak Island]. Sighted Cape Lazaref at 6:00 A.M. in north. Passed Cape Lazaref at 9:00 A.M. Sighted schooner FORTUNA at anchor off Cape Pankof. Anchored in East Anchor Cove at 3:30 P.M. in 7 fathoms in the middle of the cove. Fishermen working at getting up dories.

May 13, 1911

Anchored in East Anchor Cove. Crew working at fixing dories and making vessel ready for fishing. Schr. MAID OF ORLEANS anchored here at 2:00 A.M. from Seattle. Light south and SW wind with snow squalls to 6:00 P.M. when it blew up from the NW with snow. On that account we had to leave the Cove at 7:00 P.M. and sailed across towards Thin Point where we anchored at 10:00 P.M. in 6 fathom.

Sunday, May 14, 1911

Anchored at Thin Point to 7:00 P.M. when it blew up from the SE with snow squalls. Hove anchor and left the place at 1:00 P.M. for Cape Pankof. At 2:00 P.M. set in snowing and the wind followed up from the SE. At 3:00 P.M. started for Ikitan Bay for shelter. On account of snow thick had a hard time in picking our way. Anchored at 5:00 P.M. in 10 fathoms with both 2,000 pound anchors and 55 fathoms of cable. Blowing an ESE gale with awfully heavy snow during the evening and night.

May 15, 1911

Anchored about 3/4 mile SWxS from Ikitan Point. Blowing a heavy ENE gale and heavy snow to 3:00 A.M. when the wind moderated and at 5:00 A.M. calmed down. From then light southerly winds. From 3:00 P. M. yesterday to 4:00 A.M. today it fell about 12 inches of snow, the heaviest snow I have seen in May. Crew working at filling water and making vessel ready for sea. Blowing a fresh SE wind during the night with snow squalls. Schr ALICE is at anchor in the bay arriving from Bering Sea.

Tuesday May 16, 1911

Anchored in the same place in Ikitan Bay. Light puffs of SE'ly wind and calms in between with snow squalls and ugly looking weather. On account of calms no chance to start for the fishing grounds today.

May 17, 1911

Anchored in the same place in Ikitan Bay, calm and snow squalls during the whole day. On that account we could not get away from this place today.

May 18, 1911

Anchored in the same place in Ikitan Bay. Blowing a fresh NW wind with snow to 6:00 P.M. when the wind calmed down. On account of the wind blowing right toward the shore and we are anchored close to it, we could not get away from here.

May 19, 1911

Hove anchor and left the place for Cape Pankof at 9:00 A.M. when a very light SW wind sprang up. At noon off Cape Pankof. As the MAID OF ORLEANS is anchored in the old place where I used to anchor, we had to anchor about 1 1/4 miles SExE from Cape Pankof Reef in 25 fathoms Gr B. at 3:30 P.M. Schr ALICE passed out at 7:00 P.M. bound for Bering Sea. Blowing a fresh to strong S'ly wind with snow squalls during the afternoon and night.

Saturday, May 20, 1911

Anchored about 1 1/4 miles SExE from Cape Pankof Reef. Blowing a fresh S and SSW wind with rain and snow squalls. Dories out fishing at 5:00 A.M. and arrived on board at 6:00 P.M. with 3885 fair cod.

May 21, 1911

Anchored in the same place off Cape Pankof, blowing a fresh SSE and SE wind to 6:00 A.M. From then wind increased from fresh to a storm with rough sea and rain. Payed out the second scope of the cable in case we had to slip. Blowing a strong SExS storm with rain and awful rough seas. The 21st day must be storm day as last year we had to slip the cable that day in a heavy SE storm and this 21st of May a heavy SE'ly storm, the highest Barometer as I have seen in a SE storm.

May 22, 1911

Anchored in the same place off Cape Pankof. Blowing a heavy SExE storm with rain and awful heavy seas to 1:00 A.M. when the wind moderated some. At 4:00 A.M. fresh SE wind. From 6:00 A.M. light SE wind with fog. Hove in the second scope of the cable at 1:00 P.M. Schr MAID OF ORLEANS hove up and sailed into East Anchor Cove at 3:00 P.M. Light SSE to SE to S and SE with fog and rain and misery.

May 23, 1911

Anchored in the same place off Cape Pankof. Blowing a fresh SEly wind with fog and rain. From noon to 7:00 P.M. light SE'ly wind. From then light easterly wind and raining. No fishing today on account of undesirable weather. Steamer DORA passed west at 8:00 P.M.

May 24, 1911

Anchored in the same place off Cape Pankof. Very light E'ly wind and mist to 2:00 A.M. From then to 6:00 A.M. light SE'ly wind and fog. At 8:00 A.M. blew up to a fresh SE wind with rain.

At 11:00 A.M. wind changed to SSE blowing fresh to strong during the afternoon. Dories out fishing at 4:30 A.M. and on account of strong wind arrived on board at 9:00 to 11:00 A.M. with 3243 fair cod. Str. CORWIN passed west at 4:30 P.M.

May 25, 1911

Anchored in the same place off Cape Pankof. Blowing a fresh to strong SE wind with rain squalls to 4:00 A.M. From then the wind moderated and changed to south. Very light south wind during the afternoon. Dories out fishing at 6:30 A.M. and arrived on board at 6:00 P.M. with 3724 cod.

May 26 1911

Anchored in the same place at Cape Pankof. Very light easterly wind, fog and rain to 7:00 A.M. From then to noon fresh to strong SE wind with rain and mist. At 6:00 P.M. wind changed to south and SxW. At 8:00 P.M. blowing a gale. At midnight blowing a SSW gale. I payed out the second scope of the cable at 8:00 P.M. Dories out fishing at 5:00 A.M. and on account of strong wind arrived on board at 11:00 A.M. with 1995 cod. Schr VEGA arrived here at noon and anchored about 3/4 mile SW from us.

May 27, 1911

Riding in a SxW storm in the same place off Cape Pankof. Blowing a SxW storm with very high seas and rain to noon when the wind changed to SW and moderated some. At 7:00 P.M. hove in the second scope of the cable. Very light WSW wind during the night. Number of cod on board only 12,847. Schr VEGA commenced dragging during the morning and fetched up when 1 1/4 miles NW from us. Schr FORTUNA passed in to East Anchor Cove at noon.

May 28, 1911

Anchored in the same place off Cape Pankof. Light SW'ly wind and fresh wind in the squalls with very rough choppy seas. Light SW'ly wind during the evening and night. Dories arrived on board at 5:00 P.M. with only 2955 cod. Schr VEGA hove up anchor at 5:00 A.M. and moved out about one mile and anchored. Schr FORTUNA started for the westward at 9:00 A.M. U.S.C.G.S. PATTERSON passed west at 3:00 P.M. and U.S.R.C. MANNING passed east at 5:00 P.M.

May 29th 1911

Anchored on the same place off Cape Pankof. Light SW wind and bad choppy sea during the day. Light SW wind with rain during the evening and night. Schr MAID OF ORLEANS passed out of East Anchor Cove at 3:00 P.M. and started to the westward. Dories out fishing at 4:30 A.M. and arrived on board at 6:00 P.M. with 3712 cod.

May 30, 1911

Anchored in the same place off Cape Pankof. Light to fresh SW wind with rain to noon. From 1:00 P.M. it blew up from the NNW to a moderate gale. Dories out fishing at 5:30 A.M. and arrived on board at 6:00 P.M. with 3847 fine cod.

May 31, 1911

Anchored in the same place off Cape Pankof. Blowing a NWxN gale to 2:00 A.M. From then the wind moderated and at 5:00 A.M. calmed down. At 10:00 A.M. very light south wind. At 4:00 P.M.

blowing up from the SSE with rain and mist. Weather is getting ugly toward the 1st of June as usually. Dories out fishing at 5:00 A.M. and arrived on board at 6:00 P.M. with 3962 fine cod.

June 1 1911

Riding in a SExS storm on the same place off Cape Pankof. Blowing a fresh SSE wind to 4:00 A.M. From then the wind increased to SSE storm with rain and mist and rough seas. June month for the last 6 years came in with the storm and ugly weather which is very remarkable. The wind increased some during the evening. Payed out the second scope of the cable at 5:00 A.M.

June 2, 1911

Riding in a SSW gale on the same place off Cape Pankof. Blowing a SSW gale with rain and snow squalls. At noon the wind changed to the south blowing a storm with ugly squalls and wintry weather. Cold and miserable indeed.

June 3, 1911

Ridding in a SSW storm in the same place off Cape Pankof. Blowing a SSW storm with rain and snow squalls to 4:00 P.M. when the wind moderated somewhat blowing a strong SSW wind with rain squalls and ugly weather during the evening and night. Number of cod on board 26,523.

June 4, 1911

Anchored on the same place off Cape Pankof. Blowing a strong SSW wind to 10:00 A.M. From then the wind moderated. Light SSW wind during the night. Hove in the second scope of the cable at 6:00 P.M. Schr FORTUNA left East Anchor Cove at 5:30 A.M. bound for the eastward.

June 5, 1911

Anchored in the same place off Cape Pankof. Light SSE wind with rain to 7:00 A.M. From then to 10:00 A.M. fresh SE wind with heavy rain and mist. From 10:00 A.M. to 5:00 P.M. strong SSE wind with heavy rain and mist, and ugly weather indeed. From 5:00 P.M. strong south wind rain and mist. Str. DORA passed east at 4:00 A.M. Dories out fishing at 4:30 A.M. and on account of strong wind arrived on board at noon with 3387 cod.

June 6, 1911

Riding in a south storm on the same place off Cape Pankof. Blowing a strong south wind to 3:00 A.M. From then to 8:00 A.M. it was blowing a S storm with rain and rough seas to 6:00 P.M. when the wind changed to SW blowing harder with rain squalls. Last June and this June is the worst June months for weather as I have seen in my life. Payed out the second scope of the cable at 6:00 A.M.

June 7, 1911

Riding in a WSW to SW wind and SSW gale on the same place off Cape Pankof. WSW-SW and SSW gale with rain squalls and rough seas. This stormy weather do not seem to be any end this summer. The USS PATTERSON passed east at 6:45 A.M.

June 8, 1911

Anchored in the same place off Cape Pankof. Blowing a strong SW wind and to 4:00 A.M. when the wind moderated and changed to WSW. At 9:00 A.M. it breezed up from the SWxS with rain squalls. At noon it was blowing a strong SSW wind. At 6:00 P.M. strong SSW wind and ugly looking weather. Hove in the second scope of cable at 8:00 A.M. Dories out fishing at 5:30 A.M. and arrived on board from noon to 5:00 P.M. with 5745 fair cod.

June 9, 1911

Anchored in the same place at Cape Pankof. Blowing a SW gale to 5:00 A.M. when the wind calmed down and left us to lay in the trough of the rough sea. Rolling the rails under, filling the deck with water, shipping and washing away everything available around. It was same thing awful calm and rough seas with snow squalls to 6:00 P.M. when it blew up from the NW with snow squalls and very cold and Godforsaken weather.

June 10,1911

Anchored in the same place off Cape Pankof. Blowing a strong NW wind with snow squalls and very cold during the whole day and night. This is the tenth of June and we have only one full day of fishing. That beats any previous record in the stormy days in my fishing experience in 10 years. U.S.R.C. MANNING passed west at 5:00 P.M.

June 11, 1911

Anchored in the same place off Cape Pankof. Blowing a strong NWxN wind to 8:00 A.M. From then the wind moderated to a light breeze from the NNW. Dories out fishing at 8:00 A.M. and arrived on board at 6:00 P.M. with 3665 fine fish.

June 12, 1911

Anchored in the same place off Cape Pankof. Very light wind with calms between during the day. At 8:00 P.M. it blew up from the NW. Hove in the first scope of cable at 8:00 A.M. Found the 25 fathom cable damaged to such an extent that we had to remove it and put in 20 fathoms new cable in its place. Albert Smith and K Evenson took one dory and ran away from the vessel about 5:00 A.M. Deserted without our knowledge. Dories arrived on board at 6:00 P.M. with 4445 fine cod.

June 13,1911

Riding on a NW storm on the same place at Cape Pankof. Blowing a NWxN gale to 1:00 P.M. From then NW storm with rain squalls and cold during the evening and night. A salmon seine gasoline boat passed west at 8:00 P.M.

June 14, 1911

Riding in a NWxN gale in the same place off Cape Pankof. Blowing a NWxN gale with cold and cloudy sky.

July 15, 1911

Riding in a NW gale in the same place off Cape Pankof. Blowing a NW gale to noon. From then it was blowing NNW wind. A.U.S.R.C. passed west at 8:00 P.M. I considered June last year the limit for stormy weather, but surely this June puts it in the second. First it was blowing from the NW and God only knows when it will end.

June 16, 1911

Anchored in the same place off Cape Pankof. Blowing a strong NNW wind to 8:00 A.M. when the wind moderated some but at

1:00 P.M. it blew up again to a strong NWxN wind. Dories started out fishing at 9:00 A.M. and arrived on board from 1:00 to 5:00 P.M. with 2113 cod. Poor fishing today.

June 17, 1911
Anchored in the same place at Cape Pankof. Blowing a strong NWxN wind to 6:00 A.M. when the wind calmed down. Calm from 10:00 A.M. Foggy during most of the afternoon. Calm and fine weather during the evening and night. Number of cod on board at date, 45,947. Dories out fishing at 6:00 A.M. and arrived on board at 5:00 P.M. with only 2069 caught. Poor fishing here now. The first chance we have, we will go in and fill water and then start for the Sanak Banks.

June 18, 1911
Anchored in the same place off Cape Pankof. Dories out fishing at usual time and arrived on board at noon with 1404 cod. At 3:30 P.M. when we hove in and sailed into East Anchor Cove and anchored there at 5:00 P.M. in 11 fathoms sandy bottom for to fill water. Blowing a fresh to strong SWxW wind with heavy fog. Calm to 4:00 A.M. when a light SW wind to 3:00 P.M. From then fresh SWxW wind and fog. SWxW wind. Strong SWxW wind and heavy fog during the evening and night.

June 19, 1911
Anchored in East Anchor Cove. Blowing a fresh to strong SWxW wind with fog and rain to 8:00 A.M. From then light SWxW wind and rain and foggy. Commenced to fill water at 9:00 A.M. and at 3:00 P.M. had the water on board. But on account of heavy fog on the outside we could not start for the Sanak Bank this evening.

June 20, 1911
Anchored in East Anchor Cove, Calm and foggy to 11:00 A.M. when it breezed up from the east with heavy fog and rain. At 8:00 P.M. it was blowing an east gale with rain and fog and gave her 2nd cable, 65 fathom altogether. The most ugly night I have seen with strong high seas and thick and the heaviest rain I have seen in my life. As we could not get away from here on account of the fog, we had the dories out from 5:00 A.M. to noon. Days catch 2207 cod.

June 21, 1911
Anchored in East Anchor Cove. Blowing an east gale with rough seas and very heavy rain to 5:00 A.M. when the wind moderated, but the rain and fog is keeping up. We are anchored about 1/2 mile off the shore but still without sight of the land to 9:00 P.M. This awful weather do not seem to take any end this summer. At 9:00 P.M. it blew up from the ENE. Hove anchor and got out at 10:00 P.M. heading north to mid night. Blowing a strong ENE wind, rain and thick.

June 22, 1911
Under sail beating off Ikitan Point, blowing an ENE gale with rain and thick. Took in the spanker and outer jib at 6:00 A.M. As it is thick and blowing a ENE storm, I considered it to be dangerous under sail in between the rocks in such a thick and stormy weather. We anchored at 10:00 A.M. in 28 fathoms on hard bottom, by reckoning about 4 miles SW from Umga Island and 8 miles SSE 1/2 E from Amagat Island. [Umga is spelled correct and not to be confused with Unga]. At 4:00 P.M. sight of

the island and found the position true. Blowing a heavy ENE storm to 4:00 P.M. when the wind moderated some. What an awful midsummer day. (May God have pity on us.) Blew up again to an ENE storm at 6:00 P.M.

June 23, 1911
Riding in an ENE gale, 4 miles SW from Umga Island. Blowing ENE gale with heavy rain and thick. The most ungodly weather as could be and do not seem to end. This is Sankt Hans Eve as we from the old country used to celebrate as mid summer. The most gloryes weather and when everything around was in its glory. But here it is something else. Storm, rain, thick and most Godforsaken ugly weather.

June 24, 1911
Riding in a heavy ExN gale, 4 miles SW from Umga Island. Blowing a heavy ExN gale with rain and thick to noon. From then strong ENE wind and rain. The roughest since Wednesday as I have seen for years. The DORA passed us at 11:00 A.M. going west. (This is Saturday)

June 25, 1911
Anchored about 4 miles SW from Umga Island to 6:00 A.M. when we hove anchor and started for Sanak Bank. Light NW wind and rain. The schr VEGA hove up at 6:00 A.M. and left Cape Pankof for filling water. At noon about 3 miles west from Midway Rock. Very light WSW wind and rain squalls. Anchored at 5:00 P.M. on 28 fathoms of gravel bottom about 3 miles east from Whale Point, Caton Island. Dress gang had good fishing from the deck during the evening.

June 26, 1911
Anchored about 3 miles east from Whale Point, Caton Island. Very light easterly wind to 8:00 A.M. From then light and fresh wind and rain. Schr FORTUNA arrived here from West Anchor Cove at 4:00 P.M. and anchored about 1 mile NW from us. She reports with 68,000 cod. Days catch including dress gang catch 4711 fine cod.

June 27, 1911
Anchored in the same place off Caton Island. Light and very light southerly wind. Calm in between and rain and mist. Very strong tide during the morning. Dories out fishing at 5:00 A.M. and arrived on board at 6:00 P.M. with 3991 fine cod.

June 28, 1911
Anchored in the same place off Caton Island. Very light SE'ly. E'ly and NE'ly wind with rain to 8:00 P.M. From then light NE wind and rain. The tide during the morning is running too strong to fish in. Dories out fishing at usual time and arrived on board at 7:00 P.M. with 3637 fine cod.

June 29, 1911
Anchored in the same place off Caton Island. Light to fresh north wind to 8:00 A.M. From then to 2:00 P.M. calm and pt. cloudy. From 2:00 P.M. to 8:00 P.M. calm and fine weather. The finest afternoon we have had this summer. Owing to strong tide, did not start out fishing before 8:00 A.M. and arrived on board at 7:00 P.M. with 2989 fine cod.

June 30, 1911

Anchored in the same place off Caton Island. Blowing a light to fresh NW to W to SW wind with fog during the afternoon. Schr FORTUNA left here at 3:00 P.M. for Pinnacle Rocks, Sandman Reef to finish up the trip with big fish. She needs only 15,000 more. Poor fishing today caused mostly by very strong tide, as we could do no fishing during the forenoon on that account. Days catch only 1941 cod.

July 1, 1911

Anchored on the same place off Caton Island. Blowing a light to fresh W'ly wind with fog and strong tide to 11:00 A.M. From then a light N'ly wind and calm with pt cloudy to 5:00 P.M. Number of cod on board at date, 68,684. Owing to strong tides, fog and wind, dories did not start out fishing before at noon and arrived on board at 6:00 P.M. with 1757 fine cod.

July 2, 1911

Anchored in the same place off Caton Island. Blowing a light ENE wind with rain squalls to 11:00 A.M. From then the wind increased to a strong ENE wind with rough cross seas sweeping the deck. Rain squalls and very ugly weather. Only 13 dories was out fishing during forenoon and a short time during the afternoon and brought in 1878 good cod.

July 3, 1911

Riding in a NExE gale in the same place off Caton Island. Blowing a strong ENE wind to 4:00 A.M. From then it was blowing a NExE gale with snow squalls and rough seas. At 6:00 P.M. the wind changed to NNE blowing a gale with rain and rough ENE seas. Schr FORTUNA passed west inside of Caton Island at 10:00 A.M. Payed out the second scope of cable at 5:00 A.M..

July 4, 1911

Anchored in the same place off Caton Island. Blowing a NNE gale to 10:00 A.M. when the wind moderated and changed to N. At noon light north wind and rain and rough ENE seas causing heavy rolling. From 5:00 P.M. to 7:00 P.M. calm very light westerly wind during the evening and night. Hove in the second scope of cable at 1:00 P.M.

July 5, 1911

Anchored in the same place off Caton Island. Calm and very light SW'ly winds and cloudy. Very light airs of easterly winds during the evening and night. Heavy ugly looking clouds. Schr FORTUNA came out from harbor and anchored at 12:00 A.M. about 1 1/2 miles NNW from here. Dories out fishing at 5:30 A.M. and arrived on board at 6:00 P.M. with 5470 fine cod. The best catch so far this summer.

July 6, 1911

Anchored in the same place off Caton Island. Blowing a light ENE wind with very heavy rain to 6:00 A.M. From then the wind increased in force to 10:00 A.M. when it was blowing a strong wind with heavy rain and thick. The wind changed to NE and north during the evening and night. Rain and heavy mist during the day and night. Dories out fishing at 5:30 A.M. and owing to strong wind and arrived on board at 9:00 A.M with only 1271 cod.

July 7, 1911

Anchored in the same place off Caton Island. Blowing a light N to NNW wind to 8:00 A.M. From then it blew up to a strong NW wind. The wind moderated and changed to W during the evening. The FORTUNA hove up and sailed into harbor last night. Came out and anchored at noon again but drifted off. She hove up again and stood toward NE. Dories out fishing at 5:00 A.M. Owing to strong winds all dories except one arrived on board at 11:00 A.M. with 1502 cod. Sent 2 dories with 6 men out to look for the dory as failed to arrive on board. The 2 dories arrived on board at 5:00 P.M. without having seen sign of the lost dory or the man. The dory must have been loaded too heavy and swamped by the seas.

July 8, 1911

Anchored in the same place off Caton Island. Light westerly and SW'ly winds cloudy and pt. foggy. Number of cod on board at date 82,629. Dories out fishing at 6:00 A.M. and arrived on board at 6:00 P.M. with 3824 fine cod. Two men deserted, one man we lost yesterday and 1 man laying sick, so we surely have had bad luck with men.

July 9, 1911

Hove in anchor, fair wind and left this place at 8:00 A.M. and moved about 2 miles ENE and anchored at 9:30 A.M. in 28 fathoms of water. Very light westerly and NNW wind and cloudy. Dories out fishing at 10:00 A.M. and arrived on board at 6:00 P.M. with 3951 fine cod.

July 10, 1911

Anchored about 5 miles east of Whale Point, Caton Island. Blowing a fresh WNW wind to noon when NW wind and rain. Blowing a strong NW to NNW wind during the evening and night. Very cold weather! No fishing today on account of fresh wind.

July 11, 1911

Anchored in the same place off Caton Island. Blowing a strong NNW wind today to 1:00 P.M. when the wind moderated to light NW'ly winds during the evening and night. Put out the second scope of cable at 5:00 A.M. Hove in the second scope at 2:00 P.M.

July 12, 1911

Anchored in the same place off Caton Island. Light NW'ly winds and cloudy with very strong tide during the forenoon, interfering a great deal with the fishing. Very light SW'ly winds and foggy during the evening and night. Two of our best fisherman are laid up on account of sickness, but on account of the strong tide some of the dories did not start out fishing until 8:00 A.M. and arrived on board at 6:00 P.M. with 5925 fine cod including the dress gang catch.

July 13, 1911

Anchored in the same place off Caton Island. Calm and very light S'ly winds with fog and very strong tides during the forenoon. At 3:00 P.M. it breezed up from the ENE. On account of strong tides, dories did not start out fishing before 9:00 A.M. and arrived on board at 7:00 P.M. with 3302 fine cod.

July 14, 1911

Anchored in the same place off Caton Island. Light east'ly wind to noon. Light fresh easterly wind with rain squalls and rough cross seas and rolling during the evening. Dories out fishing at 6:00 A.M. and arrived on board at 6:00 P.M. with 3254 fine cod.

July 15, 1911

Anchored in the same place off Caton Island. Light NE'ly wind with cloudy during the forenoon. Fresh ENE wind and rough cross seas and nasty weather during the evening and night. Number of cod on board at date 100,856. Only 12 dories started out fishing today. The rest of them stayed in for the rest. The 12 dories catch 1795 fine cod.

July 16, 1911

Anchored in the same place off Caton Island. Blowing a strong ENE wind with rain and nasty weather. A wonderful high barometer we have for this kind of weather.

July 17, 1911

Anchored in the same place off Caton Island. Blowing a strong ENE wind with rain and mist during the day and evening and fresh wind during the night.

July 18, 1911

Anchored in the same place off Caton Island. Blowing a fresh ENE wind to 4:00 A.M. From 4:00 A.M., light and very light NNE wind to 11:00 A.M. From then calm and partly cloudy. This is the finest afternoon we have had this summer. Owing to fresh wind, dories did not start out fishing before 9:30 A.M. and arrived on board at 7:00 P.M. with 4016 fine cod.

July 19, 1911

Anchored in the same place off Caton Island. Calm and cloudy to 7:00 A.M. From then it breezed up from the SW to a fresh to strong wind with rain and misery. Dories out fishing at 6:00 A.M. and arrived on board at 5:00 P.M. with 3212 fine cod.

July 20, 1911

Anchored in the same place off Caton Island. Blowing a fresh SW wind. From then a light SSW wind. No fishing today, cause the wind not from the right direction to suit the fishermen.

July 21, 1911

Anchored in the same place off Caton Island. Very light NNW wind and NW wind with fog to 10:00 A.M. From then to 3:00 P.M. light NW wind and p'tly cloudy. From 3:00 P.M. to 6:00 P.M. very light SW wind. From 6:00 P.M. light to fresh NW wind during the evening and night. This afternoon we have had very fine weather but none of the dories started out fishing. It looks as if the fishermen don't want any more fish. We had good fishing weather the last two days.

July 22, 1911

Anchored in the same place off Caton Island. Blowing a light NW wind to 5:00 A.M. From then it was blowing a strong NW wind and cloudy. Owing to strong wind only 4 dories was out fishing for a few hours and they found poor fishing and no fresh bait to be had from the vessel as we have caught plenty of mackerel from this vessel.

July 23, 1911

Anchored in the same place off Caton Island. Blowing a very light W and SW wind and fog to 10:00 A.M. From then light SSW wind and rain to noon. From then it blew up from the SE with awful heavy rain. A very ugly night with SSE wind, rain and rough sea with bad rolling. On account of the fog only 14 dories started out fishing at 8:00 A.M. and arrived on board at 4:00 P.M. with 2548 fair cod. Some of the dories struck fair fishing about 2 miles ExS from here.

July 24, 1911

Anchored in the same place off Caton Island. Blowing a light to fresh SSE wind with rain and fog to 6:00 A.M. From then SSW wind, raining and rough seas. From 8:00 P.M. blowing a strong SSW wind. Payed out the second scope of cable at 10:00 P.M. Mackerel is plentiful around here today. On account of fresh wind and fog and rough sea, no fishing today. The hope for good weather this summer is fast disappearing.

July 25, 1911

Anchored in the same place off Caton Island. Blowing a SSW gale with rough sea and awful strong tide. From 2:00 to 7:00 A.M., the vessel was laying in the trough of the sea, filling the deck with water to dangerous point, tearing dories adrift and smashing things up. It was an awful night. At noon the wind moderated and changed to south with rain and ugly weather. We had to dump about 100 sacks of salt overboard in order to save the vessel from smashing up dories.

[Note: Each sack would hold 125 pounds of salt. These sacks were probably stored on top of the after house. This was done near the end of the season to provide room in the hold for the last of the cod and the salt would be used on the last days.]

July 26, 1911

Anchored in the same place off Caton Island. Blowing a fresh south wind with rain and mist and fog, strong tide and rough seas to 11:00 A.M. From then the wind moderated and changed to SW to 4:00 P.M. when the wind changed back to south. Light wind during the afternoon and evening. Hove in the second scope of cable at 11:00 A.M. No fishing today.

July 27, 1911

Anchored in the same place off Caton Island. Light south wind and rain squalls, mist and strong tide to 10:00 A.M.. From 10:00 A.M. to 2:00 P.M. light SSE wind. From 2:00 P.M. fresh SSE wind with rain and mist to 8:00 P.M. From then it was blowing a strong SSE wind and heavy rain, mist and misery. Dories out fishing at 10:00 A.M. and on account of rough weather arrived on board at 4:00 P.M. with 3115 cod including the dress gang catch.

July 28, 1911

Riding in a SSE gale on the same place off Caton Island. Blowing a SSE gale with rough sea, strong tide and awful heavy rain. At noon the wind moderated and changed to SSW. From 5:00 to 8:00 A.M. the vessel was laying in the trough of the sea and rolling and filling the deck with water. I have been in hope of getting some good weather this summer, but it looks as a disappointment. Payed out the second scope of cable at 6:00 P.M.

July 29, 1911

Anchored on the same place at Caton Island. Very light SW'ly wind with calm in between and rough south swells causing bad rolling. Number of cod on board 119,631. dories out fishing at 5:00 A.M. and arrived on board at 6:00 P.M. with 5884 fine cod.

July 30, 1911

Anchored in the same place off Caton Island. Calm and light east wind with fog to 6:00 A.M. From 6:00 to 10:00 A.M., blowing a fresh east wind with fog and rain. At 11:00 A.M. the wind changed to SE and moderated. Fog and rain during the day and evening. Dories out fishing at usual time and arrived on board at 6:00 P.M. with 4106 fine cod.

July 31, 1911

Anchored in the same place off Caton Island. Light SE wind with rain and fog to 8:00 A.M. From then fresh SE wind, rain and fog to 6:00 P.M. From then light SE wind and fog. Sixteen dories started out fishing at 5:30 A.M. and owing to fresh wind arrived on board at 10:00 A.M. with 2083 fine cod.

August 1 1911

Anchored in the same place off Caton Island. Very light SE'ly and southerly wind, rain and fog to 1:00 P.M. From then awful heavy rain, mist and light ESE wind. Owing to fog dories did not start out fishing before 7:00 A.M. and arrived on board at 6:00 P.M. with 3083 fine cod. 17 dories out fishing today.

August 2, 1911

Anchored in the same place off Caton Island. Blowing a fresh ESE wind with rain and rough sea. Owing to fresh wind and rough sea, no fishing today.

Aug 3, 1911

Anchored in the same place off Caton Island. Very light S'ly and SW'ly wind with calm in between, and rough SSE swells and foggy with rain as usual this summer. Dories out fishing at 5:00 A.M. and arrived on board at 7:00 P.M. with 4604 fine cod.

Aug 4, 1911

Anchored in the same place off Caton Island. Calm and foggy to 4:00 P.M. From then fresh ENE wind and rain and fog. We have not had one whole fine day yet this summer. Dories out fishing at 7:00 A.M. and arrived on board at 7:00 P.M. with 4963 fine cod.

Aug 5, 1911

Anchored in the same place off Caton Island. Very light easterly wind, rain and mist to 8:00 A.M. From then to 2:00 P.M fresh to strong SSE wind, heavy rain and rough sea. Number of cod on board at date 140,358. 15 dories started out fishing at 7:00 A.M. and account of rough weather arrived on board at 1:00 A.M. with 1878 fine cod.

Aug 6, 1911

Anchored in the same place off Caton Island. Blowing a strong SSE wind with heavy rain and fog with a rough sea and misery. No fishing today on account of rough weather.

Aug 7, 1911

Anchored in the same place off Caton Island. Light NW to NNW wind with rain squalls to noon. From then very light NNE wind and pt cloudy sky to 6:00 P.M. when the weather changed to east with rain and mist. At 10:00 P.M. SSE wind, rain mist and misery. We had 6 hours summer today! Had an observation at 3:40 P.M. for to compare the chronometer and found it to have gained at the rate of 0.84 sec daily. Daily rate from Seattle 0.5 gaining. Dories out fishing at 6:00 A.M. and 7:00 A.M. and arrived on board at 7:00 P.M. with 5007 fine cod.

Aug 8, 1911

Anchored in the same place off Caton Island. Blowing a fresh ESE wind with rain and mist to 6:00 A.M. when it was blowing a strong SSE. Rain, mist and rough sea. Very ugly and miserable weather. Owing to strong tide no fishing today

Aug 9, 1911

Riding in a SSE gale on the same place off Caton Island. Blowing a strong SSE wind with rain and fog to 4:00 A.M. From then it was blowing a SSE gale with rain, mist, and very rough sea sweeping the deck. Awful weather this is. At 6:00 P.M. wind changed to SSW blowing hard with rain and fog and heavy rough sea. This is an awful year with blowing and rain and rough weather without one whole fine day during the summer. Payed out the second scope of cable at 4:30 A.M.

Aug 10, 1911

Anchored in the same place off Caton Island. This day came in with light SSW'ly wind and rain, fog. rough sea and very strong tide to 10:00 A.M. From then easterly wind and heavy rain and rough S swells. This summer we have had the most Godforsaken weather imaginable. At 3:00 P.M. the wind changed to the S blowing fresh with fog and rain. Hove in the second scope of cable at 6:00 A.M. Owing to strong tide and rough swells, dories did not start for fishing before 10:00 A.M. and arrived on board at 5:00 P.M. with 3200 fine cod.

Aug 11, 1911

This day commences with a strong south wind, rain and fog and very rough sea on the same place off Caton Island. At 1:00 P.M. it blew up to a heavy SxW gale with heavy fog and rain. The weather seems to be getting worse right along, awful – awful. Strong SW wind and fog and rough seas during the evening and night. Payed out the second scope of cable at 0:30 A.M.

Aug 12, 1911

Anchored in the same place off Caton island. This day commences with strong SxW wind fog and rain. The wind moderated some at noon, but the fog and rain still keeping up. We have been fighting storms, rain, and fog during the whole spring-summer and come we have fall and still no change to the better. [writing not very clear.] We need about 12,000 more cod to fill the vessel but it seems to be a hard proposition to get it.

Aug 13, 1911

Anchored in the same place at Caton Island. This day commenced with fresh to strong SSW wind, heavy fog and strong tide causing the vessel to lay in the trough of the sea, filling the vessel's deck with water right along. This is surely a Godforsaken weather as the Arabian Knight. We are laying about 4 miles off Caton Island and have had no sight of the sun since Monday, Aug 7. At noon we had the highest barometer I have seen since Sept 12th 1907. A sight [of the sun] was very rare this summer. Hove in the second scope of chain at 1:00 P.M.

Monday, Aug 14, 1911
Anchored in the same place at Caton Island. This day commenced with a light SSW wind and pt foggy. At 4:00 P.M. it blew up from the SSW to a strong wind with rain squalls and thick. 17 dories started out fishing at 7:00 A.M. and arrived on board at 6:00 P.M. with 3577 fine cod.

Aug 15, 1911
Anchored in the same place off Caton Island. This day commences with fresh SW wind and fog and rain. The wind moderated at 7:00 A.M. but breezed up again at 10:00 A.M. to a fresh SW wind with heavy fog. At 2:00 P.M. the wind moderated to a light breeze. At 6:00 P.M. it blew up to a strong SW wind with fog. Wind moderated some toward the midnight. Owing to fresh wind and fog, dories did not start out fishing before 8:30 A.M. and arrived on board at 7:00 P.M. with 4175 fine cod.

Aug 16, 1911
Anchored in the same place off Caton Island. This day commenced with a light SW wind and fog. From 6:00 A.M. very light W'ly and SW'ly with rough south swells and pt cloudy. 17 dories fishing at 7:00 A.M. and arrived on board at 7:00 P.M. with 5343 fine cod. Have room and salt left for only about 1500 fish.

Aug 17, 1911
Dories out fishing at 8:00 A.M. and arrived on board at noon with 1285 cad, all the fish we have salt for. Number of cod on board 162,931. Dressing fish and making ready for sea, from noon to 4:00 P.M.. Hove anchor from 5:00 to 8:00 P.M. We had a hard time in bringing up the anchor as the chain was jamming on the whelps of the windlass. Left 4 miles east of Caton Island at 8:30 P.M. for Seattle.

Aug 18, 1911
This day commenced with light WSW wind and rain squalls. 9:00 A.M. Fine light WxS wind and cloudy. Noon position: 53:37N, 160:00 W. 8: 00 raining.

Aug 19: 1911
This day commenced with light airs of the WxN wind, rain and thick. 5: 00 A.M. rain and very light airs of NW'ly, winds changed to the N and NNE and then back to WNW at 10:00 A.M. with rain squalls. Noon Pos: 52:53N, 158:03W. 4:00 P.M. ohs long. 157:37 W.

Aug 20, 1911
This day commenced with a very light ESE winds and rain squalls. 8:00 A.M. wind changing to E and ENE. Tacked ship at 11:00 A.M. Noon pos: 53:01 N, 156:08W. 4:00 P.M. Obs Long 155:58 w. 10:00 P.M. Very light airs of NE wind, rain and rough S swells causing heavy slatting.

Aug 21, 1911
This day commenced with very light airs of NE wind and rain and rough south swells causing awful slatting. When we are on the fishing grounds we had plenty of wind but now when we are sailing and need wind we get calm. On account of calm and awful slatting we had to lower the spanker and drop the fore and main peak at 7:00 A.M. At 9:00 A.M. the steamer NORTH STAR of Astoria passed east toward Astoria. Noon pos: 52:25 N, 153:30 W. At 3:00 P.M. a very light ESE wind sprung up, set all the sails at 3:30 P.M. We are pounding up against a heavy NE swell. Contrary weather we have had the whole summer and it still keeping up.

Aug 22, 1911
This day commenced with a fresh to strong ExN wind, rough cross seas and rain and contrary weather A ship passed us at 2:00 A.M. bound east. Took in the flying jib at 3:00 A.M. A very heavy squall struck us at 8:30 A.M. From then ENE changing to east and than back to ENE, awful hard rain and awful rough seas. Noon pos: 51:26N, 154:25W. At 1:00 P.M. on account of rough sea and very light air of wind causing awful slatting we had to lower the spanker. Awful heavy slatting during the afternoon and evening and night

Aug. 23, 1911
This day commenced with calm and rough cross swells from NE and SE causing the vessel to roll and slat something frightful. A very light air of S wind sprang up at 8:00 A.M. but on account of very rough swell we could not set the spanker before 10:00 A.M. Noon pos: 51:18N. 153:50W. At 1:00 P.M. the wind changed towards the east again. Obs long at 4:00 P.M. 153:35. Took in the flying jib at 8:00 P.M., blowing a strong ExS wind, rain and rough sea.

Aug 24, 1911
This day commenced with a strong ESE wind and rain and rough seas. At 2:30 A.M. the wind changed to SSE blowing hard. The wind changed to south at 8:00 A.M. Noon Pos:51:32 N, 150:05W. Set the flying jib at 4: 00 P.M. Obs lat at 4:00 P.M. 149:05 W.

Aug 25,1911
This day commenced with a very light air of SSE wind, rain and rough swell causing bad slatting. On that account we had to lower the spanker at 4:00 A.M. Noon pos: 51:14 N, 147:40 W, 1:00 P.M. calm and rolling.

Aug 26, 1911.
This day commenced with calm and choppy S swell and rolling. At 5:30 A.M. a very light air of south wind sprang up and at 6:00 A.M. we set all the sails. We now have had a 26 hours calm, the longest calm we have had this summer. Noon owing to slatting we had to lower the M T staysail. Noon pos: 51:05W, 146:40 E. At 1:00 P.M. very light air of WxS with, choppy south swell, rolling and slatting as usual. Obs Long at 4:00 P.M. 146: 23W. In order to keep the sails full we had to steer ESE from 4:00 P.M.

Aug 27, 1911
This day commenced with a very light air of SW wind and cloudy. Sighted a ship at 5:00 A.M. bound for Frisco or Astoria and at 7:00 A.M. sighted another ship bound for Sound. Wind changed to south at 8:00 A.M. At 9:00 A.M. to SSE with rain and

ugly weather. Noon pos: 50:35 N, 144:35 W. At 7:00 P.M. blowing a strong SE and SSE wind with heavy rain and awful rough cross sea.

Aug 28, 1911

This day commenced with a SSE gale, heavy rain and awful rough seas sweeping the deck. Noon pos: 49:54 N, 139:35W. 5:00 P.M. blowing a fresh SW and SSW wind, rain and mist.

Aug 29, 1911

This day commenced with a fresh SSW wind and rain and mist. Set the MT staysail at 10:00 A.M. Noon pos: 48:55 N, 135:55W. We had a poor sight of the sun through the fog and rain at noon. Obs long W at 4:00 P.M. 134:34 W.

Aug 30, 1911

This day commenced with very light S'ly wind, fog and rain. On account of slatting we had to steer ExN and E to 9:00 A.M. from then NExN in order to keep the sails from shaking to pieces Awful. Noon pos: 48:28N, 132:00W. Owing to heavy slatting we had to lower the spanker at 1:00 P.M. Obs at 3:20 P.M. 131:55W.

Aug 31, 1911

This day commenced with o'cast, light air from north with fog. Set the sails at 3:00 A.M. Very light air of N wind. Noon pos: 48:28N, 130:25W. Obs long at 4;00 P.M. 130:06W. At 6:00 P.M. Calm and fine fishing weather now we don't need it. But it is poor weather for sailing.

Sept I, 1911

This day commenced with calm and pt'ly cloudy and fine weather. Noon pos: 48:24N, 129:30W. A very light air of W'ly sprung up at noon.

Sept 2, 1911

This day commenced with a light W x N wind, fog and rain. Sighted Vancouver at 5:00 A.M. in N direction Obs Long at 8:00 A.M. 127:00W Noon pos: 48:35N, 126:34W. At 1:00 P.M. heavy fog hiding the land from sight. Obs long at 4:20 P.M. 126:04W.

Sept 3, 1911

This day commenced with calm, fog and rain running before the WSW swell to 1:00 A.M. when we on account of thick weather decided to wait until daylight. Sounded at 1:00 A.M., 70 fathom. Passed about 70 miles SSW from Cape Beal at 6:00 A.M. a light air of SW wind, fog and rain. Sighted Swiftsure Lightship in ENE at 10:00 A.M. Noon pos: 48:34N, 125:00W. At Swiftsure Lightship at 1:00 P.M. drifting at the lightship this afternoon in calm. 8:00 P.M. drifting around in calm, heavy fog and very rough WSW swell. Rolling, slatting awful. Lowered the spanker at 9:00 P.M.

Sept 4, 1911

This day commenced with a very light west wind and fog. At Clallam Bay at 4:00 A.M. Sighted 2 schooners and 1 barkentine about 2 miles west of us at 8:00 A.M. bound in. From A.M. drifting out with the tide. At 10:00 A.M. light west wind sprang up. Passed Clallam Bay at noon. Passed Port Angeles at 7:00 P.M. Passed Dungeness at M.N.

Sept 5, 1911

This day commenced with a light SW wind and rain. At 3:00 A.M. at Middle Point. Wind calm and the tide took us out again. At 8:00 A.M. off Protection Island At 9:00 A.M. sent a dory to Port Townsend to try to get a tow boat to tow us up. Could get only 2 gasoline boats. Passed Point Wilson at noon. Left Port Townsend in tow of 2 gasoline boats at 1:00 P.M. Passed Point No Point at 6:00 P.M. At Apple Cove at M.N.

Sept 6, 1911

In tow of gasoline boats At 5:00 A.M. when going in to the dock we went aground with the bow at West Seattle City Dock. Left West Seattle at 2:30 P.M. in tow of MYSTIC for Poulsbo and moored at the P.C.C.Co. Plant at 7:00 P.M. So ends this miserable trip.

In this log, Captain Grotle many times mentions the vessel is "slatting." This is a term used to describe the vessel undergoing severe rolling with no wind in the sails to steady them, and the gaff on the upper edge of each large sail swinging from side to side. At this time there is great strain placed on the after leach of the sail, that edge reinforced with a heavy rope that connects the boom on the lower side with the gaff on the upper side. Should this rope or "leach" break, the sail would be torn from side to side and possibly also up and down. The sail would require major repair work, most likely beyond the capacity of the crew. Further, the gaff, now having lost restraint, might cause additional damage.

Appendix III

Charts of the Alaska Peninsula and Aleutian Islands

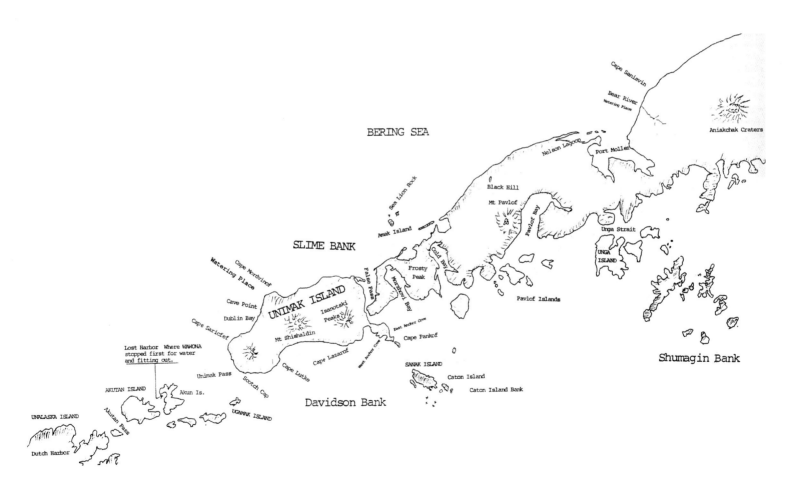

Alaska Peninsula, Aleutian Islands, and Shumagin Islands.

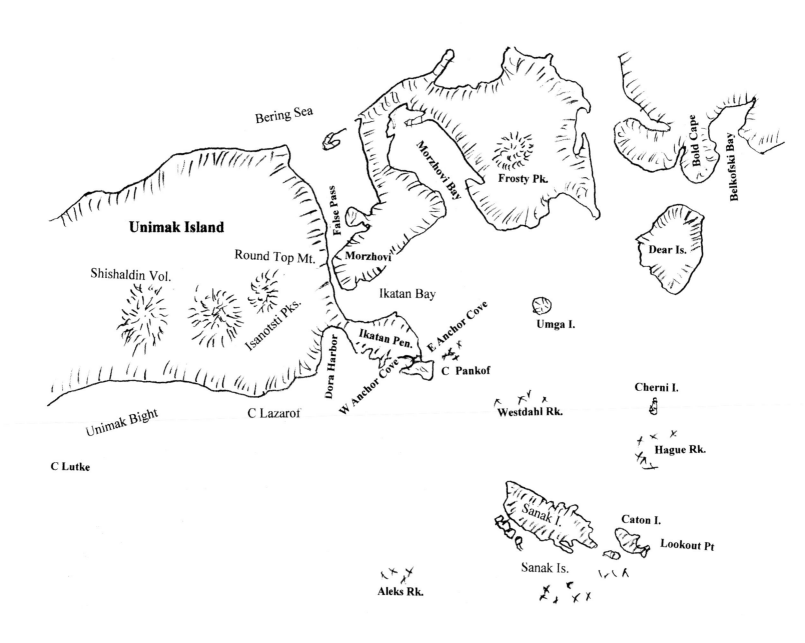

Bering Sea

Unimak Island

False Pass

Round Top Mt.

Shishaldin Vol.

Isanotsti Pks.

Dora Harbor

C Lazarof

Unimak Bight

C Lutke

Morzhovi Bay

Frosty Pk.

Morzhovi

Ikatan Bay

Ikatan Pen.

E Anchor Cove

W Anchor Cove

C Pankof

Umga I.

Westdahl Rk.

Aleks Rk.

Bold Cape

Belkofski Bay

Dear Is.

Cherni I.

Hague Rk.

Sanak I.

Caton I.

Lookout Pt

Sanak Is.

Aleutian Islands

230

KOROVIN ISLAND

UNGA STRAIT

KOROVIN STRAIT

Unga Spit

Zachary Bay

Pirate Cove

Little Harbor

Sand Point

Dark Cliff

POPOF ISLAND

Egg Is.

Red Cove

UNGA ISLAND

Popof Straight

Popof Head

Delarof Harbor

Unga   Halfway Rk.

Acheredin Bay

Baralof Harbor

Unga Cape

Acheredin Pt.

Shumagin Islands

Appendix IV

Captain Ed Shields' Master's License

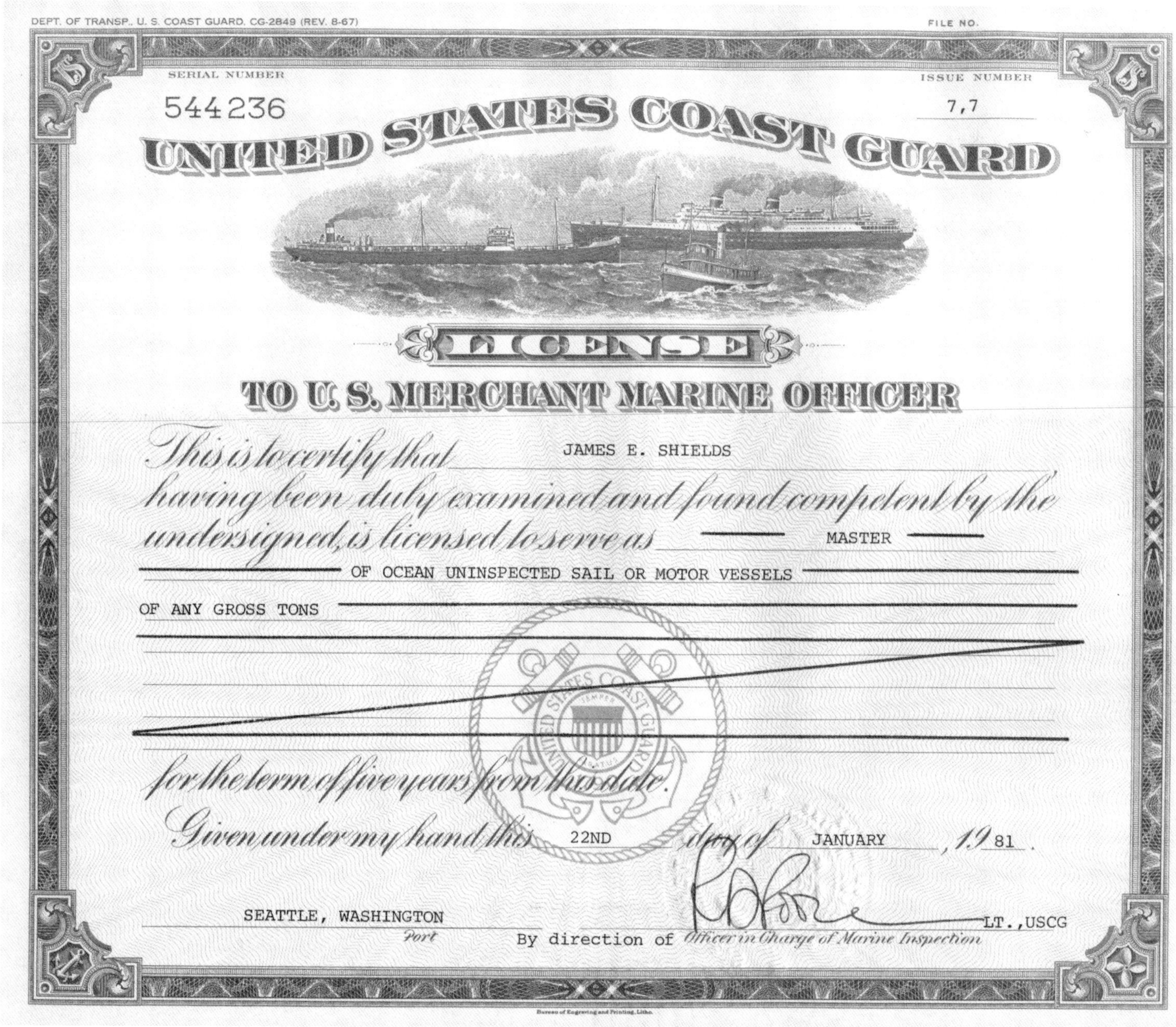

DEPT. OF TRANSP., U. S. COAST GUARD, CG-2849 (REV. 8-67)

FILE NO.

SERIAL NUMBER 544236

ISSUE NUMBER 7,7

UNITED STATES COAST GUARD

LICENSE

TO U. S. MERCHANT MARINE OFFICER

This is to certify that JAMES E. SHIELDS *having been duly examined and found competent by the undersigned, is licensed to serve as* MASTER OF OCEAN UNINSPECTED SAIL OR MOTOR VESSELS OF ANY GROSS TONS

for the term of five years from this date.

Given under my hand this 22ND *day of* JANUARY, 1981.

SEATTLE, WASHINGTON
Port

LT., USCG
By direction of *Officer in Charge of Marine Inspection*

Bureau of Engraving and Printing, Litho.

PHOTO CREDITS

James A. Cole 217

Harry Dring 179, 180, 195, 202

Captain Harold Huycke 8

Hewitt Jackson 218

Gordon Jones 18, 19, 20, 55, 77, 78, 150, 176, 177, 182, 194

Harry Kirwin 82 108, 109, 126, 164, 165, 166(R), 168, cover photos

Marine Digest, Seattle 52

Museum of History and Industry, Seattle 34, 35

National Maritime Museum, San Francisco 26, 27

Art Oien 5, 22, 23, 36, 39

San Francisco Maritime Museum Library, Fort Mason 12, 76, 91

Seattle Times 134

Ed Shields 37, 41(L), 58, 60, 61, 87(L), 89, 92(L), 93, 94, 95, 96, 110, 115, 116, 118, 119, 120, 121, 122, 123, 125, 127, 128, 129, 130, 131, 132, 146, 147, 149, 154(L), 157, 158, 160, 162, 166(L), 167, 172, 173, 186, 196, 197, 198, 205

Ed Shields Collection 21, 24, 25, 28, 29, 31, 32, 38, 40, 41(R), 42, 43, 44, 46, 47, 48, 50, 51, 53, 54, 56, 57, 62, 64, 65, 69, 70, 71, 74, 80, 84, 86, 87(R), 92(R), 102, 103, 104, 105, 107, 114(L), 133, 135, 136, 137, 144, 154(R), 161, 163, 174, 175, 184, 187, 188, 189, 190, 191, 192, 193, 200, 201, 206, front flap

Jeremy Snapp back flap

Mrs. Trafton 114(R)

Trafton Brothers 170

University of Washington John Cobb Collection 15, 16, 17

Joe Williamson Collection 29, 67

INDEX